NEWTOWN

A history of Newtownards

Trevor McCavery

The White Row Press

NEWTOWN

A history of Newtownards

Trevor McCavery

The White Row Press

First published 1994 by
The White Row Press
135 Cumberland Road
Dundonald, Belfast BT16 OBB

The publishers would like to record their grateful thanks to the Mladek family of
Crepe Weavers, and the Ards Borough Council, for their sponsorship of this book.

Cover: Market Square, Newtownards, & View of Newtownards, by J.W. Carey
(1906), from an illuminated address presented to Mr Alexander Love on the occasion
of his retirement, after forty years teaching in the Londonderry Schools,
Newtownards; reproduced with the kind permission of Mrs Dorothy Russell.

A catalogue record for this book is available from the British Library

ISBN 1 870132 70 X

Typeset by Island Publications, Belfast
Printed by W & G Baird Ltd., Antrim

Contents

Preface

To tell the story of Newtownards is, in a sense, to tell the story of Ireland in miniature. Newtownards is one those places whose history consistently mirrors that of its region and country, for the groups of people who have shaped the country have also figured prominently in the history of this locality. The first settlers, who hunted and gathered around Strangford Lough, Stone Age farmers, Celtic kings, early Christian monks, Viking raiders, Norman conquerors, Gaelic chieftains, British planters, United Irishmen, tenant farmers and the entrepreneurs of Ireland's Industrial Revolution – all have left their mark.

Perhaps because it has such a fascinating story to tell, the people of Newtown and Newtownards have always had an interest in the history of their town and district. This is seen, for example, in the work of William Montgomery whose *Manuscripts* sought to relate the activities of his grandfather and other members of his family in the founding, or re-founding, of the town in the seventeenth century; in the many lectures given on the history of the area in the nineteenth century; in the concise histories that have always been part of the Official Guides that have appeared from time to time; in the pioneering work of the late Ted Griffith; and the informative publications of the Ards Historical Society.

The aim of this book is draw some of this work together in one place and to fill in a few gaps with original research. If it has succeeded it is due in no small measure to the advice, information, and help given by the following: the staff of the Historic Monuments branch of the Dept. of the Environment, Newtownards and Bangor Libraries, Library Headquarters, the National Trust, Hugh Brown, William Brown, Lady Mairi Bury, Peter Carr for his inspired assistance during the edit, Jonathan Coates, Dr. Peggy Donaldson for her work on the evolving script, Billy Ervine, Malcolm Fry, Eddie Hanna, Dr. William Harvey, Tom Maddock, Hilary Maginnis, Dr. Bill Maguire, Scott Mawhinney, Douglas Mayne, Brian McDonald, George McConnell, Jimmy McGuigan, Dr. D.B. McNeill for his comments on the first draft, Frankie Mottram for her line drawings, Trevor Parkhill, Bert Thompson and finally to my wife, Mandy, to whom this book is dedicated.

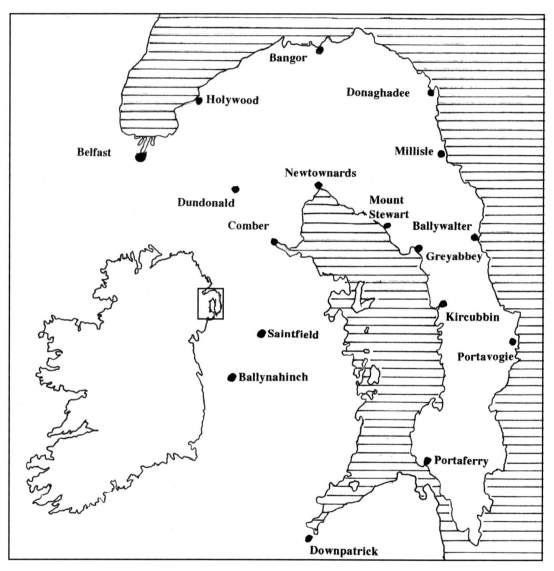

Location of the town of
Newtown, alias Newtownards,
County Down.

1

Earliest Times

Like the proverbial cat, or the hero in modern computer games, the area we know as Newtownards has had many lives and has been home to many different peoples and cultures. It was attractive to the Stone Age hunter-gatherers who fished and foraged along the lough shore, to the early farmers who cut the first fields out of its thickly wooded hillsides, and to the mysterious peoples of the late Bronze Age, the rcmains of whose village can still be traced on Scrabo Hill. In historical times it has been the hub of a Celtic lordship, an influential monastic settlement, an Anglo-Norman administrative centre and more recently, if we can call the seventeenth century recent, a Scots plantation town.

Newtownards owes its prominence to its geography. It is a natural regional centre. The town sits at the head of Strangford Lough and nestles at the foot of an amphitheatre of hills ranging from craggy Scrabo to the southeast, Cairngaver to the northwest and Conlig to the north. To the west lies the Dundonald Gap and Lagan Valley. To the east the drumlin covered Ards Peninsula juts southwards into the Irish Sea.

The name Ards derives from one or other of these geographical features

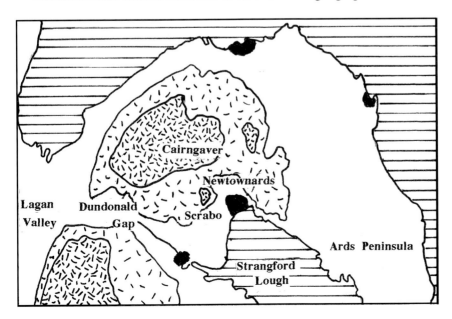

The lough before it, the hills behind. The geography of Newtownards.

Above: flint tools.

Below: worked flints found at Ardmillan, Strangford Lough. 1,2 blades; 3 core from which flint tools were struck; 4 scraper.

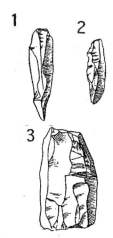

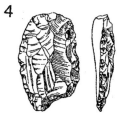

– but the question is which? The earliest reference to the area comes in the late seventh century A.D. when it was called *Aird*, a name linguists have translated as 'promontory', which would suggest the peninsula as the source of the name. However, the Scots Gaelic word *aird*, can be confused with *Ard*, which means 'heights', and the author of *The Life of Comgall*, writing in the early twelfth century, refers to the area as *altitudo Ultorum*, the 'heights of the Ulstermen', which seems to favour the hills as the source! By the late fourteenth century the *Ard* form was almost always used. We can perhaps reconcile the two by suggesting that, at first, Ards was named after the peninsula but over time became associated with the heights.

Hunters and gatherers: the Mesolithic period 7000–3500 B.C.

The first people to settle in the area were probably hunter-gatherers from what is now northwest England or the Isle of Man. Britain and Ireland were closer then, and the journey between the islands would have been nothing to an experienced boatman. On reaching the sheltered lough they would have found in it, and on the shores around, abundant resources: fish, seals, shellfish, wildfowl and their eggs. Dense forest then grew right up to the water's edge and would have held a healthy population of wild pig, small animals and birds and yielded fruit, berries and nuts in season.

Given that they lived here for some four thousand years, almost half of the district's inhabited history, these nomadic people left behind almost nothing which might enable us to begin to get to know them. As good ecologists, their waste was bio-degradable, apart from the highly prized commodity that was at the centre of their technology – flint. There have been significant finds of worked flint implements at Ardmillan, Rough Island, Castle Espie, Reagh Island, Ringneill and Mahee Island, and inland along the shores of the former Lough Maroney (now a marshy hollow, just south of the Kempe Stones Road), Mount Alexander, and Ballymaglaff. The location of so many sites on the shores of Strangford Lough shows how important the area was to these ingenious, undervalued peoples.

The first farmers: the Neolithic 3500–2000 B.C.

Gradually, however, hunting and gathering gave way to farming. At Ringneill the bones of a domesticated ox, pig, sheep or goat (it proved difficult to be precise!) were found and were dated by radiocarbon to 3420 B.C. This was a highly significant discovery for it tells us that the new culture, which originated in the Middle East, and was based on growing crops and raising domesticated animals, had reached the area by then. Some archaeologists believe these changes were the result of the spread of new techniques; most, though, believe that they were due to the arrival of new peoples, and that the two groups probably co-existed for many

Artist's impression of the Neolithic harvest. The area's light soils attracted these early farmers.

centuries before the agriculturalists, or at any rate their lifestyle, finally prevailed.

The northeast of County Down would have been as attractive to these new peoples as their predecessors, for it offers the low technology farmer relatively easily workable soils. These soils are a legacy from glacial times. At the end of the last Ice Age a huge lake – 'Lake Lagan' – formed in the Lagan Valley, draining eastwards through the Dundonald Gap into Strangford Lough. This coated the Triassic sandstone floor of the Gap with fertile fluvio-glacial deposits. This combination has produced light and medium loams in the area between Dundonald, Newtownards and Comber. The forest cover would have been removed by burning or ring barking in order to establish both pasture and crop land. The Palaeozoic shales and grits elsewhere in the Newtownards area yield slaty soils which warm up quickly and favour arable husbandry.

Another benefit to the intending farmer would have been the absence of drumlins in the immediate Newtownards area. Although an attractive and prominent feature of the rest of County Down, these small hills would have been a barrier to the first settlers because they were originally forested and badly drained, and their hollows were filled with lakes and bogs.

With the focus of settlement moving from the loughshore to the land, one particular feature will have assumed central importance – Scrabo Hill, standing like a sentinel at the head of Strangford Lough. This imposing hill, beloved of artists through the ages, owes its existence to a geological accident. It is thought that some sixty million years ago, intense heat and pressure from a great depth pushed molten lava upwards and, as it came into contact with the pre-existing sandstone, it hardened and changed it to give us the varied colours and textures of Scrabo stone. At the top of the hill the lava formed a thick dolerite sill which has protected the sandstone beneath from erosion. The earliest reference to it comes as early as 1275 when it was called *Scraboc,* which comes from the Irish *Screabach* meaning 'rough' or 'scraggy', a reference, probably, to the summit's thin cover of soil. However, its name belies its agricultural value, and Scrabo's warm sunward and seaward slopes of dry sandy soil must have been a magnet to these early farmers. Also, the hill provided settlers with natural protection from attack and allowed surveillance of the surrounding area. The large number of arrow heads, scrapers, knives and polished stone axes that have been found here tell us that the hill has been more or less continuously inhabited since the Stone Age.

Scrabo once boasted an impressive Neolithic cairn and dolmen-type burial chamber, which was unfortunately destroyed in the early 1850s. However, though no trace of the monument itself remains, a good account of its appearance, and disappearance, was published in the *Ulster Journal of Archaeology* in 1855, shortly after its removal. According to the account's author, the cairn stood four hundred yards northwest of Scrabo Tower, on what is now the Scrabo Golf course, and overall the site occupied an area thirty yards square. Inside this area stood a burial chamber constructed of enormous blocks of stone, four of them sunk three feet into the ground and standing five feet above it. The chamber was in the form of a rectangle five feet long by three feet wide. Apparently it had once been covered by a huge capstone but this had collapsed and rolled some way downhill. Inside the cairn was a pile of charred bones surrounded by a mixture of soil and wood charcoal, and the remains of a decorated bowl, the base of which was the size of a large saucer. This type of pottery is usually dated to about 1500 B.C., long after the construction of the dolmen, suggesting that the tomb retained its status as a sacred site for many centuries.

The remains of similar monuments can still be found at Greengraves, about one and a half miles to the northwest of Newtownards, and at Cairngaver Hill, two and a half miles to the northeast. The Kempe Stone at Greengraves is a beautiful example of a Neolithic portal dolmen. Like the lost dolmen on Scrabo, it dates from around 2250 B.C. and was also formerly enclosed by a protective cairn, traces of which can be seen in the monument's base. When it was excavated, around 1830, by labourers acting for the Rev. John Cleland, the scourge of the United Irishmen, human bones were found.

The name of the townland offers intriguing clues about the site's history. Peter Carr tells us that Greengraves was formerly known as Ballycloughtogal – 'the town of the raised stone', from *tochar* which can also mean a causeway, perhaps, in this context, the causeway to an after life. He continues:

The origin of the name [Kempe Stone] is uncertain. It may derive from the Norse *kampsten*, or 'big stone', but then again, *kempe* means 'warrior ' in Anglo-Saxon, and according to local legend the dolmen is the grave of a giant slain by one of his

rivals... The name Greengraves may come from *Grainne gaireach*, 'Grainne's grave or bed', as the eloping lovers Dairmid and Grainne are said to have spent a night there on their way to Scotland.

The extremely fine Kempe Stone dolmen, created by the people of the area over four thousand years ago.

The cairn at Cairngaver, from the Irish *Carn Gabhair*, meaning 'goat's cairn', at the top of Cairn Wood, is the youngest of those in the Newtownards area and, strictly speaking, is probably of early Bronze Age vintage (c. 2,000–1800 B.C.). It appears to have been one of three cairns here. All trace of the others has gone. The last vestiges of one of them was removed about thirty years ago, and it is now difficult to say even where they stood. In its time the hill top was undoubtedly an extremely important funereal site. Carr has described these cairns as north Down's 'suitably humble equivalent of the pyramids of Giza', an importance matched by the splendour of the site, which offers truly spectacular views across southern Antrim and the plain of Down. Standing at a majestic 720 feet, Cairngaver is the highest hill in the parish.

This leads us to the question of the purpose which the monuments on Scrabo, Greengraves and Cairngaver served. They were certainly burial chambers, but even that leads us to speculate that they were ceremonial and religious centres and therefore focal points for the community. Their scale tells us that the community in the Newtownards area, or at least its upper echelons, then lived well above subsistence level, for how else would they have had the time and energy needed to gather and transport

Decorated food vessel found at Greengraves.

the materials and then construct such megaliths? These monuments offer tantalising clues as to the lifestyles of these early farming peoples, but all detail of their lives eludes us.

The Bronze Age village 2000–300 B.C.

The move from a stone to a bronze and then a copper-based technology further enhanced the strategic importance of the Newtownards area. Two miles to the north of the modern town there is a copper outcrop at Conlig which would have provided a vital source of raw material for the new technology. Possession of it would have conferred enormous economic power. A lot of the ore seems to have been worked locally. The area is one of the most prolific in County Down in terms of yields of copper and bronze artefacts and it seems likely that the ores for most of them came from the Conlig area, which for most of the early and middle Bronze Age, must have been well known for its mines and miners.

The fruits of their industry are everywhere around us. At Whitespots, a flat axe, halberd blade and dagger have been found. Not far away, at Cotton, three halberd blades were discovered. Two of them were analysed and their composition was found to be consistent with the ores at Conlig. Flat axes from the period have been found at Cotton and Donaghadee (two, one of them decorated and flanged), and four decorated flat axes and a spear head were picked up on Scrabo. Socketed axes have been turned up at Kircubbin and Newtownards, and a socketed knife was found long ago in 'The Ardes'. Swords have been found at Ballycroghan, Groomsport and Scrabo – the latter was turned up when the railway was cut through the foot of the hill. The most impressive Bronze Age artefact to have been recovered from the area, however, was probably the battered cauldron retrieved from a bog near Donaghadee. The production of such a vessel was a considerable achievement in its day as bronze ingots had to be repeatedly hammered and annealed to produce sheets large enough to mould into the required shape. Understandably, only the wealthy could

Bronze Age flat axe found on Scrabo. The hill is rich in prehistoric material.

afford cauldrons, and possession of one would have been a status symbol, just the thing to show off at a wedding or banquet.

Much less explicable, however, are the standing stones which were being put in place towards the middle of this period. In appearance, they are straightforward: the eight standing stones in north Down are all between four and seven feet tall, and two to four feet thick. Are they grave stones, boundary posts, altars, time pieces, markers on a route through the area? Regarding the latter theory, it was once thought that the location of the stones – at Ballybeen, two at Ballyoran, Killarn, Conlig, Ballycroghan and Portavo – would take the traveller from the Dundonald Gap, and hence the Lagan Valley, to the coast near Donaghadee, at a point where he could make one of the shortest sea crossings to the sister island. On the other hand, materials such as bones and funereal pots were found at the foot of the stones at Ballycroghan and Portavo, which would suggest that the standing stones could simply have been burial sites, an interpretation favoured by archaeologists. They remain amongst the most enigmatic of our Bronze Age remains.

Our Bronze Age ancestors left us pottery as well. Decorated food vessels have been found at Greengraves and Ballyvester, and when a cairn on the Mount Stewart estate was opened in 1776, during the course of so-called 'improvements', it produced a fine collection of pottery, most of which was promptly 'torn to pieces by the men on the supposition that it contained hidden treasure.' (Templeton, 1804). Altogether sixty to seventy small rough stone 'boxes' or cists were discovered, in which not treasure, but small amounts of 'blackish granulated earth' were found. Some of the urns were preserved but their whereabouts are now, alas, unknown. 'Bee hive' shaped urns from the remarkable Bronze Age cemetry in Ballyrogan, midway between Newtownards and Dundonald, met the same fate. This fascinating 'assemblage of tumuli' had been more or less completely ransacked by the end of the eighteenth century. All trace of it has since disappeared and even its precise site is now unknown.

Thankfully, however, the desecration of the district's Bronze Age cemeteries in the eighteenth century did not remove all trace of its Bronze

Middle Bronze Age bowl from the Mount Stewart cairn, dismantled in the eighteenth century. One of the few to survive the greedy intentions of treasure hunters.

Age peoples. The remains of one of the most important sites have (mostly) survived. This was on Scrabo, straddling the area now occupied by the Scrabo Golf course. The site was long known as being of some significance but no-one knew exactly what. In the lease of the golf course from the Londonderry Estates in 1908, for example, there is a clause which says that there should be as little disturbance as possible of the 'Druid's Circle'. The value of the remains only began to be appreciated in the 1930s when flints were found on the site which enabled it to be dated as Late Bronze Age (c.900–300 B.C.).

Ted Griffith's study of the site revealed four huts grouped together in a circular enclosure, a hundred feet in diameter. At the northern end of the site, was a second enclosure which contained a single large hut. This enclosure stood apart from the rest, and was sited on a raised basalt platform. Could it have been the house of the community's leader, some kind of fort, or even the Bronze Age equivalent of a church? Outside the enclosure were further huts. It is impossible to know exactly how many huts were originally in this unenclosed group; in the 1960s it was just possible to discern two. Finally, close to the present Tower, there were the remains of a pair of hut circles, the northern being twenty feet, and the southern some thirty feet in diameter. Traces of only one of these are

Scrabo golf course 2,500 years ago, when the hilltop was the site of an important Late Bronze Age settlement.

discernible today. Nowadays, the remains of the village, a group of low earthen banks and piles of stones blending into the rough grass of the golf course, pose as much of a challenge to golfers as archaeologists. The Scrabo village is one of the largest known Bronze Age settlement sites in Ireland.

The Iron Age fort 300 B.C.–500 A.D.

It is tempting to link the Bronze Age settlement to the district's last great prehistoric site, the Iron Age fort which was situated at the very top of Scrabo Hill. The fort's site can easily be identified from the modern town because in 1857 the Londonderry Monument (Scrabo Tower) was built in its centre.   The fort was oval shaped, three hundred feet long and one hundred and twenty feet wide and was surrounded by a bank and ditch (now partly filled). At the southern end of the site the rock outcrop has been cut away, perhaps to make a ditch or make access easier.   When lightning conductors were being added to the Tower in recent times, animal bones and pottery were found. The pottery is known as Continental 'E' type and this enables us to date the fort to about 500 A.D. This date opens the possibility that this impressive hill fort was the home of the rulers of the first people known to have lived in the area in historical times, the Uí Blathmac.

2

The Monastic Settlement at Movilla 500-1177

The kingdom of Blathmac

In the early historic period the district at the head of Strangford Lough was known as Blathmac, a name derived from the Irish *Blaeth*, which is a contraction of *baile ata* , meaning 'the town of the ford', a reference perhaps to the way in which the head of the lough can be forded at low water. The area takes its name from, or gave its name to, a seventh century king of the Dál Fiatach, Blathmac, the 'son of the town of the ford', who reigned from 646-656 A.D. Blathmac seems to have covered an area comprising the modern civil parishes of Dundonald, Holywood, Comber, Killinchy, and much of Bangor and Newtownards, and its people were known as the Uí Blathmac.

Blathmac was a *tuath* or small kingdom which was itself a component part of a larger one, known as Dál Fiatach, which in the eighth century encompassed much of modern County Down. Dál Fiatach, in turn, was part of Uladh, or Ulster, and for most of this period the Dál Fiatach were successful in retaining the kingship of the Ulaid, the Ulster people.

The neighbours of the Uí Blathmac were the Uí Eachach Arda on the Ards Peninsula, and in 642 it is recorded that Ferdoman, son of Imoman, was 'the red-weaponed king of the Ards of Ulidia'. Ferdoman seems to have been either a great warrior or a ruthless killer, and one cannot but suspect that amongst the people he bloodied his weapons on, would have been members of the Blathmac.

Given its situation, the area around Newtownards must have been the scene of many a skirmish between the people of Blathmac and the Uí Eachach Arda. The relationship between the over-lords of Dál Fiatach and the lesser kings was confirmed by the exchange of gifts. Thus an ancient source tells us that the king of the Ulaid gave 'eight bondmen, eight steeds with silver bridles to the King of Uí Blathmac... Eight ships and eight bondmen and eight steeds and eight horns and eight cloaks to the king of the Ards'.

Could it be that the king of Blathmac held court in Scrabo's hill fort? It

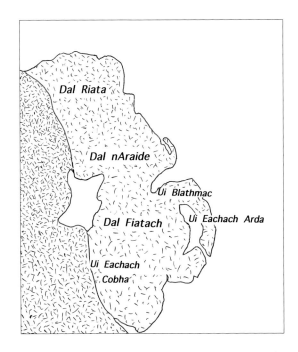

Blathmac and its neighbours.

certainly commands views of almost the whole *tuath*. The strategic importance of the hill, plus the existence of what was an inauguration site for the kings of the *tuath* at Mag-Bile (the name means 'the plain of the sacred tree'), would suggest that the 'capital' of the Uí Blathmac was not far from Scrabo.

'Erin's choicest son': Finnian and the foundation of Movilla

The monastery of Movilla was founded in 540 by Finnian, whose name means 'white headed', either from the fairness of his hair in youth or its whiteness in his august old age. The *Calendar of Cashel* calls him 'Finnianus the White'. Finnian's credentials were (suspiciously) impeccable. He was a local man, a member of the royal family of Dál Fiatach. His sponsor was his grandfather, Ailill, a brother of Dichu, who had given Saul to Patrick. Finnian was educated at Nendrum, founded by Mahee, who was the first man to whom Patrick gave a Gospel. Finnian furthered his studies at the monastery at Candida Casa, now Whithorn, in Galloway. This had been founded by Ninian in 398 and modelled as closely as possible on the celebrated White House at Marmoutiers, established by Martin who is regarded as the founder of western monasticism. Thus Finnian's intellectual pedigree can be traced via one line of thought through Ninian to Martin, and through another from Mahee to Patrick.

Finnian's illustrious career nearly came to nothing. While at Candida Casa he played a prank (nature unknown) on Princess Drustice, the daughter of a Pictish king, who was in the ladies' section of the monastery. He was expelled from the monastery, and perhaps had he not been so well connected, his clerical career could have been in ruins. However his fortunes soon recovered and, after spending seven years in Rome, he was ordained a Presbyter. His education completed, he returned to his home to start a great monastic school at Movilla, or Mag-Bile, one of the holy sites of the Uí Blathmac. The monastery was built about a mile from the shore, on a gentle slope overlooking Scrabo, Cairngaver, and the silvery expanse of Strangford Lough, then Loch Cuan, the 'lough of the harbours'.

In their sponsorship of Movilla, the Dál Fiatach would have been anxious to promote Christian culture and scholarship – to the glory of God, and of course the Dál Fiatach kingdom, for there is no reason to suppose that their motivation was any purer than that of other men before or since. One historian, E. James, has offered a particularly materialistic interpretation of the motivation of the sponsors of monasteries:

A monastery was, for an aristocratic family, a reservoir of wealth and land which could be borrowed and which, since church land could not be alienated, would not suffer from the partition or fragmentation like most of a family's estates. It could provide hospitality and suitably grand surroundings in which to display the family's power; it could accommodate elderly, incompetent or dangerous relatives; it could provide the family with saints to increase its prestige; and it could become the religious centre of an entire district attracting the local population and further increasing the family's reputation.

So the creation of a monastery was both an act of devotion and an act of self-interest. Movilla's geographical position is interesting too. It was strategically located, lying on the border of Uí Blathmac and Uí Eachach Arda. The aim of the over-kings of Dál Fiatach, in siting their foundation here, may have been to reconcile their warring under-kingdoms, Uí Eachach Arda and Uí Blathmac, or at least to create a neutral space between them. Certainly the Dál Fiatach were firmly in control of Movilla, and used that

Finnian's chamber pot? Unfortunately not. This clay urinal was found at Movilla during the excavation of 1980-1, and is decorated, and covered with an olive green glaze. It is the only such item known from Ireland, and is thought to have been imported from the continent.

power to install influential members of their family as abbots. The links between church and state were confirmed in the eighth century,when celibacy ceased to be a requirement for ecclesiastics, and their position could be inherited by their children. Movilla would have had a residence available for the kings of the Dál Fiatach when they chose to stay there, and from which they could keep an eye on the nobility of Blathmac and, with the exception of miscreants like Ferdoman, the leaders of the Ards.

The monastery was soon flourishing, not least because, according to a ninth century tradition, Finnian brought a copy of Jerome's Bible, the *Vulgate*, back with him from Rome. It was the first time the Bible had been seen in Ireland. According to another account, Finnian copied it from an exemplar at Candida Casa, brought from Rome by Ninian. Either way, Finnian was credited with making the Word of God accessible to the Irish Church. It was a brilliant coup for the Irish Church – and for Finnian, Movilla and the Dál Fiatach!

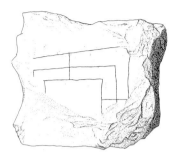

All work and no play? Not at Movilla. This curious, flat stone object, twelve inches in diameter, is thought to have been a gaming board. It was discovered during the 1980-1 excavations.

One measure of the book's importance was the number of stories or superstitions it attracted. It was said that any person swearing a false oath on Finnian's copy of the Scriptures would be instantly struck dead or become mad. Finnian was very possessive of his Bible. It is said that Fintan, a student at the neighbouring, and rival, Dál nAraide monastery at Bangor, had long requested Finnian to lend him his Bible, but that the latter had steadfastly refused. Comgall the abbot encouraged his student to have faith in God and that his request would eventually be granted. Soon afterwards a message came that pirates had attacked Movilla and were on their way to Bangor. Comgall posted Fintan and some others to watch the coast from under a large tree. When the pirates' boat appeared they fled, but a sudden gust uprooted the tree and it fell on the pirates. Encouraged by this seeming act of God, Fintan and his companions returned and amongst the plunder in the boat discovered Finnian's legendary copy of the Scriptures.

The medieval hagiographers, to whom we owe the above story, created elaborate mystiques or cults around Finnian's Bible, and, of course, around Finnian himself. One such story concerns the monastery's mill. Finnian ordered his foreman builder to build a water mill. But the builder noticed there was no water to power it. 'I wager my life,' he said, 'you will never get water to turn that mill.' But Finnian prayed and a torrent came, ploughing up the earth before it, and so drowning the hapless builder. However, this fate was thought a little harsh, so Finnian prayed for him and raised him from the dead. The mill also had the distinction of not working if the corn it was grinding was stolen. Life at Movilla must have been very dangerous for the dishonest or disrespectful!

Any who cursed Movilla's bell suffered a fate similar to those who swore falsely on Finnian's copy of the Scriptures – instant death or insanity. Once, when he was an old man, Finnian visited his great near contemporary Comgall, abbot of Bangor. Comgall welcomed his honoured guest. As they dined, Comgall suggested that perhaps Finnian would like to drink some milk, on account of his age and weakness, as their meal consisted only of bread, water and vegetables. Before that time, milk was not brought into Bangor's monastery. Comgall, though he knew that there would be no milk, sent to the store for some. But a jar of milk was mysteriously found there. When Finnian ordered it to be passed round, it was found to have enough to satisfy them all. By this miracle, Finnian convinced Comgall that henceforth milk should be given to the old and sick in his monastery.

At the time of Finnian's death in 579, Movilla was recognised as a great monastic foundation. The *Book of Kilkenny* says that Finnian was 'buried in his own town of Mag-bile'. Another ancient text, *The Life of Comgall*, gives him this obituary: 'the man of venerable life, St. Finbarr, the bishop, who sleeps amid many miracles in his own city of Maghbile.' He became the patron saint of the Ulaid and one of their most famous sons. As one ninth century poet wrote:

> The body of red gold with purity
> Comes hither across the sea;
> Erin laments her choicest son,
> Finnian of Maghbile.

This curved field boundary, to the north of the Movilla Road, marks the probable perimeter of Finnian's illustrious foundation. The site is now covered by the Abbeydale estate.

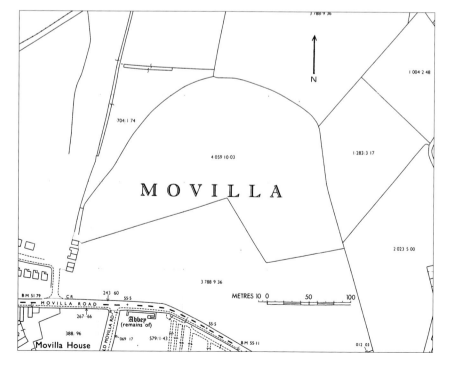

The dove of the church

One of Movilla's most famous students was Columba or Colum Cille ('dove of the church'). He was born about 521, and called Crimthann. Because he was born in the royal family of Uí Neill, he was allowed as a boy the privilege of playing outside the monastery with local children from the 'town' one day a week. The boys used to wait outside the gate and when they saw him approaching they would shout, 'Here the dove of the church comes forth.' When Finnian heard of this he believed it was God's will that the boy should be called by that name. Colum Cille's reputation grew to equal that of his great teacher. As a ninth century poem puts it:

> The descendants of Niall are under the shelter of Colum
> It is not the shelter of a bramble;
> Behind the back of Finnian of Maghbile
> The descendants
> Are all the Ulidians.

Colum Cille rose to become an influential political churchman, both in Ireland and in eastern Scotland, where he is credited with founding several religious houses, the most celebrated being Iona, the establishment of which created important links between the Ards and that country. He also actively involved himself in temporal affairs, mediating between kings, and making a less than successful attempt to turn the great pagan harvest festival *Lughnasa* into a Christian celebration, 'The Feast of the Ploughman'. The idea did not catch on.

At Movilla Colum Cille supposedly performed a miracle which many would wish to see repeated: he turned water into wine. His biographer of the late seventh century, Adomnan, records that on a certain occasion Finnian needed wine and bread for the Mass. Colum Cille was sent to the well with a cruet for water. He blessed the water, it turned into wine and was put into the Mass chalice. O'Laverty asserts that the well was situated in a field north of the church, and that the owner of the field deepened the well about 1830 and put in a pump. However the water which once tasted agreeable was found to be bad, thanks no doubt to the farmer's presumption, and the well was filled up. Ted Griffith in an article in the Ards Historical Society's *Further Glimpses of the Ards* records that a field to the north of the remains of the Church, now part of the Abbeydale estate, was known as the 'well field'. When these houses were being built the remains of an old stone-lined well were uncovered. Could the site of Colum Cille's miracle have been in Abbeydale?

It is thought that the first wrangle over copyright occurred at Movilla. After many years Colum Cille returned to visit his old teacher and asked if he could spend some time examining the precious copy of the Scriptures. He was keen to have a copy of his own. However, he knew that Finnian

An early medieval grave slab found at Movilla during the last century. The inscription reads 'Say a prayer for Dertrend'. Dertrend is otherwise unknown.

would not permit him to copy it, and so began to transcribe it without his permission. He had almost completed his task when Finnian caught him. Finnian insisted that Colum Cille surrender the 'pirate' copy, but Colum Cille refused. The case went before Diarmaid, the high king of Ireland. He pronounced his famous verdict: 'To every cow belongs her calf, to every book its copy. The copy belongs to Finnian.' Colum Cille returned his copy in bad grace.

The story of Colum Cille's 'Bible' does not end here, though. The copy passed to a branch of the Uí Neill later called the O'Donnell's, who accorded it the status of a sacred relic. It left Ireland with Daniel O'Donnell after the battle of the Boyne and at his death was deposited in a monastery in what is now Belgium. It lay there until 1816, when it was examined and found to be a portion of the Psalms, written in a small, uniform but rather hurried hand!

The 'city of Mag-bile'

The brief literary references suggest that, in its prime, the 'city of Mag-bile' was an extensive settlement. The archaeological evidence has tended to confirm this. In 1980-81, R.J. Ivens and M.J. Yates excavated the area near the Movilla Road, before it was re-aligned. Yates says that in the pre-Norman period the monastery extended over the area now covered by the cemetery, Movilla Road, and Abbeydale:

The density of this early occupation is shown by the pieces of coarse, hand-made pottery that were found scattered about in their thousands, as well as other everyday objects... Traces of timber structures, built and re-built many times, were also uncovered.

The period between the death of Finnian and the arrival of the Vikings has long been regarded as a Golden Age. Ireland became the intellectual and cultural centre of western Europe – 'the land of saints and scholars.' The monastic schools became centres of great scholarship. Many came from England and France to study in them. Movilla would have attracted its share, and we may perhaps think of the settlement at this time as a sort of 'university town', of international importance.

What went on at Movilla? Much energy would have to have been expended in maintaining the everyday routines of life: processing food, preparing meals, washing and building; maintenance work on the churches, huts, school, kitchens, refectory, barns and workshops; feeding, herding and milking livestock. Only a small number of the inhabitants of Movilla would have been full-time religious men, and these were usually recruited from the nobility of the Dál Fiatach. Many who were associated with the community would have been farmers and specialist craftsmen, who may not have lived within the confines of the monastery.

Appropriately, the curriculum of the school was based on the Latin Bible. Each student was expected to learn the Latin Psalter by heart. The students aimed to understand the Bible in its entirety. Greek and Latin classical literature was also studied. A feature of the scholarship carried on by the monks in this period was the formulation of penitentials for clerics. Finnian's are known as the *Canons of St. Finnian* and are fifty three in number. These were lists of sins with the appropriate punishments. The monasteries also concerned themselves with manuscript illumination, sculpture, art and craftsmanship. The excavations of Yates and Ivens suggest that Movilla was also a centre of fine-quality metal and glass working:

Without doubt the most important finds from the early monastery were those illustrating the skills of the craftsmen, who worked in iron, bronze and glass. There was much industrial debris: lumps of slag, broken pieces of crucible and fragments of scrap metal, all informative but perhaps not very exciting. But a few objects do stimulate the imagination. For example a trial-piece, on which the bronze-smith rehearsed his designs of triangles, scrolls and arcs and a glass headed pin, decorated with discs and trails of different coloured glass. The technical and artistic sophistication of such objects is certainly at variance with the impression of material poverty given by the simple timber houses and rather

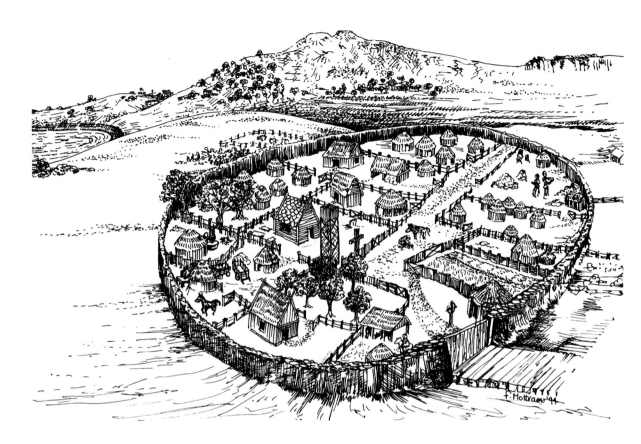

Artist's impression of Movilla monastery (after Robin Carson).

crude pottery... The excavation of a very small part of what was once an extensive monastic settlement has thus given... an insight into the skills of the early Christian craftsmen.

Another sign of the importance of Movilla is the fact that there are relatively few raths here, probably because the monastery did not allow its tenants to live in fortified enclosures. The few raths we have are found on the fringes of the parish, at Killarn for example. In 1958 Killarn's was excavated. Remains of hut circles were found inside the enclosed area, probably a dwelling place and out-houses for a single family. Pottery and part of a bracelet were also found. The rath at Killarn was not typical in that it may have been entirely roofed. The area also boasts a crumbling stone rath, or cashel, at Ballymagreehan, a quarter of a mile from Ballyalton House on an east facing slope. It is seventy feet in diameter and its dry stone walls are in places six feet thick.

Viking attacks

In 823 the monasteries of Bangor, Downpatrick and Movilla were attacked by the Vikings. The raiders on Movilla could either have come up the lough or overland from Bangor. As it was the custom to build Irish monastic structures of wood, even though stone was available, the raid would have been catastrophic, and would have meant having to re-build most of the settlement. Flannabhra, the abbot of Movilla, was probably killed in the Viking raid, for the entry of his death in the Annals is placed beside word of the raid. Because of Movilla's vulnerable position, scholars and scribes may have deserted the settlement in order to pursue their work in more secure monasteries elsewhere. Certainly the Vikings of Strangford knew the value of these specialists for they took monks captive in raids on Armagh in 876.

We can be sure that the Vikings settled near our area. At Strangford, they established a small trading settlement which gave its name to the lough. This Viking community was a colony of the Norsemen of Dublin, who in turn looked for support to the Norsemen of the Scottish Isles. Viking fleets in Strangford Lough were attacked by the Irish in 926. There is a Viking burial site on Ballyholme beach, and a collection of Viking coins was discovered on Scrabo in 1855. Perhaps the most telling indication of their influence in the Ards area is the fact that the ancient petty kingdom of Uí Eachach Arda was nearly obliterated in the ninth century, subsumed in the colony centred at Strangford. We know that Viking towns exercised considerable jurisdiction in their hinterlands. Invariably, the Vikings integrated with local Irish. For example, in the 1170s, the son of Movilla's abbot was called Amhlaeibh (Olaf), a distinctly Norse name.

The abbot taken hostage: Dál Fiatach and Movilla in decline

We cannot be sure of the course of the history of the small kingdom of Blathmac in the period between the Vikings and the Normans, from c.800 to the mid 1100s. By the beginning of the eleventh century the struggle between rival families within the nobility of the Dál Fiatach was probably costing more lives than the attacks by the Norsemen. For example, in the first decade of the century, there were no less than five different kings of the Ulaid, and the abbot of Movilla, Mael brigte Ua Crichidein, was taken hostage but was released through the efforts of Brian Boru. The instability of these years, however, did not hinder the education of Marianus Scotus, one of the greatest chroniclers of the Middle Ages, which took place at Movilla in the second quarter of the eleventh century. Nine years after Scotus had emigrated to Cologne, in 1065, Donnchad Ua Mathgamna, king of the Ulaid, was killed in the oratory (or church) of Bangor 'by his own people', the 'Uí Blathmaic'. His death was avenged by Ua Flaithri, king of the Ulaid, with a great slaughter of the men of Blathmac and the Ards.

This king's victory was said to have been the result of supernatural intervention by the founder of Bangor, Comgall, dismayed by the Blathmac's breach of the sanctuary. A series of 'tit-for-tat' murders took

Neglected and abandoned: Movilla in the nineteenth century.

place in the course of the remainder of the century. As late as the 1170s, Amhlaeibh, the son of Movilla's abbot, acting with the king of the Ulaid, plundered the monastery at Saul. The Nevins, or Uí nAebain, were the noble family who ruled Blathmac in the eleventh century.

In the early twelfth century the main concern of the Ulaid was resisting the expansionist policies of the Cenél nEógain of Tyrone, ruled by the MacLochlainns. In 1113 Domnall MacLochlainn intervened in Ulaidh's fratricidal politics and installed 'half-kings' by dividing the Ulaid between its two leading factions. This kept them weak. In 1130 Cenél nEógain plundered 'both laity and church' of the Ulaid as far as the Ards peninsula. In 1149 Movilla was again plundered by the Cenél nEógain as they swept into south Down. Undoubtedly, Movilla's fortunes were at a low ebb. The monastery never properly recovered from this series of shocks – Norse raids, internal feuding and attacks from Cenél nEógain. Although the abbey may have enjoyed a new lease of life when, in the early twelfth century, it adopted the Augustinian rule, it never recovered its former glory. In 1306 the monastery at Movilla had the one of the lowest valuations of church property in the area, at two and a half marks. Movilla was so poor that the Anglo-Normans had no interest in taking it over and left Irishmen as abbots.

By the 1160s MacLochlainn, king of Cenél nEógain, was supreme in

Ireland. His ally was Dermot MacMurrough, king of Leinster. But he did not remain at the top for long, and it was the king of Dál Fiatach, indirectly, who unseated him. On Easter 1166, MacLochlainn took the king prisoner and blinded him. This was a gross violation of an earlier solemn agreement, and caused outrage throughout Ireland. It was the cue for MacLochlainn's and MacMurrough's enemies to rise up against them and by the end of the summer of 1166 MacLochlainn was dead and MacMurrough had been forced into exile. He decided to seek the help of Anglo-Norman lords. This changed the course of the history of our area and indeed the history of Ireland.

3

The Anglo-Norman Town 1177-1400

De Courcy's conquest

At the beginning of February 1177, outside the campaigning season, an Anglo-Norman knight, John de Courcy, made a lightning strike from Dublin into the Ulaid with a force of seven hundred. De Courcy, from Stoke Courcy in Somerset, was an official in Henry II's entourage when he came to Ireland in 1171. It seems that Henry had then, half-jokingly, granted to de Courcy 'Ulster, if he could conquer it'. Now he was here to do just that. After a short campaign the Irish were routed and the area passed into new hands.

John de Courcy then set about consolidating his conquest by settling the families of his followers in the area. The Savage, White, Riddell, Chamberlain, Stokes, Mandeville, Jordan, Stanton, Logan, Russell, Copeland, Martell, Fitzsimon, Crowley and Benson families all made their homes in what are now north Down and the Ards.

Over thirty mottes were constructed in County Down – large earthen mounds topped with a wooden tower or palisade. In the Newtownards area there are mottes near Castleavery, Donaghadee, Mount Stewart and Dunover. De Courcy ruled with the independence of a sovereign prince. He created barons from his chief tenants and distributed manors to them,

The priory has always been a burial place. Important patrons were buried in the church, friars in the cloister. This fragment of a Norman coffin lid, measuring twelve inches in length, was found in 1951 in the premises of George Walker & Co., Flax Spinners.

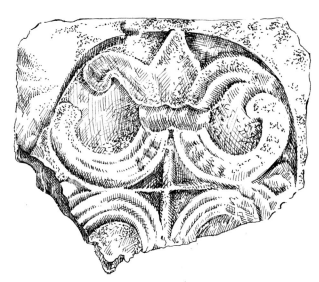

the area around today's Newtownards being part of the powerful manor of Dundonald.

All this, of course, could not last; de Courcy was becoming too powerful and had to be curbed. King John entrusted Hugh de Lacy with the task and when de Lacy finally brought de Courcy to heel in 1205 he was granted de Courcy's lands and made Earl of Ulster, the area around Newtownards becoming part of the new earldom.

However, Hugh soon proved as much of a problem to King John as de Courcy had been. So in turn his lands were confiscated, most of them, probably including the Newtownards area, being retained by the Crown and administered by Roger Pipard, the King's representative or seneschal. In the early 1220s, de Lacy was causing trouble elsewhere and it was deemed expedient to bring him back and again build him up as a bulwark of English power by reinstating him as Earl of Ulster, and restoring him to all his former lands. This took place in 1227.

Nove Ville

Sometime between the creation of the Earldom in 1205 and de Lacy's death in 1243, and probably before 1226, the town of Newtown was formed. It was intended as an important administrative centre for the new earldom, and its foundation guaranteed that, from now on, Newtownards would be more than a purely ecclesiastical centre. The year 1226 is significant because by then the Earldom of Ulster had been divided into five bailiwicks. Two of these were 'Newtown of Blathewyc' (covering north Down), and 'Art' (covering the Ards Peninsula). These two bailiwicks were merged by 1333, creating a larger unit also known as Newtown of Blathewyc, which comprised the baronies of Lower and Upper Ards, Lower and Upper Castlereagh and Dufferin. It was centred on New Town, as the Normans called it, or to be more precise, *Nove Ville de Blathewyc*. It was referred to in Latin as *Villa Nova*. The Irish called it *Baile Nua* – New Town. Interestingly, locals still called the town 'Ballyno' as late as the eighteenth century. The Normans chose to associate the town with the ancient kingdom of Blathmac rather than with the more recent Irish name of Lisnevan. Perhaps this was to snub the local Irish Nevins, who would probably have been prominent local opponents of the conquest.

Why did the Anglo-Normans choose this site for their new town? Katharine Simms points out that Anglo-Normans tended to settle 'at a pre-existing population centre with economic potential, normally one of the larger ecclesiastical settlements of pre-Norman Ireland.'

Here we have some clues. The presence of the once great monastery of Movilla and the settlement around it was an important draw. Then there was the agricultural potential of the surrounding area. Simms says that eastern Ireland at this time changed from a subsistence to a market economy. Surpluses were produced and marketed through the towns, and beyond to England and the Continent. It is likely that Nove Ville de Blathewyc served as such a market centre because of the fertility of its hinterland and the fact that it was, in Ted Griffith's words, 'a natural meeting place of routes', which he identifies as:

...from Comber round the foot of Scrabo, from County Antrim and Belfast by the gap between Scrabo and Craigantlet, from Holywood by the valley of the present Clandeboye Road, and from Bangor, Donaghadee, the central Ards Peninsula and Portaferry by a fan-like series of routes across the low undulating plateau of the peninsula.

What is interesting about the Norman town is that, for the first time in perhaps four thousand years, the centre of settlement moved down from the hills (the Bronze Age village, the Iron Age fortress, and Movilla had all been on upland locations) to the loughshore and the site of the present town, which is also the confluence of the routes outlined by Griffith. For the first time we can begin to deal with a place that is recognisably the ancestor of modern Newtownards.

The arrival of the Black Friars

The town must have been fairly well established by the mid-thirteenth century because the Dominicans set up a priory in Newtown in 1244, dedicated to Columba. The earliest foundations of the mendicant orders in Ireland were associated with the important Anglo-Norman towns, further evidence that Nove Ville was growing before 1244.

Carved head: Dominican priory. (DoE)

Old Church, Newtownards

Newtown priory. By the late nineteenth century the roofless building had been laid out with paths and shrubs.

The key piece of background to the priory's foundation was the death of the Earl of Ulster in the previous year. The town passed to the Earl's widow, Emeline de Ridelsford, and to bolster the settlement at a vulnerable time, one of the most prominent of the local Anglo-Norman families in the Ards area, the Savages, acted as sponsors for the new religious order. On the other hand, of course, their motivation could have been religious for as E.C. Rae says:

There was apparently little preaching of any kind in churches at the end of the twelfth century. But in the growing towns people were asking questions and seeking answers. Heretics were increasing in number. Thus the stage was set for the arrival of St. Dominic and St. Francis. The orders they founded, Dominican (1216) and Franciscan (1223), differed markedly from most in their emphasis on evangelism, on preaching, meeting the world on its level and lifting it up. Preaching the Christian doctrine was a special aim of the Dominicans... The friar preachers came to Ireland in 1224 settling first at Dublin and Drogheda. Because of their evangelizing mission to lead men to a better state of being through preaching, the hearing of confession, and general concern for the people, the ideal location for a friars' house was considered to be close to a town of importance, or even within it.

The ruin of the priory is in Court Street. It is a classic example of its kind in scale and design. It was 96 feet in length and 24 feet wide and was originally one storey high. The cloister and conventual buildings, now disappeared, were behind the south wall of the nave and traces of the roof of the north cloister walk can be seen on the outer face of the south wall, in the property now owned by British Telecom. But as Rae says:

...the friary church did not often long remain a simple, long rectangle. If well

*This mysterious, almost
iconic carved head is [...]
into the priory wall. ([...]*

located, the community of friars and the congregation of the people tended to
increase... The usual way of adding to the area of the nave was to construct an
aisle on the side away from the cloister... Beginning in the late thirteenth century
more spaces for altars were afforded by another kind of extension – a single
transept arm placed usually near the east end of the nave, again away from the
claustral buildings.

This was the case with Nove Ville where a north aisle was built in the
early fourteenth century, and it is likely that a north transept was also
added. The only departure from the norm was in the fact that the nave
itself was extended ten feet *westwards* at the people's end, rather than the
usual east or friars' end. Does this peculiarity tell us something about the
popularity of the black friars in Nove Ville or, perhaps, the rapid expansion
of the town? Or are there external reasons? The extensions as a whole may

The priory was used as a place of worship until the eighteenth century. This inscription from above the doorway arch is a quotation in old English from the Bible: 'Keep thy foot when thou goest to the house of God'.

well be connected to the fact that national conferences of the entire order in the British Isles met in the priory in 1298 and 1312. This was a great honour for both the town and the priory. As the historian O'Laverty puts it, the priory at Nove Ville 'became celebrated among the Dominicans.'

The rise of the vigorous new priory did not signal the death knell of Movilla, but its status did diminish. The Abbey Church of Movilla was built at this time. (Its ruin is what is visible today). It seems to have served as the parish church of the area, for thirteenth century coffin lids have been found around the building. The ancient monastery was also re-constituted as an Augustinian foundation, further evidence that the town was well developed, for Augustinian monasteries were usually situated near existing communities.

The late medieval town

Hugh de Lacy left no heirs, and on his death in 1243 the great bulk of the lands reverted to the Crown. However, Hugh's widow, Emeline de Ridelsford, retained as her dower Dundonald, the castles of Antrim and Dundrum and the sheriffdoms of Down and Nove Ville. When the Countess Emeline died in 1276 the area around Newtownards was not included with the lands held by the new Earls of Ulster, the de Burghs. It, along with her other dower lands, was retained by the Crown. And so we learn that in 1276 the Crown appointed William Fitzwarin as sheriff of Nove Ville, followed in 1281 by William de Mandeville. Only in 1283, when the King gave the town as a wedding present to Richard de Burgh, was the area united again with the extensive possessions of the Earls of Ulster.

The new owners, the de Burghs, were amongst the most powerful families in Ireland. The de Burghs brought peace to eastern Ulster and during the last quarter of the thirteenth century and the first decade of the fourteenth the town flourished, enjoying a sustained period of security and prosperity.

That it was chosen to host prestigious religious conventions is another indicator of its stability and relative importance. The priory's rise owed

A citizen of ancient Nove Ville glowers out at those who disturbed his/her peace. (DoE)

much to the interest taken in it by Richard de Burgh, who is thought to have financed its extensions, a gesture probably made possible by the economic health of the town, from which he would have drawn sizeable revenues. All this highlights the interdependence of priory and town. Their fortunes were tied and it is likely that they rose – and fell – together.

The town had one good century but its prosperity was not to last. Edward Bruce's campaigns of 1315-18 devastated the local economy. They coincided with a general north European famine which caused many

deaths in Ireland. Cattle murrains were recorded in the years 1321, 1324 and 1325. Smallpox and influenza epidemics claimed many lives in 1327 and 1328, particularly amongst town dwellers. Harvest failures in 1320, 1330 and 1331 compounded the region's difficulties.

Movilla grave slab. From the shears, we can tell that this stone marked the burial place of a woman.

Political factors also hastened the decline of the town. Richard de Burgh died in 1326 and his strong hand was now removed from Irish affairs. He was succeeded by his grandson, William de Burgh, then a minor of fourteen. Deprived of leadership, there was a resurgence of friction between the English and the Irish, and amongst the English themselves.

The new owner of Nove Ville, William de Burgh, when he came of age, appears to have been a man of promise. He might have arrested the decline of the whole Anglo-Norman lordship – but one can only speculate, for on 6th June, 1333, after setting out from Nove Ville on a journey to Carrickfergus, the twenty one year old Earl was ambushed and murdered at Le Ford (Belfast). The assassination triggered off a war in the area and north Down was again laid waste. The young Earl's lands passed to his baby daughter, who later married the King's son, Lionel of Clarence and so his estates were returned to the Crown once again. Nove Ville suffered absentee landlords for many decades.

The Inquisition of 1333 provides an inventory of all the land and income of the Earldom of Ulster at that time. In its entry relating to the County of the New Town of Blathewyc there is no record of many of the townlands which surround the town. This would tend to confirm that much of this land then belonged to the two religious houses. It would seem that only the land on which the town was built was left to the Earldom. In 1333 the Earl received '3s 4d from burgages held in fee in the New Town of Blathewyc'. It would appear that this burgage rent was actually a nominal figure, the result of a deal struck between Richard de Burgh and the abbot in 1297. This is unfortunate, for we cannot use the figure to calculate the size of the town. Normally each burgage paid one shilling of rent. The Inquisition also mentions that 'a monthly court is held at the New Town, the pleas and perquisites of which are worth 6s 8d.' This would have been the normal criminal court with appeals to the main court of the Earldom at Carrickfergus. The Earl's interest in the town would have been looked after by the sheriff, John de Mandeville.

Unfortunately, little survives from the medieval town. Apart from the ruin of the priory, no medieval buildings survive. Though we can guess at its likely boundary, its customs and routines and even its street pattern are unknown. Some Norman pottery has been found in the area of the present electricity showrooms in High Street. A small Norman coffin lid was found in Greenwell Street and human skeletons have been found in the area between Castle Street, Greenwell Street and Market Street. Until 1975, there were two ponds in the grounds of Castle Gardens Mill. These were thought to have been the monks' fish ponds, but when the Post Office acquired the site they were filled in and covered with tarmacadam.

One of the most interesting survivals from the late medieval town was unearthed in August 1977 when four workmen, clearing the site for the new electricity showroom in High Street, discovered a hoard of fourteen coins. All the coins were minted in London or Edinburgh in the period 1300-71. Archaeologists believe the hoard was probably hidden about 1380, a period of anxiety and unrest. The hidden hoard is symbolic of the whole town in the late fourteenth century, by which stage Nove Ville would have been very much a community under stress, with its population of merchants, clerics, labourers and artisans facing declining standards of living and an uncertain future.

During the late medieval period the priory and the abbey at Movilla owned the greater part of the land surrounding Newtownards. Movilla

Approximate border of the Norman town. The Normans would have appreciated the railway embankment that effectively 'walled' the northern and western approaches to the town in the century after 1850. They had to be satisfied with, at best, a much smaller bank and water-filled ditch. The exact size of the medieval town is unknown.

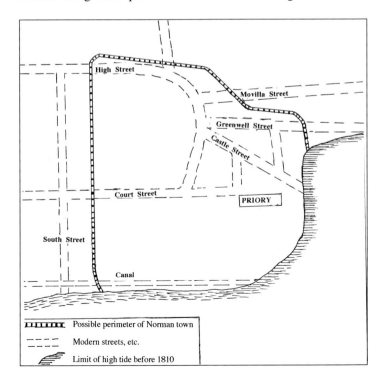

⬛⬛⬛	Possible perimeter of Norman town
- - - -	Modern streets, etc.
⬃	Limit of high tide before 1810

Abbey was the major landowner. When it was suppressed in 1542, it surrendered to the Crown the townlands of Movilla, Ballyharry, Ballyhenny, Drumhirk, Ballyalicock, Loughriscouse, Ballywatticock, Ballyreagh, Ballyhaft, Cunningburn, a large part of Ballyblack, Craigantlet, Killarn and Ballyrogan, in addition to lands in other parishes.

The Dominican Priory was also a significant owner. At its dissolution, it gave up the townlands of Scrabo, Ballycullen, Killynether, Ballybarnes, Tullynagardy, Whitespots 'and all the lands in the township and plain of Lissnevan.' The latter was probably the area known today as Gregstown. It is thought that the outlying townlands of Cronstown and Crossnamuckley were also part of the priory's property. However, the priory only had the tithes from Scrabo, Ballycullen, Killynether, Ballybarnes and New Town itself; the tithes of all the others went to Movilla.

Medieval window, Movilla church.

It is not difficult to understand the extent of such ownership in the case of Movilla. Early Christian monasteries were usually generously endowed. The size of the priory holding is more puzzling. Dominican friars are not normally associated with land ownership. Poverty was at the heart of their appeal and success. They devoted themselves to the spiritual needs of urban localities and they were supported by the charity of those that they helped. However, the Dominicans' influence declined in the late thirteenth century and this may have been due in part to their increased worldliness.

What happened to the Norman name of 'Nove Ville de Blathewyc'? The town was still called by that name, or one rather like it, in 1345 when Robert de Halywoode was appointed sheriff of 'Nove Ville de Blawico.' However, a reference in the Patent Roll of 1400 granted the office of sheriff of 'the *Ardes* in Ulster' to Robert FitzJordan Savage. Thus we might conclude that Newtownards got its modern name, Nove Ville de Ards – New Town Ards, and dropped its associations with Blathmac, sometime between 1345 and 1400, a period which coincided with the waning of Anglo-Norman influence in Nove Ville and the locus of Norman power moving south-eastwards into the Ards. In 1449 the Great Council of Ireland enacted that the town be walled. There is no evidence of these walls and it is likely that the order was never carried out. By this stage the Earldom of Ulster was collapsing and had shrunk to a small area around Carrickfergus, the Upper Ards and south-east Down. North Down was falling under the control of the Clan Aedhe Buidhe.

4

The Gaelic Revival 1400-1605

The rise of Clan Aedhe Buidhe

The Clan Aedhe Buidhe, 'the people of Hugh the yellow haired', (pronounced 'Clan ee boy', giving us modern 'Clandeboye') was a branch of the Tyrone O'Neills who migrated east of the Bann, conquering the Ballymena area in the mid fourteenth century. By the early 1500s, the Clan Aedhe Buidhe had become one of the most powerful groups in Ulster with a lordship which extended from mid Antrim (North Clannaboy) to north Down (South Clannaboy), including the northern part of the Ards Peninsula to the River Blackstaff ('the Great Ardes'). The area south of the River Blackstaff, known as the 'Little Ardes', remained in the hands of the Anglo-Norman Savage family, now thoroughly gaelicised and according to an account of c.1540, 'so environed that [they were]... almost expulsed out of the country'.

Although most of the lands around Newtown were 'spiritual' lands, the property of Movilla Abbey and the Dominican Priory, this did not prevent their absorption into Clannaboy. Technically, after the dissolution of the monasteries in 1541, Patrick O'Dornan, the last prior, and James McGuilmere, the last abbot, surrendered their lands and tithes to the Crown. In fact, they became part of Clannaboy, and the O'Neills expressed their ownership in the bluntest of terms – by building a tower house in the grounds of the priory.

The lands that they took over were of good quality. South Clannaboy was described in 1586 and 1597, at a time of timber shortages, as 'for the most part a woodland' and the Great Ardes as a 'champion and fertile land'. However they seem to have been relatively sparsely populated. In 1593, the Chief Justice of Common Pleas commented that Antrim and Down were 'very slenderly inhabited, and a great part thereof very good and fruitful land do lie desolate'. Raymond Gillespie estimates that in Antrim and Down there were only about twelve hundred adult males. Sir Henry Sidney writing on the state of Ulster in 1575 also commented on its meagre population:

...the Ardes: much impoverished, but in good hope of recovery for there are many freeholders of English race, of ancient habiting there [referring to the Savages]. County [country] of Clandeboy: utterly disinhabited.

'Utterly disinhabited' here probably means 'uninhabited by English'. To be Irish was to count for little, to be beyond the civilised pale. To have

A sixteenth century Irish chieftain (right) and his retainer. Note the chief's anglicised clothing. Woodcut from The Image of Ireland *by John Derricke, 1578. (Mansell Collection)*

43

voluntarily become Irish was even worse and made one fair game for mockery. As one poem had it:

> The Ards of Uladh
> Where Savage hath, nor bread, nor herds, nor flocks
> But lives by scraping limpets of the rocks

The rise of the Clannaboy O'Neills alarmed the government greatly, so much so that on the death of Hugh McNeill Oge O'Neill in 1555, it tried to split the lordship into two parts, giving the northern portion to a cousin and the southern to a brother of the late lord. Both men protested strongly at the division of their inheritance and for their pains were promptly thrown into prison! The lordship passed as a whole to a pro-English, younger brother of one of the lords, Brian McFelim O'Neill.

Brian McFelim was the last Clannaboy O'Neill to be lord of all Clannaboy. He became rich, possessing 30,000 cattle, and in 1567 he was knighted for aiding the Crown. He seemed secure in Clannaboy. His main internal rival was his cousin, Con, who had been lord of South Clannaboy for a few months in 1555 but had since been a prisoner in Carrickfergus Castle. But the real threat was external. In the words of the historian, O'Laverty, 'hungry adventurers were looking with greedy eyes on his rich and extensive territories.' Before the mid 1560s the English sought to make peaceful compromises with the local native lords. But the Lord Deputy, Sir Henry Sidney, and Queen Elizabeth, were giving thought to a more economical method of controlling the Irish. Instead of maintaining expensive garrisons, they came to believe that lasting stability could best be achieved by planting English settlers on conquered territories, at their own expense, of course. Moreover, the expanding and prospering gentry in England were looking for investment opportunities, and what could be better than the underpopulated lands of Ulster. These ideas crystallized in what became known as the 'Enterprise of Ulster' or the 'Ulster Project'.

The first of these adventurers was Sir Thomas Gerrard, who appeared in Down in 1570. Living up to her reputation for being stingy, Queen Elizabeth refused to help finance his venture, and it came to nothing. Next year, in 1571, Captain Browne and Captain Borrowe petitioned the Queen for the Ards Peninsula and north Down to Belfast Lough. However, their petition was rejected in favour of a scheme proposed by the Queen's principal Secretary of State, Sir Thomas Smith, in early 1571.

The expeditions of Sir Thomas Smith

Sir Thomas was one of the most eminent and cultivated men of his age, an intellectual whose interests included political science, law, economics, and the history of earlier voyages of discovery. His interest in the Ards was more prosaic, however. He wanted the lands for his illegitimate son,

East Down in 1572. From a map supposed to have been engraved for Sir Thomas Smith.

also Thomas Smith.

Sir Thomas had some novel ideas. He had made a detailed study of colonisation and his petition stressed that the project's success would depend on its leader being allowed sweeping powers in his new domain. He also insisted that a town should be quickly established. 'I reckon that you can do nothing till you have a strong town, as a magazine of victuals, a retreat in time of danger, and a safe place for the merchants.' Churches were to be built in each parish and lands set aside for clergy, schoolmasters and constables. The Irish leaders and their military forces were to be driven out, but the labouring population was to be retained as a helot class to work the land.

In October 1571 the Queen granted land to Smith 'in the Great and Little Ardes in Clandeboye, which lieth to the south of the castle called Belfast' and north of this into Antrim. There was the promise of more in central Ulster if Smith was successful. In the next six months the two Smiths conducted a widespread and original publicity campaign and were able to assemble nearly eight hundred investors, or 'adventures' at Liverpool in May 1572.

Of course such publicity also had its effects in Ireland. Sir Brian McFelim O'Neill was aghast at his betrayal by the Queen. The Governor of Carrickfergus backed him. Sir Brian was 'captain of this country, appointed by the Lord Deputy, and as yet hath, at all time, continued a loyal and true subject.' Sir Brian appealed to the Queen. One letter of March 27th, 1572 reminded the Queen of his loyalty, and that his family had possessed Clandeboye 'above fourteen descents'.

He was also supported by the new Lord Deputy, Fitzwilliam, who disapproved of the whole policy. Being resident in Ireland he had a more accurate picture of the situation and advised the English Lord Treasurer Burghley (who had put £300 of his own into Smith's scheme) that, 'Mr Smith's grant will bring the Irish into a knot to rebel.' He persuaded the English government to delay the expedition until July.

Thomas Smith waited until August 30th, and with his numbers significantly, and fatally, reduced to about a hundred, set sail for County Down. He arrived the next day. On September 25th, 1572, the Lord Deputy wrote to the Queen:

Thomas Smith is now at length come to the Ardes. He came to me on the 16th of this present. I wish his numbers such as were able to help and not as such as shall need help; for if it be a full hundred it is not many more.

Lord Deputy Fitzwilliam put forward another plan. This involved pretending to release the dreaded Con McNeill Oge O'Neill, held prisoner since 1555, in order to frighten Sir Brian into acquiescence. As he explained to Burghley:

...[this] dangerous fellow is so well followed in that country that I believe he would soon turn Sir Brian out of it... I mean not to let him go... for so perilous a fellow he is that he cares not what or how many of his friends do perish so that he may be at liberty.

Sir Brian now felt that the time for talking was over and he called the Lord Deputy's bluff by taking an English soldier, Thomas Moore, as a hostage and forming alliances with other Irish chiefs whose lands were included in Smith's grant. Sir Brian then adopted a 'scorched earth' policy. Moore's superior officer, Malby, who was himself attempting to plant a colony in mid Down, wrote to the Lord Deputy:

Sir Brian hath come into the Ards with all his force and took all the prey [livestock] and set fire upon some towns where one Henry Savage was killed by his special appointment... A horseman of mine who came from Sir Brian doth tell me that he hath burned the abbeys of Newtown, Bangor, Movilla, Holywood and sundry other places...

These places were the only buildings that could have provided shelter for the would-be colonists as the winter approached.

In spite of these set-backs, Smith and his company established a base some miles south of Newtown, perhaps at Ringhaddy, which they called Newcastle Comber. After a hard winter in 1572-3, and with some defections from his force, he still managed a few successes in the spring of 1573. Sir Thomas Smith bolstered his son's position by obtaining the wardship of John White, heir to the Dufferin, which lay beside the Ards, and by having a preacher in his son's retinue appointed Bishop of Down. Smith also obtained command of the Newry garrison. But then his luck began to run out. Sir Thomas sent reinforcements from England in March but they never arrived.

Affairs became more complicated still when the Queen granted virtually all of County Antrim to the Earl of Essex. Of course this overlapped with the grant made to the Smiths, and both parties to the existing dispute –

*A scorched earth policy.
'Sir Brian... hath burned the
abbeys of Newtown, Bangor,
Movilla and Holywood.'
From* The Image of Ireland.

Smith and Sir Brian – hoped to enlist the Earl of Essex as a friend in order to crush his enemy.

The Earl of Essex had arrived at Carrickfergus in mid August 1573, and placed garrisons at Belfast and Holywood. Sir Brian was not able to secure his support and when the Earl stole his cattle, he resumed his offensive. In October, he arranged to have some Irishmen who worked in Thomas Smith's household at Newcastle Comber assassinate their master. Smith was shot in the head. The colony was now doomed. His followers, 'finding his house scant guardable', sent to Essex for help. Essex set out with 100 horse and 300 foot to assist personally in the relief of the remains of Smith's colony. But when he arrived, he learned that Smith's followers had already made their escape over to the Little Ardes, passing through Newtown on their way. On Essex's return home, he was met by 'Brian and all his power' near Belfast and they engaged in a two hour battle. Essex won, killing over a hundred of Sir Brian's men, and that night, as he encamped on the other side of the river, he 'heard their cries, after their country's fashion, for the loss of them that were dead.'

Sir Brian was now anxious to make terms with Essex. He pleaded with the Queen that he might be a tenant in Clandeboye, giving 1,500 cattle in the first year as rent, 'with promise to increase the same yearly as I and my people grow more plentiful in this worldly wealth.' Essex and the Queen agreed to this in May 1574 and Sir Brian was pardoned.

But Smith had not given up yet. In August 1574 a third Smith expedition set out from Liverpool and Workington. It consisted of 150 men led by George Smith, Sir Thomas's brother, and George's three sons. The

Walter and Robert Devereaux, father and son, in turn, were unsuccessful in their attempts to make a fortune in Ulster. Robert, second Earl of Essex.

colonists re-established themselves at Newcastle Comber and met with the war-weary Sir Brian, somehow obtaining from him his provisional recognition of the Smith title to the Ards. If this colony had succeeded, the history of the area would have been very different. It would not have been a Scots colony but perhaps an English one, with a very different character.

But it was not to be. Several months after making their accord, Sir Brian, his family and retinue were invited to spend a few days with the Earl of Essex at Belfast. After three days, as they were 'agreeably drinking and making merry', the Earl and his men seized Sir Brian, his wife and brother and had 115 of their followers put to the sword. The prisoners were brought to Dublin where they were executed and quartered. Essex maintained that he did this acting on information that Sir Brian was about to rebel, but the Queen's representative thought that the treatment was brutal and excessive.

Essex's actions were the signal for a rising led by Niall McBrian Fagartagh O'Neill, the chief Clannaboy O'Neill in the Great Ardes. He attacked Newcastle Comber and once again the settlers were driven out to the Little Ardes. In July, Essex and Niall made peace, and it was agreed that the latter would be lord of South Clannaboy while the North would go to Shane McBrian, son of the late Sir Brian. But Niall's lordship of South Clannaboy was short-lived as in that same year, 1575, Con, imprisoned for the last twenty years in Carrickfergus, made his escape and was immediately recognised by the clan as the new lord of all Clannaboy. The Lord Deputy intervened and insisted that the lordship be divided as before, with Con having South Clannaboy. To placate his nephew, Niall McBrian Fagartagh, Con had him placed again in the Great Ardes.

The Smiths did not give up their claim. Although Sir Thomas died in 1577, he left his lands in the Ards to his nephew, William Smith. In June 1579 William landed with forty men to make yet another attempt, but the Dublin government called him to the capital and refused him permission to proceed, probably on the grounds that his uncle's grant had become void, as, under its terms a permanent colony had to be established by March 1579. The four invasion attempts had cost the family over £10,000, and they continued as late as 1700 to petition the Crown for 'their' lands.

The decline of the Clannaboy O'Neills

For a while it seemed that the Clannaboy O' Neills had retained their hold on the area. Con McNiall Oge continued as lord of South Clannaboy, and on his death in 1589 he was succeeded by Con, the son of his nephew whom he had placed in the Great Ardes.

The Irish footsoldier sporting the traditional long fringe, or glib. *From* The Image of Ireland.

In 1601 Con made a mistake which cost him and his people dearly: he joined the rebellion of Hugh O'Neill, the head of the Tyrone O'Neills. The war impoverished Con and his lands, as the Crown forces destroyed his food supplies. For example, on the Castlereagh Hills two Crown officials witnessed:

...a most horrible spectacle of three children (whereof the eldest was not above ten years old) all eating and gnawing with their teeth the entrails of their dead mother, upon whose flesh they had fed twenty days past, and having eaten all from the feet upward to the bare bones, roasting it continually by a slow fire, were now coming to the eating of her said entrails in like sort roasted, yet not divided from the body, being as yet raw.

By 1603 Con was heavily in debt with the Crown rent on his land. His participation in the war also cost him the goodwill of those representing the English government in the area. In the words of a contemporary, 'he betrayed all the trust committed to him.' Sir Arthur Chichester, whose father had been killed by the Irish in the recent war, was particularly displeased with Con's betrayal, and in 1601 it was noted 'that Sir Arthur makes dainty [absolutely sure] to hang him before he hath your lordship's [the Lord Deputy's] warrant.' The hanging never did take place, but Con's days as lord of South Clannaboy were numbered.

Chichester got his revenge in 1603. Con was holding a party at Castlereagh and he sent his servants out to Belfast to bring in more wine. The servants encountered some English soldiers who took the wine. The servants were drunk themselves and were no match for the soldiers even

'We spare none of what quality or sex soever, and it hath bred much terror in the people.' Sir Arthur Chichester, the ruthless conqueror of Down, sworn enemy of Con O'Neill.

though they outnumbered them. They returned empty handed. When Con heard their story he flew into a rage and demanded they avenge the affront to him and themselves. The servants duly met the soldiers again and a fight ensued which resulted in some of the Irish being killed and the rest put to flight, all under the gaze of Con and his guests who had come out to watch. But one of the soldiers was also badly wounded and he died later that night. Within a week Con was arrested and charged with levying war against the Queen. He was thrown into prison at Carrickfergus Castle. Chichester intended that Con should lose his life and that he should receive his lands.

A contemporary described Con as a 'drunken, sluggish man', but his wife as a 'sharp nimble woman.' She calculated that it would be better that Con should preserve his life with only a part of his lands than risk a prejudiced trial in which he would almost certainly lose everything. She resolved to get help. She approached Hugh Montgomery, the laird of Braidstone in Ayrshire. He had trading connections with Carrickfergus and had sought to purchase lands in Ulster for some time. Moreover, he had connections at the court of King James I, himself also a Scot. Con's wife negotiated with Montgomery, agreeing that they would be happy with one third of the ancestral lands of South Clannaboy, and that he could have two thirds if he could procure a pardon for her husband. Montgomery agreed provided that she managed to get Con out of Chichester's hands and into his keeping.

The story begins to resemble fiction rather than fact at this stage. Montgomery arranged for a friend to court the gaoler's daughter, and Con's wife, on one of her visits, brought in a large rope concealed in a cheese. He let himself down the castle walls into a boat which Montgomery had arranged, and was ferried across Belfast Lough to Bangor, where he hid in a church steeple until it was safe to proceed to Ayrshire where he met with Montgomery and confirmed the bargain.

To obtain the pardon Montgomery was forced to use another Scot, James Hamilton, who was closer to the King than he was, and in return Montgomery had to agree that Hamilton should have half of his share. And so the lands of South Clannaboy were divided with a third each going to the Scots and the remaining third only to Con O'Neill; and so, ironically, the struggle for control that had begun between the Irish and the English finished with the Scots winning the biggest prize.

5

The Creation of the Scottish Town 1605-30

Con O'Neill was to be humiliated even further when the King specified how the lands of South Clannaboy were to be carved up. Hamilton and Montgomery were to have the coastal areas, with Con to be confined inland, providing the government with, in the words of Perceval-Maxwell, 'a safe beachhead in Ulster from which expeditions might be launched quickly to control rebellions that broke out elsewhere in the province'. Weekly markets were to be established in the main centres and Hamilton and Montgomery were to 'inhabit the said territory and lands with English and Scotch men.'

The Plantation historian Philip Robinson has remarked that:

Through these grants to Montgomery and Hamilton, foundations were laid for the most concentrated and substantial colony of British to arrive in Ulster during the first half of the seventeenth century.

Montgomery worked hard at trying to attract Scots to his new territories in north Down. His wealthiest tenants, men such as Thomas Nevin, David Boyd and Patrick Montgomery, were already landowners in Scotland. Being a landowner himself, he was able to attract tenants from his Scottish estates. In contrast to Hamilton, Montgomery deliberately tried to attract substantial tenants, who would create under them a class of sub-tenants, who would become, in time, gentlemen. Gillespie has noted that in the muster roll of 1630 a high percentage (20%) of the settlers on Montgomery's lands had snaphance weapons, a sign that they were men of some substance. However, it is likely that a considerable number of his and Hamilton's colonists were landless labourers or even criminals fleeing from the law in Scotland. The son of a minister who had accompanied some of the new immigrants, described them as:

...generally the scum of both nations, who for debt, or breaking or fleeing from justice, or seeking shelter, came hither hoping to be without fear of man's justice in a land where there was nothing, or but little, as yet, of the fear of God. And in a few years, there flocked such a multitude of people from Scotland that these northern counties of Down, Antrim, Londonderry, etc., were in a good measure planted, which had been waste before; yet most of the people... made up a body who seemed rather to flee from God in this enterprise than to follow their own mercy. Yet God followed them when they flew from him – albeit at first it must be remembered that they cared little for any church... Their carriage made them to be abhorred at home in their native land insomuch that going for Ireland was looked on as a miserable mark of a deplorable person – yea, it was turned into a proverb, and one of the worst expressions of disdain that could be invented was to tell a man that Ireland would be his hinder end.

We must allow for some exaggeration here as the author may wish to paint as black a picture as possible so as to make a favourable contrast between the settlers when they arrived and the community which existed when the source was written. The Scottish settlers came from Lanarkshire, Renfrewshire, Stirlingshire, Argyllshire, Bute, Arran, the Borders, Kirkcudbrightshire and Dumfries. People with the following surnames appear to have settled in the first dozen years: Adair, Agnew, Aicken, Allen, Anderson, Barkley, Bracklie, Boyle, Cathcart, Catherwood, Cowper, Craig, Crawford, Cunningham, Fraser, Harvey, Harper, Hunter, Kelso, Kennedy, Logan, Martin, Maxwell, McDougall, McIlveen, McMackene, Moore, Mowlen, Neill, Orr, Peacock, Sempill, Shaw, Spiere, Thompson, Williamson, Wilson, Wylie, and Wymis.

What made them leave Scotland? They were, in effect, pushed out of south-west Scotland by a rising population which had caused food prices

North Down was quickly transformed into a replica of the Scottish Lowlands. This map shows the planters' places of origin.

and rents to rise. When the collection of tithes was put back into the hands of the church in 1617, the increased efficiency of the new system also drove many out. James VI brought more authority into the Borders and Isles in the late sixteenth and early seventeenth centuries, and potential rebels were evicted to make way for loyal tenants. Even the strengths of the Scottish economy assisted the colonisation process. The expansion of trade, improvements in agriculture and a relatively long period of uninterrupted peace had allowed some to amass capital for which there was little scope for investment in Scotland.

But there were also 'pull' factors. Eastern Ulster offered considerable scope for investment. The land was cheap and fertile, with woods and fishing at hand. Sir Brian O'Neill's 'scorched earth' policy of 1572 and a repetition of the policy thirty years later, at the end of the Nine Year's War, had left the whole of Montgomery's lands under-utilised. According to the author of the *Montgomery Manuscripts*, there were less than thirty houses in the three parishes of Newtown, Donaghadee and Greyabbey.

The new colony was blessed with abundant harvests in 1606, 1607 and 1609, so that there was a surplus available to sell to the new colonists as they arrived. Linen and woollen manufacturing was also begun. Merchants from Belfast and Scotland were only too keen to supply the needs of the new community. Indeed there seems to have been a regular flow of travellers from Portpatrick through Donaghadee. In the summer months of 1607 merchants came several times a week from Stranraer as well, staying two or three hours and returning home the same day.

Blessed with this fine start, it was reported that Montgomery had, in 1610, one thousand able bodied men available for service in a militia should they be needed. It was estimated that there were 2,000 adult males in north Down as a whole in 1614, a figure that had increased by 40% sixteen years later. J.C. Beckett has said that 'within a generation a great part of both counties [Antrim and Down] had been transformed, in population and way of life, into a sort of extension of the Scottish lowlands.'

The second 'new town'

Montgomery had plenty to do. He arrived at what remained of Newtown in the spring of 1606, to find that the priory and abbey were roofless, and the tower house owned by Sir Brian was only a stump. Montgomery had wisely brought masons, carpenters and smiths with him, and temporary dwellings were soon erected. Montgomery made the old tower house habitable for himself while he made the creation of the town an urgent priority. The establishment of an urban community was, after all, more profitable than the letting of agricultural holdings; besides, as Sir Thomas Smith had pointed out, the fate of any new colony depended on the establishment of successful towns.

Montgomery turned his attention to the potential of the remains of the priory. During the the summer of 1606 he got the native Irish to cut timber for its repair. The planters contributed their money, skills and labour too, so that by the autumn of 1607 the chancel was turned into a church, and by 1618 the claustral walls on the south side were converted into a house for Montgomery's own family. A seventeenth century source spoke of:

...the walls, and other large additions of a gate house and office-houses, which made three sides of a quadrangle (the south side of the church being contiguous, made the fourth side), with coins and window frames and chimney pieces and funnels of freestone all covered: and the floors beamed with main oak timber and clad with boards; the roof with oak planks from his Lordship's own woods and slated with slates out of Scotland and the floors laid with fir deals out of Norway, the windows were fitly glazed and the edifice thoroughly furnished within.

However, not everyone viewed these changes as progress. A Franciscan friar, travelling in the area in 1643, noted:

At the town called Newtown, where there was even in my day, a monastery of St. Dominic, which some years ago, Mogumrious [Montgomery] the Scotchman

'Sir Hugh... brought with him divers artificers as smiths, masons, carpenters, etc.' The door of Newtown church, engraved for Montgomery.

converted into a secular dwelling; such is the propensity of impious heretics to obliterate all memory of what has been deemed sacred.

However, Montgomery's own religious preferences were far from being neglected. He brought some clergy with him from Scotland and because he took their tithes, he paid them stipends, gave them glebe land and arranged for them to have fees for marriages, christenings, burials and Easter offerings. The first minister in the town was a kinsman, Robert Montgomery.

The development of the town proceeded apace. In 1611 government inspectors reported:

Sir Hugh Montgomery, Knight, hath repaired part of the abbey of Newtone for his own dwelling and made a good town of a hundred houses or thereabouts, all peopled with Scots.

To crown his work, the town was created a borough in 1613 with Montgomery himself as its Provost (Mayor), and the power to send two representatives to the Irish parliament in Dublin.

Montgomery prospers

Sending representatives to Parliament was only a small part of the new Corporation's work, as there were only eight parliaments throughout the whole of the seventeenth century, each lasting only a few months.

The Corporation's main business was to run the town and it usually ran it the landlord's way. As well as a Provost, the charter named twelve other burgesses drawn from a list supplied by Montgomery himself – so much for local democracy! These wealthy townsmen constituted the Common Council of the Corporation. The Provost was to be elected annually – a formality of course – while the burgesses held office until their death, unless removed for misconduct or any other reasonable cause. When a vacancy occurred in the office of burgess it was filled by co-option.

This exclusive, self-electing oligarchy ran the town. The Corporation was empowered to acquire, hold and dispose of lands within the borough, make bye-laws and hold a court each Friday to deal with cases of debt, covenant, trespass, detention, contract and demand. Its fines and costs went to the magistrate – Montgomery. The Corporation could form merchant guilds which alone were entitled to issue licenses for merchants and craftsmen to carry on their business. The town's market was also under the control of the Corporation, the Provost being the clerk of the market, and entitled to collect tolls on every item sold. Market day in Newtown was Saturday, and special Fair Days were held on 23rd January, the second Saturday in March, 14th May, and 23rd September. Only the harvest fair survives today.

As landlord, Hugh Montgomery would have enjoyed other perquisites.

Young love in old Newtown. This date stone was placed in a house built for Hugh Montgomery, a kinsman of Sir Hugh Montgomery, who had brought his bride, Jean Herriot, from Scotland. The house stood on the site of the present NIE showroom in High Street.

The Plantation re-established Newtown as a market town. This photograph of the Market Square was taken about 1900.

There were the rents from the buildings and the town parks or fields which were part and parcel of each property. Town fields, which were considered necessary in case a poor harvest left no surplus available for the townsfolk, were regulated by the Corporation on the landlord's behalf. Montgomery cleverly gave the building plots in freehold, to attract the settlers, but gave the accompanying parks on a short lease, so that, at the end of the term, the tenant had to agree to a rent increase on the parks or else lose both the building and the parks. By these means Montgomery and his successors were able to increase the rents from 1s. per acre per year to 10s. by the end of the century – an average annual increase of 10%! The landlord would also create a 'pound' where stray animals were placed, and out of which they could only be redeemed by the payment of a fine. Today's Pound Street indicates its likely site. The manor mill was the landlord's, and farmers on his lands had to use it to have their grain milled. One was built in 1622 at the end of Mill Street, in what is now the housing estate between John Street and Mill Street.

Because of this variety of sources, Newtown and similar towns could generate a sizeable percentage of a landlord's total income. These sources of income, together with the rents from his land throughout north Down and the Ards Peninsula, raised the wealth – and prestige – of the Montgomery family. Sir Hugh was elected MP for County Down in 1613, made an Irish Privy Councillor and entrusted with the command of a company of horse and foot in 1614. In 1615 he was assessed to pay £100 toward the subsidy (a form of direct taxation on landowners) which would suggest an annual income of about £2,000, making him one of the three richest men in Ulster at that time. This was recognised when he was created a Viscount in 1622, Viscount Montgomery of the Great Ards. He also speculated in land in Clogher, County Tyrone, and purchased estates around Portpatrick between 1619 and 1628. In 1629 he was able to set up his second son, Sir James, as a landowner in Greyabbey with ten townlands there and elsewhere. At the time of his death in 1636 he was the fourth richest man in the two eastern Ulster counties of Antrim and Down with annual income from land and goods estimated at £2,615.

From plantation village to market town

Nove Ville had decayed so much since Norman times that the settlement of the early seventeenth century can almost be regarded as a new creation. Newtown was a fairly typical plantation market town of the period, having evolved quite quickly out of a 'plantation village'. Plantation villages tended to quickly flourish or die. Newtown grew rapidly. With a hundred houses in 1611, its likely population was over 500. It was one of the four largest towns in Antrim and Down.

Another central feature of the Jacobean plantation town was the Market Cross. Carrickfergus, Limavady, Omagh, Bellaghy, Comber and Coleraine all had them in their market place. Wooden market poles were found in Holywood, Bangor, Moneymore and Limavady. Newtownards has the only surviving seventeenth century Market Cross. It was built in 1636 several hundred yards to the north-west of Montgomery's house. By degrees the focal point of the town moved away from the fair green in front of Montgomery's house to the intersection of High Street and Movilla and Greenwell Streets, site of the Market House and the inn.

The role of Newtown was that of any other plantation town in east Ulster. It existed as a market for the produce of the surrounding townlands, as a provider of services, as a strong point in the event of rebellion, and as a means of civilising the countryside beyond. Instrumental in achieving the last and most wishful of these aims was Montgomery's establishment of a school. The headmaster was John Maclellan M.A. of Kirkudbright, who was to teach Latin, Greek and logic for an almost generous annual salary of twenty pounds, and he was assisted by two other teachers, one of English and arithmetic and another of music who also acted as choirmaster in the parish church. The school had a playing field for golf, football and archery.

Montgomery's County Down estates in 1622. His peerage reflected his new status as a wealthy landowner.

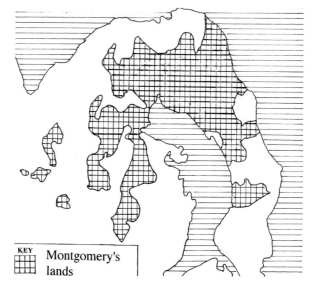

KEY
Montgomery's lands

Old Cross, 'Newtownards

Valentine's Series 26307

*The Market Cross,
Newtownards, c. 1900.
The town has Ulster's only
surviving seventeenth
century Market Cross.*

On Sundays the pupils would come into church led by the headmaster and would sit in the gallery behind the Provost and burgesses. The choirmaster succeeded in teaching the pupils to sing in parts, so that they would sing in harmony in church, and 'overruled any of the heedless vulgar, who learned thereby (at least) to forbear disturbing the congregation with their clamorous tones'. Maclellan occasionally supplied the pulpits of Presbyterian clergy in the county. He was described as:

...a most straight and zealous man; he knew not what it was to be afraid in the cause of God and was early acquainted with God and his ways...

He went on to be the minister in his native Kirkudbright, and to play a prominent part in the famous Scottish General Assembly of 1638. Later in his career he twice revisited Newtown as part of a pastoral mission sent to Ulster by the Scottish General Assembly.

The zenith of the life of the plantation market town was probably the period around 1630, and this may too have been a turning point in Montgomery's own life. His first wife, who herself had done much to further the plantation, died at the end of the 1620s. In contrast, Montgomery's second wife spent only a few months in Newtownards: she refused to live there and returned to Scotland where Montgomery visited her each summer.

When Montgomery died in May 1636 his body was embalmed and kept in a 'turret' until the funeral in September 1636. The night before, it was carried a mile outside the town and kept in a tent. The following

A lordly funeral of the seventeenth century. Montgomery was buried with great pomp in 1636.

morning an extremely elaborate ceremonial procession wound its way from the tent to the church, formerly the priory. The most eminent of the 'great and the good' in attendance included the Bishop of Down and Connor, the Dean of Clogher, Viscount Clandeboye, the Earl of Eglinton and a number of Ulster and Scottish landed gentry. Local figures, called 'servants' by Montgomery's grandson, the author of the *Montgomery Manuscripts*, but probably chief tenants, included Hugh Kennedy of Greengraves, John Boyd of Drumfad, William Catherwood of Ballyvester, Hugh Montgomery, the seneschal of the town, and Hugh Montgomery of Grangee. Mourners described as 'gentlemen and esquires' who lived locally were John Cunningham of Newtown, Hugh Kennedy of Drumawhey, William Montgomery of Ballyhaft. Montgomery left a legacy to build an extension and church steeple, which were erected within a few months of his death.

The second Viscount took up residence at Newtown House in 1636. His father had employed a page, Edward Betty, or Beattie, who was a dwarf, and the son had been instructed to keep the man. He must have been a character in the town in those days. The author of the *Montgomery Manuscripts* describes him as follows:

He was of blooming damask rose complexion; his hair was of a shining gold colour, with natural ring-like curls hanging down and dangling to his breast, and so exact in the symmetry of his body and limbs to his stature, that no better shape could be desired in a well carved statue. His wit was answerable to what his comely face might promise, and his cunning no less.

In the late 1630s, when the second Viscount brought his wife to live there and ladies again started to visit Newtown House, the man was frequently mistaken by them for one of the second Viscount's children: they would often take him on their knees and kiss and cuddle him. The pretence was maintained by the man and the hostess, the Viscountess, long enough for the guests to be thoroughly embarrassed when the man's true age was revealed to them!

So ended the brief golden age of the Scots market town. The *Montgomery Manuscripts* idealistically record that:

...everybody minded their trades, and the plough, and the spade, building, and setting fruit trees, etc., in orchards and gardens, and by ditching in their grounds. The old women spun and the young girls plied their nimble fingers at knitting – and everybody was innocently busy. Now the golden peaceable age renewed, no strife , no contention, querulous lawyers, or Scottish or Irish feuds, between clans and families and surnames disturbing the tranquillity of those times and the towns and temples erected with other great works done...

It was to be the calm before the storm.

6

Colony in Crisis 1630-60

'Certain factious and irregular puritans'

During the 1630s the government and the Scots settlers in Newtownards fell out. At the commencement of the settlement the weakness and poverty of the Church of Ireland, and its small membership, had allowed the new settlers gradually to introduce the Presbyterian form of worship into the areas into which they had migrated. This was not formally permitted. As early as 1621, the Archbishop of Armagh complained that:

...certain factious and irregular puritans, which I have discovered of late to be settled in the lands of Sir Hugh Montgomery, do entertain the Scottish discipline and liturgy so strongly that they offer wrong to the Church government here established.

On Thomas Wentworth's arrival as Lord Deputy in 1633, the government cracked down. A Court of High Commission was created to enforce new church discipline and the local bishop forced 'Presbyterian' clergy out of several parishes. The town's minister, the Rev. David Kennedy, was excommunicated by the Court of High Commission. In 1638 the bishop denounced the churchwardens of Ards and Clandeboye, because their churches were 'kept no better than hog sties' and that they were 'disorderly men, the very ring-leaders of the separation.'

Many of Charles I's subjects throughout the British Isles found these changes unwelcome but it was in Scotland that resistance to them was most passionate. There, many signed a Covenant pledging to oppose them. Their resistance fuelled Ulster's unrest. It was, after all, a Scottish colony: by the early 1630s there may have been as many as 1,500 Scots on Montgomery's lands. Many fled to Scotland rather than take an oath of allegiance to the episcopal church (nicknamed the 'Black Oath'). Matters were made worse by the quartering of troops in County Down. The harvest was bad in 1639 and what little grain there was had to be shared with the army. By 1640 the population had declined to the point where all of the harvest could not be brought in. It seemed that the whole colony was in danger of collapse.

The Lord Deputy, Thomas Wentworth, who did not find Newtown's Presbyterians as obedient as this scribe.

While the Covenant was signed in Holywood, it is not known if it was actually signed at Newtown. Here moderation prevailed and the majority apparently followed the lead given them by the Montgomery family. It may seem like a contradiction, but the Montgomerys were both Presbyterian and royalist. Their position was in some ways delicate and ambiguous. For example, the second Viscount helped to administer the 'Black Oath', but his Presbyterianism did not go down well in Dublin Castle. Wentworth said of the second Viscount, and his wife, 'I might hope personally very well of him, were it not for his lady and other of his friends who are extremely passionately set on the Scottish way of divine worship.'

Wentworth's point is well illustrated by the following story. When the Bishop of Down was on his deathbed in 1635 he was attended by his physician, Dr. Patrick Maxwell. When the doctor asked his patient what ailed him the bishop replied, 'It's my conscience, man!' to which the doctor answered, 'I have no cure for that!' Maxwell was also the first Viscount's doctor and when he told him the story at Newtown House, the old Viscount recommended the doctor not to repeat it anywhere else, whereupon his daughter-in-law, who was made of sterner stuff, exclaimed, 'No man shall get that report suppressed, for I shall bear witness of it to the glory of God, who hath smitten that man for suppressing Christ's witnesses', i.e. the Presbyterian clergy.

Montgomery is threatened

Though the Montgomery family owned the town and over twenty townlands in the parish of Newtown, the position of this bulwark of the plantation was actually very insecure.

The Montgomery family had to fend off a series of attacks in the courts, any one of which could have ruined them. First came the 'troubles and costly toils' offered by the great-nephew of Sir Thomas Smith who had pressed his claim from 1610-1612. This was followed by a bitter legal wrangle between Montgomery and Hamilton over the extent of their territories. Hamilton accused Montgomery of obtaining advantageous deals with Con O'Neill as the latter parted with his estates. The dispute raged, draining the energies and purses of both men – the action cost Montgomery £1,400 – and this, together with the bad 'press' it generated, undoubtedly weakened the plantation process.

This damaging legal wrangle becomes all the more ironic when we consider how close the Hamilton and Montgomery families became in the 1640s. The third Viscount Montgomery and the Earl of Clanbrassil became close friends, indeed it is related that one night while he slept at Newtown House, a ghost was alleged to have ripped off the Earl's shirt leaving only his collar and cuffs. The Scots called these spirits 'broonies' or 'brownies'. They played pranks and appreciated having clothes or food left out for them. A house that had visits from them was considered lucky. When the Earl awoke next morning and discovered his loss he was reluctant to rise. At last his nephew, Hans Hamilton of Hamilton's Bawn, came in to rouse him. The Earl pleaded with him not to tell his host of the incident as he found it all to be a great embarrassment. He persuaded his nephew to lend him a shirt but as the Earl was a fat man it did not 'reach his Lordship's navel' and he had to spend the rest of the morning being entertained in these uncomfortable conditions. The remains of the shirt were later found neatly wrapped and placed in a chamber-pot!

However, the main agent destabilising the Montgomerys' position was

James Hamilton, Montgomery's neighbour and adversary.

– paradoxically enough – the Crown. In 1636, on the death of the first
Viscount Montgomery, his son and heir found that his own rents to the
Crown were increased by 320%. He was forced to pay a renewal charge
of £103.17s.8d. and had his tenure converted to a less favourable form.
His situation of course was worsened by the fall in rents from his tenants
due to the troubles of the late 1630s. To meet his outgoings he had to sell
all his Scottish lands, and by 1640 was unable to secure any credit.

Especially sinister for Montgomery was the government's campaign to
improve the income of the church by recovering its ancient lands. By
1639 he was having to fight in court to secure his tenure to those lands
which were formerly church lands. Of course, this also made his tenants
feel insecure. If the landlord lost his lands, what security was there for
their leases? By the end of the 1630s both the great and the humble had
been alienated by government policies.

The community at war

In 1641 the storm clouds that had been gathering for decades finally burst
into a full-scale rebellion followed by civil war, then invasion by Scottish,
and finally, English forces. The whole settlement was thrown into jeopardy.

In October 1641 certain of the much put upon native Ulster chiefs rose
in rebellion. Within a month both English and Scottish colonists in Ulster
were under attack.   In desperation the Bishop of Down wrote to
Montgomery from Lisburn seeking help from Newtown:

> I pray your lordship to think of some course to be taken for making head against
> them... We cannot hold out long without help from those parts which your
> lordship commands, so in great haste I beseech Almighty God to bless your
> Lordship and to be our deliverer.

The government decided to send a Scottish army to Ulster. While
negotiations continued for this army, Charles commissioned leading planters
to raise forces in his name. Viscount Montgomery was made a Colonel,
and mustered a thousand foot and five troop of horse, largely at his own
expense. This local force was to hold out until the Scottish reinforcements
arrived.

Montgomery raised this militia from his own tenants (giving them an
allowance off their rents), and from the refugees who crowded into
Newtown. At first they were armed only with scythes, pitchforks, sticks
and a few pikes, which shows how successful Wentworth's disarming of
Ulster in the 1630s had been, for the Montgomery estate had been heavily
armed in 1630, having over a thousand weapons in total. The Viscount
bought enough muskets to arm his whole new regiment. As soon as he
had his force in some sort of order, Montgomery obliged the bishop by
garrisoning Lisburn. Then he and his brother returned home:

...to take order for securing the best we could the of the rest of the country since which time we have been in perpetual action, sometimes in one part of the county and sometimes in another, and have kept afoot, at our own charges, three or four hundred foot and two or three troop of horse, besides the drawing together oft times of our whole tenantry... The charges we have hitherto borne, being upon such a sudden, has so exhausted us that we are no longer able to endure it. Beside that, there is no rent to be had now from our people at this time.

The Newtown area was also under threat. Another Hugh Montgomery, son of the Earl of Eglinton, wrote on December 17th, 1641 from Comber:

Except speedy assistance be sent from Scotland, they will find but few of their countrymen to welcome them, for we are few and very naked for want of arms to withstand them... The rebels burn and kill every other night within a mile or two of us; neither can we help it; for what they do is in the night, and if we send out a party they have sentinels on all the hills and will not stand but retire to the woods. We are informed that they divide themselves in three: Sir Phelim O'Neill in two, whereof one part is appointed for Lisburn and the other for us; and Sir Con Magennis and MacCartan for Down.

On New Year's Eve 1641, the second Viscount wrote from Mount Alexander, outside Comber, clearly now a frontier settlement:

We are kept exceeding busy with the rebels who burn and kill within a mile and a half of this place, insomuch as from Newry to this, there is not a Scots or English dweller - this being thirty four miles; nor from Downpatrick to Killyleagh, nor from thence hither.

The long anticipated attack finally occurred in January 1642. A force of native Irish advanced from Killinchy and were met by the second Viscount's forces at Battletown outside Comber in February 1642 where they were repulsed. This was enough to stay the Irish and a stand-off was reached in north Down.

Help arrived at last in the form of Monro's ten thousand strong Scottish army which began to arrive in Carrickfergus from April 1642. One, and possibly two, regiments of this army, commanded by the Earl of Eglinton were stationed in and around Newtown. As there were over a thousand soldiers in each of Monro's regiments, the town must have been bustling with troops.

But there was a price to be paid for their reassuring presence. Payment of the army was always delayed and on January 10th, 1645 a petition was sent from the inhabitants of Newtown to the authorities in Scotland stating that:

The whole army for these seven weeks past has been eating the meal out of our mouths and now they are fallen upon that should sow the ground, which has occasioned in many parts the giving over of ploughing.

These losses could be offset by the spoils of war. In the spring and summer of 1642 the forces in Newtown joined with others in Lisburn and saw action in Kilwarlin Wood (on the south-west corner of Lough Neagh), Loughbrickland and Newry. They returned through the districts of Kinelarty and Lecale plundering four thousand cattle from the native Irish *en route*. An Englishman related the sequel to this plunder:

When the cows were to be divided many of them were stole away into the Ards and Clandeboye on the last night, and the goods so sneaked away by the [Ulster] Scots that the troop[er]s got just nothing and the foot very little which gave them too just a cause to mutiny, insomuch that I think it will be hard to get them out to march with the [Ulster] Scots again who will have both the credit and the profit of whatsoever is done or had.

Small wonder that the government in Dublin complained in June that the Ulster Scots 'do export cattle in mighty numbers'!

The second Viscount had little time to enjoy his victories. He fell ill and his son, Hugh, was sent for from England. Before he made the journey to Newtown, he called on King Charles I for a few days at Oxford. Charles had heard from his physician, the famous William Harvey, that

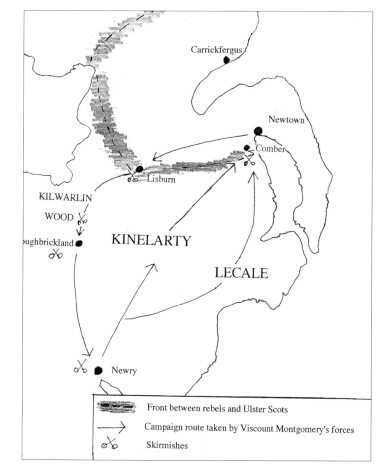

The 1642 campaign in east Down.

Charles I received Hugh Montgomery at his court-in-exile in Oxford, during the Civil War.

the young man had a peculiar feature. As a result of a childhood accident he had a large hole in his side through which his heart could be seen. The king said, 'Sir, I wish I could perceive the thoughts of some of my nobility's hearts as I have seen your heart.' Montgomery replied, 'I assure Your Majesty before God here present and this company, it shall never entertain any thought against your concerns; but be always full of dutiful affection and steadfast resolution to serve your Majesty.' His pledges were to be well tested in the future.

He then resumed his journey and was at his father's side when he died on November 15th, 1642. The dead man was just forty-five years old. Hugh, aged only twenty-two, immediately took command of his father's forces and estates as the third Viscount Montgomery of the Great Ards.

Wanted: 'two grave and learned ministers'

In the wake of the success of the Scots army came the establishment of Presbyterianism. Presbyterian clergy accompanied the troops of Munro's army as chaplains and met as a Presbytery in Carrickfergus in 1642, urging others to join.

Viscount Montgomery responded to this and played an important part in arranging to have Presbyterian clergy in the town. Earlier in the year the town had experienced the ministry of the Rev. Thomas Peebles when he served as chaplain to the Earl of Eglinton's regiment, stationed in the town. Accordingly a Session, or eldership, was ordained in 1642, with Maclellan, the former school principal, attending the ordination ceremony. All they needed now was a preacher. On July 20th, 1643 Montgomery wrote to the Scottish General Assembly expressing his regret at the lack of a 'lively ministry' in the town, though thanking them for 'sending pastors to this place by turns'. He said that there was 'a remnant of well-disposed Christians yet preserved alive by the mercy of God in these parts, yet the outward means of their salvation is altogether wanting', and concluded by begging them:

...to make choice of some two grave and learned ministers, of good and holy lives and conversations, and... recommend and send over to this country, the one for the parish church of Newtown and the other for my regiment, and by the assistance of God, they shall not want competent stipends.

Montgomery's first choice was John Greg, but Greg was already minister in Carrickfergus. So as an inducement, Montgomery granted the ministry a townland on the edge of the town (now called Gregstown). His overtures were successful. In 1650 Greg accepted a call to Newtown. It would seem that Newtown was one of the first places in Ulster to build a meeting house in which Presbyterians could worship.

Montgomery's work in nurturing Presbyterianism earned him praise

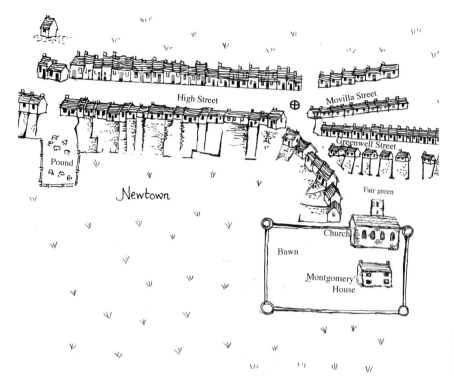

High Street

Movilla Street

Greenwell Street

Pound

Newtown

Fair green

Bawn

Church

Montgomery's House

Three streets and a church, a bawn and flankers: an artist's impression of mid seventeenth centuy Newtown.

from the clergy of that denomination but it also exposed the paradox of his position. As long as the troubles in Ireland were seen as separate from those in Great Britain it was possible for the third Viscount to be both a royalist, privately, and publicly fight with Monro's Scots army against the Irish insurgents. But the time was fast approaching when it would be impossible to espouse both royalism and Presbyterianism.

However this period of tension had its lighter moments too. The wedding of the third Viscount to his first wife in December 1648 was celebrated over several days. The bride displayed a scarf, ring and gloves as prizes and several men had to joust for them 'on horseback, with lances at their thighs, running at full career'. The author of the *Montgomery Manuscripts* records that it was a 'sight never beheld by any of the Ladies or any of the attendants before that time' and that Captain George Montgomery 'broke his lance against the garden wall at high speed'. These private festivities, which took place in the gardens behind the church and Newtown House, would have been accompanied by parties and bonfires throughout the parish.

Newtown's rebellion

The execution of Charles I on January 30th, 1649 caused a massive wave of royalist sympathy. In addition, the new Commonwealth regime in England sought complete toleration for most types of Protestant religious groups. This antagonised Presbyterians both in Scotland and Ireland, who urged a national church for everyone on Presbyterian lines. These and other sentiments prompted a rather shaky royalist-Presbyterian rising in

69

Scotland and Ulster against England's new republican regime.

Montgomery was at the forefront of this movement. In February 1649 he drew up a declaration stating support for the Covenant. This was approved by the Presbytery of Ulster and mobilised important sections of Ulster Scots opinion behind the royalist rising. King and Kirk were together again and, given his beliefs, we should not be surprised to learn that Montgomery became accepted as leader of the royalists of Ulster. A great party was held in Newtown to celebrate the proclamation of Charles I's son as 'Charles II'. The author of the *Montgomery Manuscripts*, then a pupil at Newtown School, describes the festivities:

His majesty Charles II was proclaimed king in Newtown, where I saw the claret flow (in abundance) from the spouts of the market cross and catched in hats and bowls by who could or would; the noise of six trumpets sounding levitts [or reveille], drums beating, the soldiers discharging three volleys a piece, as the brass guns also at his Lordship's house did at the healths drank to the three royal brothers; and at night bonfires in the street and illuminations of candles in the windows, and good fellows in the houses with the soldiers (to whom a largesse [generous bonus payment] was given) increasing their mirth and joy by good liquor.

The celebrations over, Viscount Montgomery proceeded to gather his forces. The author of the *Montgomery Manuscripts* described the occasion:

I remember to see great clutter of mustering and exercising of armed men at Newtown; and my father, Sir James Montgomery, going often to our Viscount and many officers also resorting hither and 'the King' and 'Colonel Monk' was in every man's mouth almost every minute.

A visitor related that there was 'a Council of War at Newtown to see what course they should take with the country and to settle all decisions amongst themselves'. Newtown was the centre of royalist rebellion in Ulster.

Viscount Montgomery took possession of most of the towns of Ulster. When Charles II, then in exile, heard of Montgomery's successes he sent an envoy, Sir Lewis Dives, to Newtown to confirm his appointment as Commander-in-Chief of the royalist forces in Ulster.

Unfortunately the King had already given this command by mistake to another. Inevitably, the two men came into conflict and Montgomery was forced to proclaim his royalism in public rather more than he wished to, or was politic. Montgomery's loyal declarations unsettled the movement's Presbyterian rank and file, and when it became clear that his master Charles was as interested in wooing Irish Catholics as Scottish Presbyterians, their concern turned to disillusion.

The final straw came in June 1649. In that month Montgomery placed Belfast and Carrickfergus under the control of royalist garrisons as he could no longer be sure of the loyalty to the King of the Presbyterians who

were in control of these towns. His true colours had now been revealed.
The alliance fell apart.

Immediately the Presbytery of Ulster warned Montgomery that:

The Lord will visit your family with sudden ruin and irreparable desolation, for
you have been so grand an instrument to destroy the work of God here. We
exhort your lordship, in the name of the living God, to whom you must give an
account, in haste to forsake that infamous and ungodly course you are now in, and
adhere to your former professions, otherwise all the calamities that will ensue will
be laid at your door. The Lord himself and all the faithful will set themselves
against you and we will testify of your unfaithfulness to all the world, so long as
the Lord will give us strength.

THE
Right Honorable
and vndaunted Warrior
OLIVER CROMWELL
Lo: Governour of
IRELAND

*'Cromwell came over,'
wrote a contemporary, 'and
like a lightning passed
through the land.' The
defeated royalist leader,
Montgomery, surrendered
to him, abjectly and in
person, in 1649.*

Just in case he missed the point, they followed this up three days later with a second blast:

You have already involved yourself already so far in the guilt of unfaithfulness to the cause of God and your own subscriptions that we cannot but testify against the course you are in, and denounce judgement upon your person, family and all your party, till the Lord persuade your heart to return.

The Presbytery forbade anyone to obey him, and by degrees their prophecy, or curse, began to be fulfilled. Montgomery was routed by English republican forces at Dundalk, and again near Lisburn in December 1649. The eldest son of the seneschal of Newtown was captured and shot, and Viscount Montgomery escaped only to surrender himself abjectly and in person to Oliver Cromwell. The royalist rising was over.

Montgomery paid a high price for his leadership of the failed rising. More royalist than a Presbyterian, he was allowed to return home in 1652 if he promised not to leave the country or act against Parliament. He was also required to pay a crippling fine. But the government was worried that the former royalist leader, once re-established in the royalist centre of Newtown, would renew his troublemaking and so they insisted that he move to Dublin. He spent the next few years in various prisons throughout Ireland. His health deteriorated, his wife's too: she died in 1655 at the age of twenty four.

Montgomery eventually returned home in 1656. The English government understandably remained deeply suspicious of the Ulster Scots. Too many still harboured loyalties in varying degrees to either the King, Presbyterianism or Scotland – some to all three – to enable them to be trusted. However, in a pioneering attempt to build consensus a new Lord Deputy, Henry Cromwell, convened a religious conference in Dublin to discuss how religious differences might be lessened. The Rev. John Greg[1], Presbyterian minister of Newtown, was one of only three Ulster Presbyterian ministers to be invited.

And so three turbulent decades came to an end. Wentworth's persecution, the 1641 rising and the collapse of the royalist rebellion, had severely taxed the young settlement. Economically and demographically this appears to have been a period of stagnation. The 'census' of 1659 records that the population of the town was 146 adult males (87 Scots and 59 Irish), and in the town and parish as a whole, there were 332 adults (207 Scots

---

1 Greg was credited with mysterious powers. He was said to have divined the location of the famous Kirkdonnel well 'in a dream'. The waters from this well (now in Knock Golf Course, Dundonald) were widely believed to have miraculous powers, and 'multitudes' flocked to it every summer from miles around, sometimes staying for several days, to drink its bitter-tasting waters. Eventually, the man who owned the land it stood on became so 'oppressed' by the numbers in attendance, he closed it off, ending the traffic.

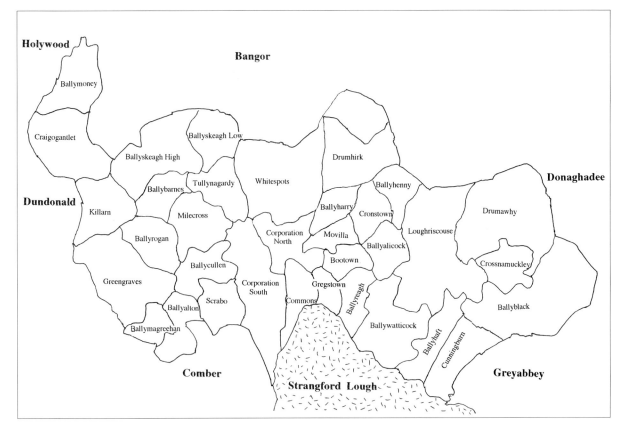

and 125 Irish). We have to be careful with this source as it would appear that it numbered only individuals who were liable for taxation. Nevertheless, it seems likely that the rapid growth of the early part of the century had not continued. How can this be explained?

An obvious explanation was the tension and conflict which characterised the area for over thirty years. These conditions dissuaded would-be immigrants. But there were also economic factors at work. An important function of a town was to enrich its landlord and if he did not re-invest, the result could be the impoverishment of the town itself. The political involvement of the Montgomerys reduced their ability and opportunities for investment.

In addition, people did not always stay in towns like Newtown. Leases were short, early plantation tenants were mobile and had yet to develop binding ties of family and place. Also, the government in Scotland, alarmed at the drain on resources, discouraged emigration, and Montgomery experienced difficulties in recruiting settlers after the mid 1630s. Some of Montgomery's problems were his own making. Many landowners in the Ulster Plantation were forbidden to take native Irish as tenants. The first Viscount had gone further, forbidding his own lessees from taking native Irish as sub-tenants: any who did lost their leases. Some of these tenants may have moved on to more easy-going landlords.

Capital too was in short supply. To these difficulties were added the shortage of cattle, horses and coin, and harvest failures in the 1630s.

The parish of Newtown by townland (with adjacent parishes); and below, its population of British and Irish, according to the 'Census' of 1659.

Townland	English & Scots	Irish
Cunyngburne	4	3
Ballyblack	6	7
Ballywitticock	5	5
Ballerea	4	6
Drumchay	3	6
Loghrescow	8	6
Movilla	10	5
Ballyhoney	4	1
Drumhirk	11	4
Couleck	8	0
Milecross	10	5
Ballyhary	4	0
Ballybairnes	1	1
Ballyskeagh	11	2
Ballymoney	4	0
Carrickgantelan	4	2
Killerny	4	0
Gnonegranes	6	4
Ballymagwoghan	1	2
Ballequillan	6	2
Scrabo	4	3

73

Confidence in the new colony was undermined. It would be interesting to know what role the Catholic Irish played in Newtown society for they stayed on in sizeable numbers. Unfortunately lack of evidence prevents us from drawing any conclusions about their position and attitudes, except that Montgomery's leasing policy suggests that they did not rent land. What was certain was that a period of peace and stability was required to consolidate and expand the new colony. It would be another thirty years before such conditions were to be enjoyed.

7

'An Improving Place' 1660-1790

Montgomery campaigned for the restoration of Charles II, and meetings to secure the restoration in Ireland were held in Newtown. As a result, when Charles ascended the throne in 1660, Montgomery's fortunes were totally reversed and he was created the first Earl Mount-Alexander. He was able to enjoy his final years in peace and prosperity. It was said:

His lordship lived in grandeur, highly esteemed and respected by all and for his ripe judgement appearing when he spoke at the House of Lords or at the Council board.

There was an unusual postscript to the political turmoil of the previous decades, involving the town of Newtown. Colonel Thomas Blood had served the King in England during the Civil War and afterwards settled near Dublin. His brother-in-law had converted him to Presbyterianism, and when the new monarch began deposing Presbyterian ministers from their Ulster parishes and restoring Catholics to their lands, Blood became a leading member of a conspiracy to overthrow the Irish government, headed at the time by the Duke of Ormonde.

Blood came to Ulster to see if he could enlist the support of Greg and the other threatened Presbyterian ministers for the 'cause on foot for God's glory', as he called it. On receiving intelligence that Blood had reached Newtown on his recruiting drive, Ormonde asked the Earl of Mount-Alexander to apprehend him. The Earl ordered his troops to have Blood arrested but he narrowly escaped.

As a precaution against any possible rising, the government rounded up all the Presbyterian ministers in the Ards area in June 1663, and kept them in Carlingford. When the authorities suspected that Blood may have actually conferred with Greg whilst at Newtown, the minister was taken to Dublin where he languished in prison for some time. On his release he continued as Presbyterian pastor, and possibly, given the climate of the times, a local folk hero, until his death in 1670.

The last years of the Montgomerys

The Earl of Mount-Alexander died in 1663. His funeral, like that of his grandfather in 1636, was attended by many of the leading figures in Ulster society. Mourners identified as leading figures within the parish of Newtown were Major William Buchanan of Scrabo Hill, Hugh Montgomery of Ballyskeagh, J. Montgomery of Tullynagardy and William Shaw, the Provost.

The funeral sermon was preached by Dr. Rust, the Dean of Down. He applauded the fact that the deceased had risen above the prejudices of his early upbringing, i.e. Presbyterianism, and had proved himself a man of principle in 1649 when he defied both government and Presbytery in his loyalty to the Crown. The author of the *Montgomery Manuscripts* says that the common people, or the 'vulgar', who were admitted to the church that day found the prayers a 'novelty' and the 'learned pious sermon' 'rare'. He meant that they were either Catholics or Presbyterians!

The town's growth was slow over the next sixty years: even by 1720 the adult male population was probably still less than two hundred. One reason for this slow growth in the early years was the extreme youth of the second Earl, who was only twelve years old when he inherited, so that it was not possible for the town to receive leadership and investment from its new landlord. In 1664 a great fire broke out in Newtown House and the building and its contents were destroyed, a disaster attributed, as ever, to the negligence of the servants. In 1672, when the second Earl came of age, he found that his affairs were in total confusion.

The young Earl found that, despite his efforts to have his affairs put in order, a £1000 debt of his father's remained outstanding. This had been borrowed from Dr. Colvill, a wealthy Anglican clergyman, to pay the fine required to get the first Earl's estates back in 1652. Now, twenty years later, the debt had to be paid. The young heir had already borrowed £2000 in the hope of obtaining a favourable ruling in a case in Chancery but the case fell through in November 1674, and he found himself in even deeper trouble. So, he sold most of the estate on November 12th, 1675 for the sum of £10,640 to Captain Robert Colvill, and retired to Mount-Alexander. Robert Colvill was Dr. Colvill's heir and already owned a large estate, Mount-Colvil, in Galgorm near Ballymena. And so, after seventy years as its masters, the history of the Montgomery family largely parts company with the history of Newtown.

Colvill and the crisis of 1689–91

Robert Colvill was one of the richest men in the county but he was an outsider and, according to the values of the time, a *parvenu*. He was also an enigma to his contemporaries, as the following extracts from contemporary sources show:

I have scarce ever known a man more variously spoken of, than this Sir Robert. Some very good men give him a great character; others, as good, shake their heads, and say they know not what to make of his principles. All agree that he has a great interest [wealth and power]; that is, a great estate. Some, perhaps, envy him for that; and some hate him for the meanness of his birth; indeed they say he has come from a very vile beginning. Sir Robert Colvill is looked upon as a very great favourer of the fanatics, though he goes to [the Established] church himself: he is a man of... at least £3000 per annum in the north of this kingdom, and was for several years of the Privy Council, till the change upon his majesty's coming to the Crown

The 'majesty' referred to here was James II, the first Catholic to become monarch for over a century. James's succession, in 1685, caused disquiet in Protestant Ulster. Whatever Colvill's feelings about the new King and his policy of de-Protestantising Ireland's army and administration, Colvill pursued an independent political line, acting for a time as a mediator between the Dublin government, headed by the Catholic Earl of Tyrconnell, and the Protestant gentry of the North. It is easy to see why contemporaries found Colvill hard to fathom. Though conservatively Presbyterian in matters of religion, he was apparently liberal in politics, hence his attempts at mediation. These, however, brought little success and earned him only the coolness of his neighbours. The extent of Colvill's isolation became apparent during the crisis of 1688-91. By the middle of 1688 the Protestants of Ulster feared, with some justification, that the government intended to overturn the plantation.

These fears appeared to be confirmed by an anonymous, semi-literate letter addressed to Lord Mount-Alexander, which was found on the streets of Comber on December 3rd, 1688. The 'Comber Letter', which some historians have dismissed as a joke or a hoax, and others have seen as an attempt to inflame Protestant opinion, warned of an imminent Catholic uprising. Whatever the intention, the letter was taken seriously. Copies were widely circulated, causing considerable alarm. In January 1689 the state of feeling was such that a junta of five Protestant gentry met at Comber to plan resistance to James II, and proclaim their loyalty to William and Mary of Orange, then on the eve of being declared joint monarchs in Britain. At first Colvill was not invited to take part, although the Covenanters pressed for his inclusion.

Tyrconel arming ỹ Papists in Ireland.

Richard Talbot, Earl of Tyrconnell, depicted as a knave on an English playing card of c.1690.

Colvill, however, was eventually admitted to the Association, perhaps as a result of the lobbying of the celebrated Scots Covenanter minister, David Houston, who was living in Newtown at the time (possibly at Colvill's invitation) and was in regular contact with Lord Mount-Alexander. In February 1689, at his own expense, Colvill raised a regiment from his tenants around Newtown which joined the confederate forces of Antrim and Down under the overall command of the second Earl of Mount-Alexander.

NO SURRENDER. REM.1690

The men of the Newtown area were at war again. Their Williamite 'army' set out to meet a large and well-equipped professional force of Jacobite soldiers coming north from Dublin. On March 14th, 1689, the two sides clashed at Dromore, the north Down contingent arriving too late to stop a complete rout of the Protestants, a debacle which became known as the 'Break of Dromore'. Sir Robert Colvill, the Earl of Mount-Alexander and most of the rest of the province's Protestant gentry promptly fled to England and at this critical time in the town's history it was left leaderless.

The government moved quickly to fill the power vacuum. Tyrconnell ordered Lord Iveagh's Catholic militia to take over the towns of north-eastern Ulster, as their regular troops had been sent north to Londonderry. Reid, the Presbyterian historian, describes Iveagh's force as:

...composed of rude and half-civilised natives from the mountains of Mourne [who] were stationed in the several towns. Their unauthorised and oppressive exactions were for a time borne in silence; the people having few arms and being destitute of a leader.

One such town was Newtown and fearing that the occupying Mourne men were about to plunder it (possibly as revenge for a similar action perpetrated on them by Newtown men in 1642), a soldier, Captain Henry Hunter, raised a force in Donaghadee and headed for Newtown in an attempt to oust Iveagh's troops. The garrison, which came out to meet his band at Cunningburn, was put to flight and the town was saved.

The early eighteenth century town

The Williamite victory at the Boyne ushered in a long period of stability, and something of a building boom. We know that by the early 1690s the town had developed as far as No.10 Mill Street as the date, 1693, can be seen at the back of the house. On the site of Newtown House, the old home of the Montgomery family, Sir Robert Colvill built a considerable home for himself:

[He] has from the foundation built up one double roofed house, stables, coach-houses and all other necessary and convenient edifices for brewing, baking, washing, hunting, hawking, pleasure-rooms and pigeon houses etc., with inner outer and back courts; and a special olitory[?], fruit and pleasant flower gardens.

High Street was still the main thoroughfare and, beyond Pound Lane,

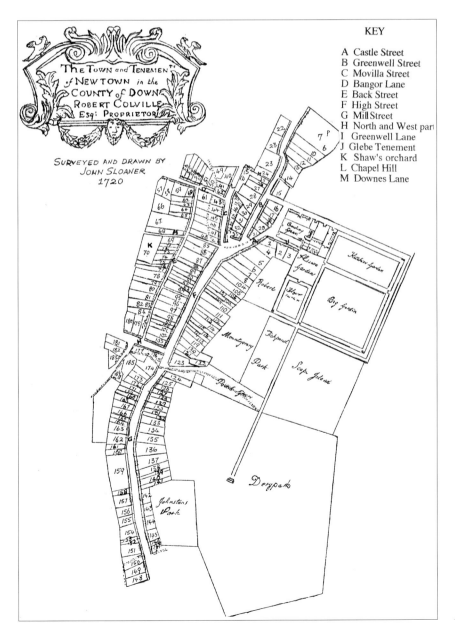

KEY

A Castle Street
B Greenwell Street
C Movilla Street
D Bangor Lane
E Back Street
F High Street
G Mill Street
H North and West part
I Greenwell Lane
J Glebe Tenement
K Shaw's orchard
L Chapel Hill
M Downes Lane

Plan of Newtown, 1720.

became Mill Street which ended at the mill. Running parallel to High Street was Back Street which stretched from about Price's Lane to near Mary Street and may have been the town's poorest quarter, lived in by labourers and servants. The general impression received by visitors, however, was one of relative prosperity. Harris, a visitor in 1744, remarked that, 'The town is well paved and has many neat houses in it.'

The Market Cross always caught the attention of visitors. In 1701 it was 'painted and gilded' and at that time was the place where 'are made public (with the town solemnities) all proclamations that come from our Chief Governor [the Viceroy] and their own town business which needs an outcry.'

In front of it, probably on the junction of High Street and today's Castle Place, was the first Market House, built in 1636. Harris describes it as a 'handsome structure, on the west end of which is erected a cupola with a public clock.' No trace of it now survives.

By 1744 the town was attracting industry. In 1728, James Bradshaw, a Quaker from Lurgan, visited Hamburg for two years and observed developments in looms, yarns and weaving styles. On his return, he built a factory at Kiltonga on the main road to Belfast. Harris reported that:

...the principal and most beneficial trade in it [Newtown] is the linen manufacture and it is especially in repute for the sale of great quantities of fine diaper linen. The Quakers have a factory in it.

Another business to prosper here was brewing, which developed because the raw materials were grown in the surrounding countryside, and its produce was sure of a ready market locally and further afield! The eighteenth century brewery was located in the yard behind the old church in today's Court Street.

Other ventures proved less successful. One was an attempt by local landowners to mine lead at Whitespots, but when the shafts were dug (by hand) they too quickly filled with water and the project had to be abandoned. The Bangor and Newtown Mining Company folded after about seven years, primarily because its founders' ambitions exceeded the technology available to them at that time. The Newtown Mining Company's search for coal was also a failure. After receiving bad geological advice, the company sank shafts at Crawfordsburn Glen, the Shore Road and the Comber Road, but nothing was found.

Those seeking after souls did better. By 1723 there were three churches in Newtown, one Anglican and two Presbyterian. The Anglicans had worshipped in the church which Montgomery had built on the ruin of the Dominican Priory, but it had become ruinous by the end of the seventeenth century. Although it still had a roof on it, most of the seats inside were destroyed, and so Anglican services were held instead in a small chapel at

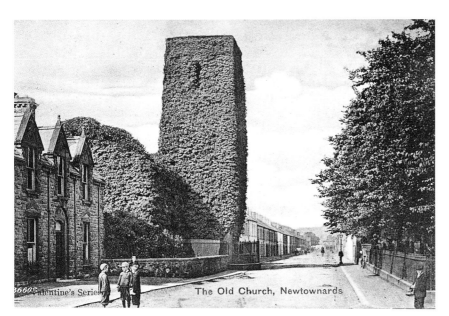

the east end of the old church, built by Sir Robert Colvill, which Harris described as 'the neatest piece of Church building inside that is to be met within Ulster.'

The district's Presbyterians could choose between a theologically conservative and a liberal-leaning ministry. This situation had arisen when the original congregation split. In 1720 the Rev. John Mairs had been installed as minister of the town's single Presbyterian congregation. Mairs had been influenced by the new liberal views on theology, called New Light, then fashionable within Scottish universities. Within two years of commencing his ministry, he was advocating non-subscribing and Arian views and was proposing to conform to the Church of Ireland liturgy. This did not go down well. The congregation complained to the Presbytery of Down, and in spite of the fact that Mairs recanted his views, the wounds were such that the congregation split and a second Presbyterian church was formed. Those preferring conservative doctrine remained with what was called the Old Light congregation and the others joined with Mr Mairs (who had apparently changed his mind again) in the New Light, non-subscribing, church.

The Old Light Meeting House was a low, thatched building situated between Greenwell Street and Movilla Street (then called Chapel Brae Street), nearer the latter, and approached by a narrow thoroughfare known as 'Dummy's Lane', a name may have come from the Irish 'Domhnach's Lane' which translated means Church Lane. It was more recently called Church Lane, before it was demolished in the 1970s. Others believe that the name refers to the Dominicans and it was so called because the monks used it as they travelled between the abbey and the priory. The New Light congregation met on the site of what is today Wright's Arcade on Frances Street.

The Quakers built a meeting-house too. Quaker numbers were small in Newtown, only twenty in 1764. Despite the small numbers, however, a

The Quaker meeting house, Kiltonga.

meeting house was built in the town in 1780. The congregation seems to have increased, for at a meeting in November 1797 there were four hundred worshippers, although paradoxically enough, given the Quakers' pacifism, this number included some soldiers who were stationed in the town at the time. The district's leading Quaker family was then the Bradshaw family, of Bradshaw's Brae who built the meeting house opposite their residence at Milecross House. The district's religious life was becoming more plural. However, because of the penal legislation of the early 1700s, this diversity did not as yet encompass any regular place of worship for the town's small, diminishing Catholic population.

The end of the Colvills

The town was only nominally under the control of the Colvills after 1701. Sir Robert died in 1697 and was succeeded by his son, Hugh. But Hugh died at the early age of twenty-five, in 1701. His young widow was left with a small child, Robert, and she re-married.

Given the size of the estate she had inherited, it is not surprising that she made what was, in material terms at least, a good match. Her new husband was Brabazon Ponsonby of Kilkenny, a powerful politician who had somehow succeeded in marrying both of his sons to daughters of the great English aristocrat, the Duke of Devonshire, Ireland's Lord Lieutenant from 1737-44. By 1744 Ponsonby had secured the title of Earl of Bessborough, and then, first for himself in 1739, and then for his second son in 1742, the lucrative and powerful post of First Commissioner of the Revenue. His eldest son was Chief Secretary to the Lord Lieutenant.

Of course it was natural in that era that Ponsonby should manage affairs for his wife – and for his own interest too. When his step-son, Robert Colvill, came of age it appears that he was suicidal, 'wild and indecent' in his conversation and 'disordered in his understanding'. In 1721, in uncertain circumstances, Robert was persuaded to make a will by which he bequeathed his vast estates in north Down to John Ponsonby, Brabazon's second son. In the meantime, from 1731-1744, Brabazon Ponsonby held the Newtown estate in trust for this son. Brabazon Ponsonby, or some other member of his family, represented the borough of Newtown in the Irish Parliaments of 1704, 1713-15, 1725-7 and from 1739 onwards.

By 1744, however, the supposedly wild and deranged Robert Colvill had come under the influence of a mistress, Martha Launders, who persuaded him to sell the estate, though it was promised to John Ponsonby. This he did in 1744, for £42,000, to Alexander Stewart. Stewart became the owner of the manors of Newtown and Mount Alexander which then consisted of about sixty townlands or 30,000 acres.

He 'lost the town by his dirt and conceit': Stewart v Ponsonby

Alexander Stewart's great-great-grandfather was a Scot who had been granted a small estate called Ballylawn, near Moville in County Donegal in the early seventeenth century. Alexander was born in 1700 and educated in Londonderry Diocesan School. As a younger son, he was not expected to inherit and so he was apprenticed to a Belfast linen merchant. Alexander established his own business, travelling to France, Flanders and the Baltic. He was a Presbyterian and an elder in Rosemary Street Non-subscribing Church, Belfast. When his older brother died in 1731, Alexander unexpectedly inherited the family's Donegal lands and was able to retire from business.

Then came the first in a series of dazzling marriages that would do so much to advance the fortunes of the Stewart family. When visiting London, Alexander met and then married his first cousin, Mary Cowan, originally from Londonderry, the daughter of Alderman John Cowan. Mary had inherited a fortune of £100,000 from her brother, Sir Robert Cowan who had been Governor of Bombay. The trustees of Mrs Stewart's marriage settlement had recommended that part of her inheritance, which was in East India stock, should be sold and invested in land. The Stewarts had been looking for suitable property and when Colvill put his estate up for sale in 1744, it provided them with just the opportunity they had been looking for. Alexander was aged forty-four when he purchased the town and manor. The new owners took up residence in the town in a 'large but not elegant' house on the corner of High Street and Castle Lane (later the Londonderry Estate Office), opposite the Market Cross, and began to put money into the town.

Mary Cowan, wife of Alexander Stewart. (Lady Mairi Bury)

Alexander Stewart had assumed that when he purchased the estate, he would have control over the borough as well, as was the custom. Consequently, when Colvill asked him to pay an additional £500 for the borough, he refused, a decision which his agent and adviser, William Macartney of Belfast (who later fell out with him) scorned, saying that Stewart had 'lost the borough by his dirt and conceit in not taking my advice and behaving like a gentleman in that matter'. In the meantime the acquisitive Ponsonby family, which had been waiting vulture-like in the wings, snapped up the offer, and thus retained control of the borough.

Stewart did not accept this without a fight. In 1747 he challenged the legality of the fact that nine of Newtownards's thirteen burgesses were not resident in the town. A fierce court battle followed, which ended in Stewart losing his case before the highest court, the British House of Lords, in 1758. To seal their victory the Ponsonbys had an Act passed through the Irish Parliament, later nicknamed 'the Newtown Act'. This Act secured the positions of burgesses on Corporations who were not resident in the borough which their corporation governed.

Thus a curious situation had emerged: Alexander Stewart was the landlord of the town of Newtown, but had no control over the Corporation which nominally ran it. The Ponsonbys continued to use the borough to return their relatives and stooges as MPs until 1788 when they sold it to James Alexander of Caledon, County Tyrone, in exchange for Banagher, King's County. James Alexander did not go out of his way to build any bridges, the introduction of his burgesses being celebrated with a dinner in the town held 'under the noses of the Stewarts'.

Deprived of his anticipated political role at a national level, Alexander Stewart, the Presbyterian outsider, the largest Presbyterian landlord in County Down, set himself up as the leader of the popular, independent interest in local politics. He chaired the first meeting of the Patriot Club which was set up in Newtown in the spring of 1756. The historian, Roy Foster, says that:

Patriot opposition at all levels concentrated on resentment of English placemen

Alexander Stewart, owner of Newtown from 1744, who rebuilt and dignified the town centre. (The National Trust)

Alexander Stewart

[in Irish government posts], the necessity of a secure settlement of lands, the need to keep the catholic threat contained, the desire for cheap government (sustained by low taxes) and for investment in certain areas of the Irish economy.

While the divorce between the ownership of the town and the control of the borough may have been advantageous to the Ponsonbys, and given Alexander Stewart a 'cause', it cannot have done much for the town and would certainly have hampered the Stewarts' plans to invest in their new possession. Being isolated from the Corporation meant that Stewart had no control over the markets, the borough magistracy, and matters such as paving, lighting and cleansing the streets, although as far as the ordinary town dweller was concerned, as long as someone was looking after these things, it probably did not worry them who it was.

In another sense too, the packing of the Corporation with Ponsonby placemen was academic as far as most of the citizens of Newtown were concerned. Most could not have sat on the Corporation even if the Ponsonbys had wanted them to, because the Test Act of 1704 barred Presbyterians from serving on borough Corporations, an Act which remained in force until 1780. The town seems to have languished in the middle years of the century. John Wesley was certainly not impressed by its condition when he visited in 1773. He described it as 'dreary Newtown... More ruined than ever and very ruinous even by Irish standards.'

The two rival authorities in Newtown, landlord and Corporation, usually kept their distance, but clashes were inevitable. One such concerned the lighting of the town. Powers were given in acts of 1727-8 to *vestries of parishes* to raise sums for paving, cleansing or lighting towns in their vicinity. However, in November 1784, the Provost, Thomas Merry, *through the Borough Court* levied the sum of £19.4s.7d. to have the town lighted, and directed Michael Rankin, his Petty Constable, to obtain the money from the town's residents. Some of them refused to pay and the Provost directed the Petty Constable to have them arrested. It appears that Stewart led the challenge to the lighting rates. He did so, firstly, because only parish vestries had the power to levy money for this purpose, and secondly, the Corporation had no power to appoint petty constables in the first place: constables were to be appointed by the Grand Jury at the Court Leet (or manor court), which was Stewart's. (The practice of appointing constables in Newtown by the Corporation had been established when the town and manor had been owned by the same person and then it had not mattered which authority appointed these officials.)

Two examples will illustrate the everyday work of the Borough Court, and cast interesting light on life in mid-eighteenth century Newtown. As the fining powers of the Borough Court were limited it would sometimes refer offenders to the next highest court, the Grand Jury. On October 14th, 1757 John Gillis of Newtown was referred for being 'guilty of pulling up

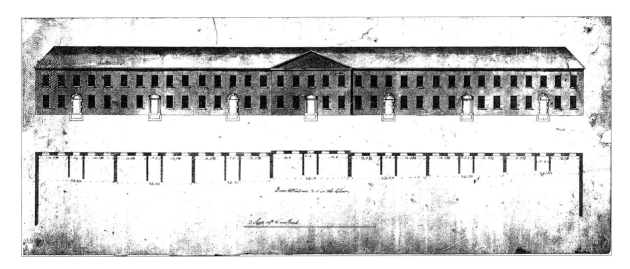

Dr. Cooper's cabbages and planting them in his own garden on the Sabbath day, commonly called Sunday.' His crimes were both theft and Sabbath-breaking. Another presentment gives us an insight into the morality of the period, that of: 'James McClurg for harbouring, entertaining and keeping in his house Katharine Barton, a woman of evil fame.'

By mid century the population of town and parish was growing rapidly. In 1764 it was reported that, although there were only fifty Catholics, twenty Quakers and sixty members of the Church of Ireland, there were 4,750 Presbyterians. A third Presbyterian meeting-house opened in 1771. This congregation was Anti-Burgher Seceder. The Seceders originated in Scotland in 1733 when a number of Presbyterians objected to allowing landlords and corporations to nominate ministers in congregations where there was a vacancy. Their theological conservatism appealed to many in Ulster who sought to hear 'the gude auld comfortable doctrines of election, reprobation, original sin and faith': one hundred Seceder congregations were started in the century after 1744. The Anti-Burgher variety was a particularly conservative group who had split from the Seceders over an oath to be taken by burghers in Scottish towns. The early services of the local Anti-Burgher Seceders were held in the open air and, as they often took place in what was strictly the parish of Bangor, it was known as 'Bangor' [congregation]. It became Second Newtownards. In addition, a congregation of the Reformed Presbyterians, or Covenanters, who insisted on fidelity to the Scottish Covenants of the seventeenth century, was set up in Conlig in 1772. This congregation took over the premises that the Secessionists had vacated when they moved into the town. A call was issued from 92 'Covenanting electors between the Bridge of Dromore and Donaghadee in the County of Down' to the Rev. William Stavely to be minister. In 1776 Stavely ministered to two congregations, one at Newtown and another at Knockbracken near Belfast.

As well as new churches, a very extensive rebuilding programme got under way in the 1770s. An impressive new Market House was built in

This elegant terrace, intended for either the east or west side of the town's new Square, was unfortunately never built. (P.R.O.N.I.)

the space opened up by demolishing part of the north side of High Street. Stewart hired one of the best architects of the day to design it, Ferdinando Stratford, who had produced highly acclaimed work in Bristol. Plans were drawn up in 1765 and work was well under way in the early 1770s. The square, which was laid out in front of the new Market House, was named Conway Square after Alexander Stewart's daughter-in-law, Lady Sarah Frances Seymour-Conway.

The opportunity was taken to completely re-orientate the town, the focus of which had drifted eastwards from the old medieval centre, the green in front of the Priory, away from the centre of the plantation town, the 'Mercat Cross' at the junction of High Street, Greenwell Street, Movilla Street and Castle Street, to the new piazza. Around it a cruciform street plan was laid, with North Street being inter-sected by East and West Streets. North Street entered Conway Square through the central archway built in the Market House, which was fitted with gates that could be closed at night. On either side of this passage were prison cells. South Street was built in the 1770s along the route to Comber. Finally, sixty new houses were built between 1769-77, bringing the total to five hundred, 'mostly built of stone or slated'.

Wesley's poor impression of the place may be partly accounted for (but only partly, as Wesley was an extremely astute observer) by this welter of demolitions and new building. When Arthur Young passed through Newtown on July 28th, 1776 he saw the town quite differently, describing it as:

...an improving place belonging to Mr Stewart who has built a very handsome Market House and laid out a square around it.

Whether Young knew the back streets as Wesley would have is unclear, but Young's observations show us that Newtown was presenting a new and impressive public face to the world. The new Market House also had Assembly Rooms which served as an important social centre. That it was finished to a very high standard is clear from the following description of its interior which appeared in the *Hibernian Magazine:*

Over the centre arch is a most beautiful room, 32 feet long and 12 feet wide, which serves for a drawing room to the larger or assembly room.   This room is most elegantly stuccoed, the walls painted a light green, and bordered with gold. A large branch for twenty candles hangs from the ceiling. The marble chimney piece is hardly to be equalled. Over one wing of the market house is the assembly room, 50 feet by 24. The walls of this room are painted a light blue and bordered with gold, the ceiling is beautifully stuccoed. From it hang three brass branches which hold twenty candles each.

Interestingly, the writer also remarked that 'the language spoken here is a broad Scotch hardly to be understood by strangers.' It may seem odd that the Scottish influence was still so evident 170 years after the start of the plantation, but it must be remembered that large scale immigration persisted right through into the early eighteenth century.

Alexander Stewart died in 1781. A contemporary, William Steele Dickson described him as a:

...man of polite and pleasing manner, a clear and comprehensive understanding and principles truly liberal in politics and religion. He had an ambition to raise his family to honour and influence in his country and for his country's good.

He was succeeded by his son Robert who was then forty-two. Robert also inherited his father's politics. In his early years he was known as a Whig, considered himself to be a 'patriot', and remained a Presbyterian all his life. Though their politics were liberal, their money was sound, and the family found itself accepted by the Anglo-Irish aristocracy. Robert's first wife, Lady Sarah Frances Seymour-Conway was the daughter of the Marquess of Hertford, Lord Lieutenant of Ireland.   His second wife, whom he married in 1775, was the eldest daughter of Earl Camden, the Lord Chancellor of England. Robert Stewart was elevated to the peerage as Baron Londonderry in 1789, taking his title from his family's connections with the 'maiden city'.

In the late 1770s, feelings in the Protestant ascendancy ran high over the inferior economic and constitutional position they had in comparison to Englishmen. When the country seemed threatened by invasion, during the American War of Independence, Protestants armed themselves into Volunteer Companies to protect the country; but when the immediate danger had passed the Volunteers used their muscle to press for commercial and constitutional reforms. Robert Stewart formed 'The Ards Independents' and attended the great Volunteer Convention in College Green in 1779.

In 1783-4 Robert Stewart took part in a nation-wide campaign for parliamentary reform.   The repeal of the 'Newtown Act' was one of the reforms sought, as it had strengthened the hands of great borough owners

and weakened the independence of boroughs. Stewart hoped that its repeal would give him control of the borough of Newtown.

These campaigns, and the generally enlightened political climate of the 1780s, radicalised Stewart's tenants. In the 1790 General Election Lord Londonderry's son, also called Robert Stewart, stood as a Whig candidate. During the campaign he pledged himself to support various popular reforming measures. There had to be some sense of shared aims and values between landlord and tenant if there was to be any chance of the landlord or his representative being returned. To make absolutely sure of victory, Lord Londonderry reputedly spent £60,000 in the campaign which resulted in 83% of his tenants voting for his son. The election severely stretched even Londonderry's finances. After 1790, the family had to live very economically and Lord Londonderry had to postpone the building of his mansion at Mount Stewart for many years.

Lord Londonderry's tenants in and around Newtown were prepared to vote for his son as MP as long as his politics were the same as theirs. But over the next few years their politics diverged, and Lord Londonderry would come to rue the love of egality and freedom that he had hitherto done so much to instil.

8

The Rebel Centre 1790-1800

For many, though, the best hope of a new life lay not through reform but emigration. Ships carried many Newtownards people away to a new life in America. There was at least one emigration agent for a Belfast shipping company located in the town in this period. The emigration helped both to defuse and develop radical politics in Ireland. It defused them by allowing the disaffected to leave the country, but strengthened them by building strong ties between the Presbyterians at home and the colonists who were challenging British rule in America. As one Presbyterian minister put it, 'there is scarcely a Protestant family of the middle classes amongst us who does not reckon kindred with the inhabitants of that extensive continent'. Another contemporary claimed that 'the Presbyterians of the north are in their hearts American'. And why might what was good for America not be good for Ireland?

America was not the only inspiration for the Presbyterian radicals of the parish of Newtownards. The revolution in France was equally heartening to Irish radicals, and though many of them were sickened by the consequent blood letting, they identified with the spirit of the new regime and welcomed new reforms like the widening of the electoral franchise, the abolition of tithes and the establishment of religious equality. The Newtownards Volunteers celebrated the 'emancipation of the French nation from the chains of despotism' with heart-felt enthusiasm. Turning to affairs in unreformed, barely democratic, rotten borough-ridden Ireland, the Volunteers resolved 'not to lay down our arms until we have accomplished the full redress of our grievances.' On February 15-16th, 1793, at a large representative meeting of Volunteers from the province of Ulster held in Dungannon, a Newtownards man, John Crawford, and Hugh Boyd of the townland of Ballycastle, near Mount Stewart, were elected on to a Committee of thirty in which the powers of the assembly were vested.

In the 1780s the reform movement had been led by landed Presbyterians like the Stewarts. In the early 1790s, this class became afraid and drew back. This gave the government room for manoeuvre, and when Britain and France went to war in 1793, the government came down hard on the reformers. The Volunteers were banned. Now radicals aligned themselves with a progressive new anti-sectarian movement called The Society of United Irishmen. The United Irishmen sought to unite Anglican, Catholic and dissenter in the cause of electoral, parliamentary and religious reform. Initially the movement was non-violent but by 1795 it had reconstituted itself as a revolutionary, secret organisation pledged to the creation of an independent, democratic republic.

The badge of the United Irishmen.

In such circumstances Lord Londonderry began to distance himself from his earlier radicalism. He adopted a tough line with his tenants. This was somewhat out of character. However, in the 1790s Lord Londonderry's prime concern was reasserting his authority. In 1792 his agent and adviser, the Rev. John Cleland, the parish's Anglican minister, began to demand the payment of tithes. Londonderry may have had a legal right to them as he was the owner of the lands, the tithes of which had previously gone to the ancient monastery and medieval priory, but according to Andrew Cooper of Milecross, who appealed to Lord Downshire for help, tithes had never been paid, except in two of the parish's townlands, since the suppression of these religious houses. His ancestors had lived in Craigantlet since the late 1600s and had never been asked to pay them. This attempt to revive an obsolete tax, its timing and its offensive nature – the imposition of tithes upon a Presbyterian community to support the ministry of the despised Anglican clergyman, John Cleland – completely antagonised local opinion and contributed to the politicisation of Newtownards.

Another thing which helped to distance Lord Londonderry from the people of the town and parish was the political career of his son, Robert Stewart, the young Viscount Castlereagh (the heir to the Londonderry title enjoyed this courtesy title). Although Lord Londonderry remained a member of a Presbyterian congregation all his life, his son was admitted to the Church of Ireland. After Castlereagh's election as MP for County Down (won on a liberal-ish platform), Lord Londonderry's second wife's father, the first Earl Camden, a member of the British government, had taken the young man under his wing, steering him away from liberal politics, and indeed for a time from Irish politics, for Castlereagh was elected MP for English constituencies from 1794-97. There, to the frustration of the tenants on his father's estate, he solidly supported the government. In 1797 Castlereagh's journey across the political spectrum was complete: he became a senior member of the Irish government in Dublin as Chief Secretary to the Lord Lieutenant, his step-mother's brother, the second Earl Camden. Castlereagh has been a misunderstood politician, given the nickname 'Bloody' and inspiring Shelley's famous lines:

> I met Murder on the way –
> He had a mask like Castlereagh.

However his niece, who saw behind the public mask, has left us the following glimpse of his personality:

The calm dignity of his manner gave an impression that he was cold, but no-one who had seen his kindly smile, or been greeted by his two hands stretched out in welcome, could have thought him so. He liked the society of young people and,

A famous but misunderstood politician? Viscount Castlereagh, after Lawrence. (The National Trust)

far from checking their mirth and nonsense, he enjoyed and encouraged it with his own mirth and cheerfulness.

By the mid 1790s, however, the Londonderrys and many of their Newtownards tenants were in opposite camps, and low level hostilities had commenced. Nearly sixty years later, the United Irish historian, Dr. R.R. Madden, wrote that Londonderry viewed anyone who differed with him on any issue as his enemy. Those who had supported or even shown friendship to his opponents were suspected as being 'turbulent or disaffected persons':

A regular system of rural espionage was the consequence, and each district was divided between sycophants, spies and family interest supporters of the rural bashaw... It is difficult to conceive the extent or the mischief of this system... at the period in question. It tended more than many of the political evils, which were the subject of general complaint, to promote the views of the United Irishmen... There certainly is no method more likely to render people disaffected than by making charges of disaffection familiar to men's minds, which is difficult to disprove, and which are felt to be injurious, however undeserved they may be.

Prominent among these 'turbulent persons' was the Presbyterian minister of Greyabbey, who was deeply concerned at the divisive and demoralising effect of these activities. The Rev. James Porter was well read in classical literature, had a great interest in science, and gave popular lectures in chemistry, optics, mechanics and astronomy. His main vice was said to be the purchase of books and scientific apparatus! By 1794 he became so concerned about local feeling that he contributed a series of fictitious letters to the *Northern Star*, the radical United Irish newspaper, which became very popular. He created comic characters called Lord Mountmumble, Squire Firebrand and Billy Bluff. These were immediately identified by the readership as Lord Londonderry, the Rev. John Cleland and William Lowry, a local farmer widely known as an informer. Through these letters, which were signed 'SYDNEY', he ridiculed the espionage system. The letters were gathered together and published as a pamphlet which ran to thirteen editions, and continued to be published as late as 1840. They gave Lord Londonderry great offence. The following is an extract:

Billy Bluff, my neighbour was up yesterday at the squire's, with his duty hens. "Well, Billy, what news? says the squire [John Cleland?].

   "Troth, sir, plenty of news, but none very good," says Billy [the informer].

   "What is your neighbour R_____ (meaning me) about now?"

   "Why, please your honour, he's railing against the war, against the tithes, and against game laws; and he's still reading at the newspapers. He is a villain and must be laid fast."

   "But what more do you know of him, Billy?

"Why, bad enough, and please your honour, him and the Popish priest drank together last market day, till all was blue again with them; they shaked hands, so they did, drank toasts and sung songs."

"Pretty work! Did you overhear them?"

"Ah, that I did so, and listened like a pig."

"What were the toasts?"

"First the priest drank 'Prosperity to old Ireland' and ____"

"Stop, Billy. The toast is infamous: the word 'old' never was, and never ought to be, applied to any country but England: and he who would apply it to Ireland is a rebel and ought to be hanged."

"He ought, an' please your honour, as round as a hoop."

"Well, what toast did the villain R____ drink?"

"He drank 'Union [unity between Catholics and Protestants] and Peace to the people of Ireland'."

"Worse and worse, Billy; a great deal worse: he who wishes union wishes ruin to the country; I say ruin to the government and that is ruin to the country. Union, forsooth! that is what never was, and never must prevail in this country; and as to peace, 'tis flying in the face of government to speak of it."

As the government hardened its attitude to reform, in north Down and the Ards ploughshares were being turned into swords – or pikes, to be more precise – and muskets from the old Volunteer companies were being dusted down. In 1797 General Lake was ordered into Antrim and Down and instructed to disarm the community. This was carried out with ruthlessness and considerable brutality. Houses were burned down, floggings and torture took place and suspects were sent to the fleet. Arrests of leaders were made, based on intelligence given by informers; some of them from a ring of informers operated by the Rev. John Cleland in the Newtownards area.

Although all the Presbyterian denominations, officially, were against the plans for a rising, two of the town's four Presbyterian ministers were associated with the United Irish movement. These were the Rev. William Sinclair of the non-subscribing, New Light congregation, and the Rev. James Simpson of First Newtownards. A third minister, the Rev. William Stavely, of the Reformed Presbyterian Church, was suspected of being involved, and was twice imprisoned, but he strenuously denied any association and nothing was ever proved.

The loyalist response

It would be a mistake, however, to think that the people of Newtownards were unanimously committed to the cause of the United Irishmen. Local men also rallied to the government, joining the yeomanry. The yeomanry was set up in October 1796 to augment the Crown's forces and was led by local landlords to keep order in their neighbourhood. In Ulster, many of

General Gerard Lake was entrusted with the disarming of Ulster in March 1797.

the yeomanry were members of the newly formed Orange Order. Londonderry tried to form a yeomanry corps in Newtownards, and Viscount Castlereagh rode around the parish persuading many to take the yeoman's oath of allegiance to the Crown. At first his attempts were met with resistance. A man was assassinated for taking the oath and there was an attempt to murder Cleland by a United Irishman. Loyal tenants feared reprisals and were slow to come forward. But early in November, Viscount Castlereagh broke up a meeting of the Ulster provincial executive of the United Irishmen at Portaferry. This gave the loyalists confidence, and by the end of the month 1,700 of them had come forward from the parish to take the yeoman's oath and the Newtownards Yeomanry was formed, comprising a cavalry and an infantry section.

In that same month, November 1796, a number of the inhabitants of the parish met to express their:

...attachment to the principles of the constitution at this alarming period, when a foreign enemy threatens our shores and suspicion and mistrust distracts the minds of people of every description.

They pledged themselves to defend the constitution – but only on the condition that the government would introduce 'ample reform in the Commons House of Parliament, including all religious persuasions,' and finished by mentioning that:

...though we have on a late occasion differed in sentiment from Lord Londonderry, we cannot omit his opportunity of declaring our attachment to his lordship as a landlord and our esteem for his character as a magistrate and as a man.

It was not the unqualified support for the authorities that had been hoped for, and their caution highlights the complexity of the locality's politics at the time. Lord Londonderry became very careful about whom he chose to arm and train in his yeomanry.

One incident that helped to unite pro-government feeling was the murder of a loyalist called Cumming at Unicarval House in February 1797. He died resisting a group of United Irishmen, who had arrived at night looking for arms. The murdered man was a member of the yeomanry, and his comrades in the Newtownards and Comber cavalry pledged a reward of 320 guineas for the capture of the killers.

This particular murder was used by some to lobby for the enforcement of the Insurrection Act of 1796 in the baronies of Ards and Castlereagh. Martial law was declared, a curfew operated, houses were searched and suspects sent untried to the fleet. Matters were coming to a head.

The 1798 Rebellion

Before dawn on the morning of Thursday June 7th, 1798, William Fox, Newtownards' schoolmaster, and an officer in the United Irishmen, climbed Scrabo Hill expecting his division of the United Irish Army to be mustering on the summit. This was to be the day of the rising in north Down. But to Fox's horror, when he reached the summit, no-one was present but himself. As he looked down on the town, he saw the lights were blazing in the Market House, the barracks of the town's garrison – a contingent of just over three hundred York Fencibles. Something was clearly amiss.

What Fox did not know was that the authorities had pre-empted him. Acting on intelligence supplied by its spy network, the government had arrested most of the county's leading United Irishmen on the eve of the planned attack. The next day, near to despair, Fox conferred with the only representative of the county's high command to have escaped arrest. Should they rebuild their support in Down or attempt to link up with the rebels in County Antrim? While they were talking, a message came through that mid-Down had risen. Fox immediately rode around the north Down area, rallying support.

Meanwhile, back in the Market House, the commanding officer of the Crown forces, Col. Chetwynd Stapleton, felt confident that the north Down rising had been well and truly stymied. So much so, that when news of the rising in mid-Down came through, he felt able to march to meet the rebels at Saintfield with a force of 270 Fencibles, and about 230 members of the Newtownards Yeomanry, cavalry and infantry. He left a small force in the Market House. His main force proceeded through Comber towards Saintfield, only to be ambushed just outside Saintfield on Saturday June 9th, where he lost almost sixty men. In some disarray, Stapleton retreated through Comber and Dundonald to Belfast.

This retreat left the tiny garrison very vulnerable. Fox had ridden on horseback to Bangor and Donaghadee and had managed to raise a force of three hundred. They decided to attack Newtownards. They rendezvoused at Movilla graveyard, and at three o'clock in the morning of Sunday June 10th – known as 'Pike Sunday' – they launched an attack on the Market House. Corporal William Sparks of the York Fencible Infantry reported seeing a large body of armed men march down North Street, led by local man, Samuel Rankin, wielding a huge sword. A second group led by William Davidson, approached from Greenwell Street. Corporal Sparks reports that he saw the rebels:

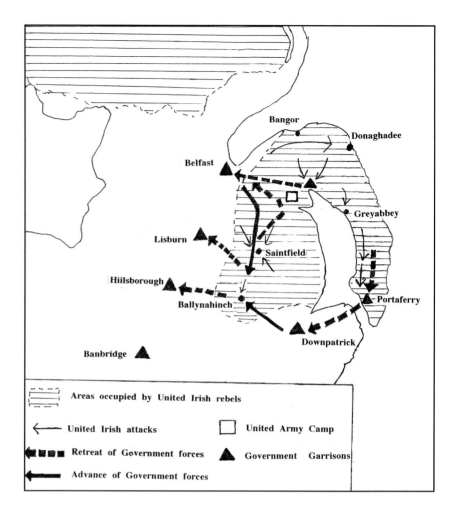

form a line before the Market House and commence an attack on His Majesty's forces stationed there. In a short time the rebels were dispersed by the fire from the King's troops.

In the dark streets, just as dawn was breaking, the two groups of attackers had mistaken each other for the enemy and had thrown down their arms and fled. No doubt they were terrified of the horrors that might befall them should they be captured, for they ran 'above a mile before... prayers, entreaties or reproaches or threats could induce them to halt.'

The insurgents regrouped at Cairngaver, then marched across to Conlig to prepare for a second assault on the Market House. By this time the little garrison had concluded that they would not be reinforced so they fled to Belfast, enabling the rebels to take the town in the late afternoon. On the same afternoon, the last government force in the peninsula, the Portaferry garrison, took ship for Strangford. The whole of north Down and the Ards Peninsula was now in the hands of the rebels.

The insurgents gathered up their forces (these small successes did wonders for recruitment) and set up camp on Scrabo Hill. One man, Hugh

Montgomery, a tailor, recalled standing at the door of his father's house at three o'clock that afternoon when he was approached by John Biers, a hosier in the town, who called on him to join the soldiers on Scrabo Hill. Biers held the rank of sergeant in the United Irish 'Newtownards Musketry', and Montgomery went promptly to the muster. But they did not have long to drill, much less weld themselves into a coherent force, when a message arrived directing them to march to Saintfield and join with the 7,000 strong army that was assembling there.   The men complained bitterly about this. It had been a long day. Many had been up since before three o'clock that morning. Fox wrote:

I was torn by a thousand vexations – which no person but one who may have been in my situation can understand or feel. However, after much flattery, I got them to begin to march off by companies and it was 11 o'clock before the rear marched off the hill.

After a disciplined night march, the force reached Saintfield at sunrise on Monday, June 11th, and since there were no arrangements made to receive them, they had to spend the next four hours lying in the Main Street. But their situation improved. They were posted to Ballynahinch and they pitched their camp in Lord Moira's grounds at Montalto. His cattle and stock were requisitioned and the women of Ballynahinch carried in oat cakes and salt beef. An almost festive atmosphere prevailed.

But it was not to last. As they rested, some fifteen hundred government troops closed in from Belfast and Downpatrick. The troops arrived late on Tuesday evening and immediately began to bombard the rebel position in

Lord Moira, owner of Montalto and Ballynahinch. Though himself an army general, Lord Moira denounced Lake's disarming of Ulster as 'the most absurd as well as digusting tyranny that any nation groaned under.'

the town. Fierce fighting began about five o'clock on Wednesday morning in the streets of Ballynahinch, involving mostly men from the north Down area and the Ards. The fighting was fierce but it was all over within a few hours. At least five hundred rebels were killed in the fighting or the bloody pursuit that ensued.

Meanwhile, back in republican Newtownards, those who had not gone off to Saintfield on the Sunday evening proclaimed the area's independence from Britain and set up a Committee of Public Safety on the revolutionary French model. This was the second time that Newtownards had demonstrated its defiance of the policies of the British government and proclaimed independence, the first being in 1649 when Viscount Montgomery declared for the monarchy against the republican government of England.

One of their orders was to requisition cattle and meal from Lord Londonderry's demesne at Mount Stewart. His lordship was not at home. He and his six children had wisely retreated to Donaghadee and taken ship. But nothing else was stolen or vandalised, though one of the estate workers was heard to say that he 'intended to live in Lord Londonderry's house next week.' The new 'administration' only lasted a few days. With the defeat in Ballynahinch on Wednesday, the whole rebel cause collapsed.

No account of the 1798 Rebellion in Newtownards would be complete without mentioning the local folk legend Betsy Gray (who was the subject of a novel written by a Bangor-born journalist, W.G. Lyttle, in 1896). Unfortunately it is very difficult to be certain of all but a few of the facts. Lyttle's book is a mixture of fact and fiction and, much as one wishes to believe it, it makes for an unreliable historical source. We cannot even be certain that Betsy Gray was from the Six Road Ends. According to another theory, she was from the townland of Tullyniskey, in the parish of Garvaghey. All that we can be sure of is that she accompanied her brother and lover to Ballynahinch, and the three of them were overtaken and shot as they fled from the battle.

The government wreaks its revenge

The authorities resumed control and a period of savage reprisals ensued. Rebels were rounded up and imprisoned in the cells below the Market House (demolished in 1969). We can get a good idea of the attitude of the authorities from a letter from a Colonel Atherton who was stationed in Newtownards. On June 20th, only a week after the rising had collapsed, he wrote from the town to the commanding officer for the province, General Nugent, that:

I have had tolerable success today... We have burned Johnston's house at Crawfordsburn mills – at Bangor, destroyed the furniture of Pat Agnew: James

Francis and Gibson and Campbell's NOT FINISHED YET – at Ballyholme burned the house of Johnston – at the Demesnes near Bangor, the houses of James Richardson and John Scott – at Ballymaconnell mills, burned the houses of McConnell, Miller and James Martin, a captain and a friend of McCullough's, hanged at Ballynahinch. We hope you will think that we have done TOLERABLY well. Tomorrow we go to Portaferry or rather to its neighbourhood.

Ought we not to punish the gentlemen of the county who have never assisted the well-disposed people, yeomanry etc.? For my own part, a gentleman of any kind, but more particularly a MAGISTRATE, who deserts his post at such a period ought to be – I will not say what. Mr Echlin of Ecclinville, Rev Hutchinson, Donaghadee, Mr Ker, Portavo, Mr Ward of Bangor, are now and now only to be found.

List of inactive magistrates, or rather 'friends' to the United Irishmen:- Sir John Blackwood, John Crawford of Crawfordsburn, John Kennedy, Cultra etc. But among others, Rev Hugh Montgomery of Rosemount who is no friend to government, or its measures, and whom I strongly suspect. I have got his bailiff.

The Rev. James Porter. His wife's pleadings could not save him.

Lord Londonderry was able to have his revenge on the Rev. James Porter too. He was arrested on June 28th and charged with intercepting a despatch from Captain Matthews, who had been in command at Portaferry. Matthews had sent his servant to Colonel Stapleton seeking reinforcements, as he knew that the town was to be attacked later that day. But as we have seen, Stapleton had already left for Saintfield and had later retreated to Belfast. As the servant was returning to Portaferry he was stopped at the Kilnatierney Bridge, just to the north of Greyabbey, and his despatch was taken from him and read.

At the court martial, it was alleged that Porter was amongst this party and had read the document. However, one witness denied that Porter was there at all. The messenger himself was unable to identify him. Only one 'witness' could be found and he was well known as a 'renegade and notorious paid informer'. Porter attempted to cross-examine him but was continually interrupted. On this sole testimony, and to the dismay of most who were present, Porter was sentenced to death by hanging. One English officer who was there said 'with tears in my eyes, I left the court.' It was clear that a great injustice had been done. Porter kept his composure, telling the court, 'I freely forgive all my enemies; may God in his infinite mercy forgive them also.'

Mrs Porter was told by the military authorities at Newtownards that only Lord Londonderry had the power of granting a reprieve. She hurried to Mount Stewart and there met one of Lord Londonderry's daughters, who had attended Porter's science classes. The daughter earnestly tried to persuade her father to have mercy. In tears she had to tell Mrs Porter that there was no hope. The Rev. James Porter was hanged on a temporary scaffold in full view of his own house and the church at Greyabbey. His wife and their seven children were left destitute. However two of his sons eventually attained high positions in America – perhaps not surprisingly in the legal profession. One became a Supreme Court judge and later represented his state in the U.S. Senate and another became the state's Attorney General.

Porter was perhaps the most celebrated of a list of men from Newtownards and district who were tried by court-martial in the town and sentenced. Others from Newtownards were: Rev. James Simpson of First Newtownards Presbyterian church – transported; Rev. William Sinclair of the New Light Presbyterian church – transported; Dr. Thomas Wilson – transportation for 14 years; Alexander Clandennon – transportation for life; John Carr – hanged; William McCormick – hanged; John Clark (alias Richard Miers) – hanged.

The following men from the wider locality were hanged following a court martial at Newtownards: Rev.Archibald Warwick of Kircubbin, Thomas McNight of Gransha, Archibald Wilson of Conlig, Robert Robinson of Ballygrainey, Robert Gowdy of Dunover (possibly a theology student), John Cuthbert of Ballyboley, Bernard Crosby and William Morrison of Donaghadee, Hugh Boyd of Ballycastle, Lambert Brice of Dundonald and James Dunlop of Bangor. David Bailie Warden of Ballycastle went into exile to America where he rose to be the American Consul-General in Paris. The seeds of Ulster-Scots liberalism were widely spread.

The 1798 Rebellion had a profound impact in the area and the scars it left would take decades to heal. *The Freeman's Journal,* a Dublin newspaper, reported on August 11th, 1798:

The magnitude of the punishment of many districts in the County of Down may be conceived from this single fact – that of the inhabitants of the little village of Ballywalter in the Ardes nine men were actually killed and thirteen wounded, victims of their folly. If such a trifling village suffered so much what must have been the aggregate loss in those parts of the country which were in a state of rebellion?

9

Regency Renovations 1800-1830

Anxious to heal divisions between himself and the many families who had suffered during, or in the aftermath of the rebellion, Lord Londonderry refrained from evicting tenants unless they were five years or more in arrears, and even some of these were forgiven in special circumstances (for example, 'This tenant has a numerous and young family and was afflicted by fever'). In times of distress he would employ extra labourers in his grounds or in Newtownards. For example, in 1816 when the harvest was bad, and in 1817 when the autumn was wet, Lord

Robert Stewart, first Marquess of Londonderry: liberal in youth, reactionary in middle age, and rather more mellow in his latter years. (The National Trust)

The flood gates at the head of Strangford Lough. Before the 1810 reclamation, the shoreline ran along South Street and Castle Gardens.

Londonderry paid men 1s 6d per day to clear the 'Canal', and 1s 1d to help build the new parish church. In 1818, at a time of economic uncertainty, he revalued his county Down estates, reducing many rents. He maintained two Lancastrian schools, one in Newtownards and one in Comber, which resulted in a high degree of literacy in the area.

What won Lord Londonderry most regard, however, was his encouragement of the custom called 'Tenant Right'. This was an interest which the tenant had in his holding. If he paid his rent then he could expect to keep his farm when the lease was due for renewal. If faced with eviction, the landlord was obliged to compensate him by purchasing the interest at its market price. If he moved, he could sell his interest to the highest bidder, and so choose his successor. The value of the tenant right depended on the value of the farm. In the Newtownards area it came to be worth £10 per acre, which made it among the highest in Ireland.

The years from 1793-1815 were boom years for agriculture. Britain was almost continuously at war with France, and so food and farm prices stayed high, facts which may lie behind the decision to build flood gates at Gregstown and reclaim two hundred acres from the head of Strangford Lough. This project was completed in 1811 at Lord Londonderry's expense. The reclaimed area was turned into farmland and was soon producing 'good crops' according to the Ordnance Survey Memoirs of the early 1830s. Indeed the same report said that the whole parish was 'well cultivated and produce[s] good crops.'

When the farmers were doing well, the town prospered too. Businesses that were related to processing agricultural produce expanded. Lord Londonderry built a new mill in 1816. The old brewery behind the Priory ruin was purchased and moved to a new site in Regent Street in 1819, and by 1837 more than 7,000 barrels of beer were being brewed each year. Malt for the brewery was made from locally grown barley.

By the 1820s, the town had about 1,300 houses and a population of about 6,000, which made it 'tolerably large' by the standards of the time. The people of the town probably would have been less *blasé*. They would have found its growth remarkable. Within a lifetime – less – the population had trebled and the number of houses in the town increased by two and half fold.

During the regency of George III Newtownards took on a shape and character that is recognisable to us today. Many of the improvements were the result of the efforts of Lord Londonderry (elevated to become Marquess of Londonderry in 1816), who had finally gained control of municipal affairs in 1800, when he exchanged his ownership of the borough of Limavady for that of Newtownards. Londonderry was the Provost continuously from 1800-1821.

In the early nineteenth century Lord Londonderry and his neighbours, the Delacherois family of Donaghadee, were keen to develop Donaghadee as Ulster's main passenger and mail port. The advantage to the Delacherois family is obvious; Londonderry's hope was that Newtownards would rise on Donaghadee's coat tails, becoming the principal town on what would be a very busy artery. Their ambition seemed likely to be fulfilled when the Irish Post Office commissioned a new coach road from Dundonald to Newtownards via Bradshaw's Brae.

The story of the Belfast-Newtownards road is an interesting (if confusing!) one. In the early eighteenth century, the road came from 'Strantown' through Dunlady, avoiding Dundonald completely, through Ballyrogan, into Kiltonga, across to Bully's Acre and down into the town via today's Glenford Road. This road was built mainly for travel on foot and horseback. With traffic between the towns increasing, it became necessary to consider cutting a new road. The idea was to make it as level as possible, even if this meant that it would meander. Local farmers objected to this, and when the new road was proposed in 1757 they threatened to use force to stop it, so plans had to be changed and a new direct route was chosen. Called the Great Road, it went through Dundonald and approached Newtownards from today's Scrabo Road, more or less along the route of the present dual carriageway. While this route makes perfect sense in the age of the motor car, as far as carts, horse-drawn carriages and coaches are concerned, a more punishing or exhausting route could hardly have been conceived of.

If Newtown was to play the leading role intended for it, its communications with Belfast would have to be improved dramatically, hence the creation of the new coach road which reverted back, to some extent, to the first route. This is the present Belfast Road which runs past Kiltonga, up Bradshaw's Brae, then down to meet up with the Great Road at Quarry Corner. It was opened in 1817 and was intended to serve the anticipated traffic of mail and passenger coaches on their way to Scotland and England, via Donaghadee and Portpatrick. This traffic would come through Newtownards and, the theory ran, would put Newtownards emphatically on the map.

'Two fine new boulevards': Regent Street and Frances Street

The new road, and the fact that it would carry traffic right through the town, necessitated changes in its street pattern. The focus of attention shifted away from the cruciform plan centred on Conway Square to an east-west axis, created by the building of two fine new boulevards, Regent Street and Frances Street.

This signified an important shift. The cruciform plan, with all roads leading equally into Conway Square, the district's communal centre and gathering place, reflected Newtown's identity as a market town. The new streets, however, tell us that the days when the market town was the capital of its own little kingdom had gone. These grand new streets, paradoxically, signify a sort of downgrading, or rather, the town's integration into the regional economy, in which it was envisaged less a place in its own right than a staging post between the region's capital (Belfast) and the packet port of Donaghadee.

These streets also reflected prevailing fashions in urban planning. Just as the Market House and Square had reflected the previous century's vogue for impressive buildings set around spacious squares, now, forty years on, in the planning of these two streets, another opportunity was taken to make a statement about the town's aspiration towards dignity and elegance. Regent Street and Frances Street are broad, straight thoroughfares which use open space to give a sense of grandeur. Their length, when taken with Church Street, which leads to Regent Street, is almost a mile. Calling one of them Regent Street also symbolised the spirit of modernity

The expanding town of Newtownards c.1830. Note Montgomery's flankers still survived, marked 'old towers'.

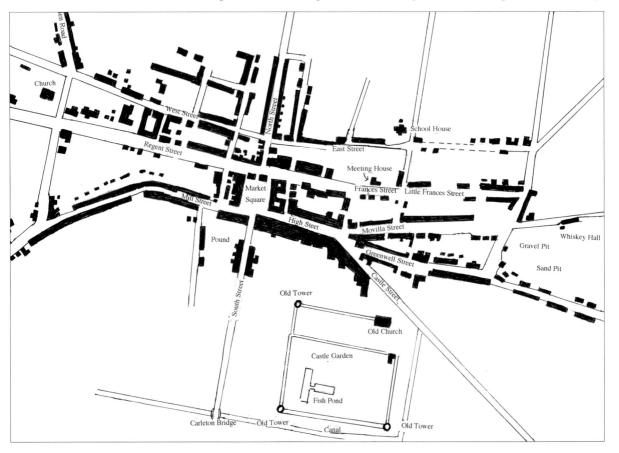

that lay behind their development. From 1811-20 the government of the United Kingdom was headed by the Prince of Wales (later George IV) acting as Regent in the name of his father, George III, who was incapacitated.

The most stately of the fine new houses erected on Regent Street was Regent House, the town's only country mansion.

The houses on these new streets, and more particularly on Regent Street, also reflect contemporary taste. There are several extremely fine Georgian doorways in Regent Street, which became particularly fashionable as a residential area, although some of the wealthiest inhabitants preferred to build their homes along the new road to Belfast. An exception is Regent House, built about 1820 by the local brewer and maltster Peter Johnston. It is one of the few examples of 'Greek revival' architecture in County Down, and at one time this once gracious dwelling (now much mutilated) was included in the Royal Institute of British Architects list of buildings acceptable for examination drawings. More recent alterations to the building have not added to its character.

Around this time the town also developed its own weavers' quarter. In the early nineteenth century cotton could be spun by steam engines but weaving remained unmechanised. This meant that there was a vast amount of work for the hand loom weaver, in weaving the cotton which was pouring out of the big cotton spinning mills in Belfast, and from the smaller spinning mills which had been established in Lisburn, Bangor and in Newtownards itself. There was one in what was then called Factory Lane, known today as Castle Place. The Ordnance Survey report of 1833 says that:

...there is a very large old unmeaning-looking house at the east end of the town facing the old fountain [i.e., the Market Cross]. It was formerly the residence of Mr Stewart whose grandson is the present Marquess [of] Londonderry. It was for many years used as a factory.

Handloom weaver at his loom. For the first half of the nineteenth century the weavers were the backbone of the town's economy.

This spinning mill gave direct employment to many and there was work also in preliminary processing and in bleaching the woven product, but it was the weaving that was most important to the town. Hundreds owned looms and weaved in their own homes. Earnings were good, better even than in Lancashire, and as one contemporary writer put it: 'a smart young cotton weaver became no slight attraction in the eyes of a country belle.'

To accommodate the weavers, the town expanded to the north of West Street. The present Robert Street was then called Shuttlefield Row, and it once contained many single and double-storied weavers' houses. The single-storey weavers' house of the time had two rooms and was built around the all-important loom which occupied the larger room, while the family squeezed in next door. Good light was important and so the workshop was sometimes lit by two windows. In the double-storey houses the ground floor living room was knocked into the workshop and the upstairs was used for living. The ceilings had to be high to accommodate the loom and so first floor ceilings were correspondingly low, with upstairs windows right under the eaves. Thomas Street also contained many interesting, if decaying, examples of single and double-storied weavers' houses until its recent redevelopment.

'Remarkable for... places of worship'

The town seems to have been prospering spiritually as well as materially, for in 1824 it was noted that, 'Newtownards is remarkable for the number of places of worship it contains, there being no less than six different

First Presbyterian Church from an old photograph. Tragically, this building was gutted by fire in 1994.

denominations, besides a Catholic chapel.'

The roof of the First Presbyterian church building became unsafe and so a new building was erected in 1815, 'pleasantly situated on an eminence' at its present site in Frances Street. It cost £3,000 to build, the money being raised by the congregation and by public contributions. A contemporary source said that, 'the interior is neatly fitted up and contains 145 seats which would hold seven persons each including the gallery.' Attendance at Sunday services was reported as averaging seven hundred to a thousand. Today's Second Presbyterian Church was then known as the Seceding Presbyterian Church, and it met in Mary Street. The town's oldest Presbyterian church, a small building, 72 x 44 feet, containing 77 seats, was occupied by the Non-Subscribing Presbyterian Church. The Reformed Presbyterian Church, or Covenanters, had moved in from Conlig and met in Anne Street. John Wesley had frequently visited the town at the end of the eighteenth century and in 1808 the Methodists were sufficiently strong to build their own meeting house. It was in Lower Mary Street, on the corner of Regent Street (in a building now used by the Reformed Presbyterian Church). It could hold 180 people and about half that number generally attended.

'The prettiest building in the town', according the officer who drew up the notes to accompany the first Ordnance Survey maps in 1833, was the new St Mark's Parish Church. This 'handsome church situated in a conspicuous point, added much to the beauty of the place.' It cost £5,446 of which £831 was a gift, and £3,692 a loan from the Board of First Fruits. The remaining £392 was a gift from Lord Londonderry. It was built to accommodate the growing Church of Ireland community. In 1764 there were only sixty adult male members of the Church of Ireland in the entire parish, but numbers increased in line with the overall population growth, and by 1816 would have been about a thousand. They had been meeting in the small chapel built by Sir Robert Colvill in today's Court Street, but by 1816 this had become unsafe. The newly fashionable west end of the town, on the Belfast side, was considered the ideal site for its successor, St Mark's. It is thought that a four-piece silver Communion Plate made in

St. Mark's Parish Church. Should it have been called St. Finnian's or St. Columba's? It has been suggested that it was named after its then Rector, Marcus Cassidy.

Dublin in the 1680s and decorated with the Colvill Crest was acquired by the church at this time as William Colvill, an indirect descendant of the Colvills, sold his remaining Newtownards property in 1817.

What about the Catholics? According to the nationalist historian O'Laverty, the Catholic Irish were either driven from the parish after 1605 or remained as labourers to the new farmers. The 1659 'Census' shows us that many Catholics stayed, probably living in difficult and straitened circumstances. Though most would have been no worse off *materially* than before the Plantation, when they would also have laboured to landowning masters for a pittance (for them it was a case of 'new lords for old'), the difference was that the *culture* was now against them and they would probably have felt little sense of being wanted by the society they lived within.

This is illustrated by the story of Killysuggan Graveyard. In medieval times there had been a chapel and burial ground called Killysuggan, opposite Kiltonga. The Bradshaw family gave the local Catholic community this small plot of land near their house as a burial ground, free of rent. It was at first unenclosed, though separated from the road by a ditch. However, graves were desecrated and mourners were forced to hoist the coffin over the ditch to get the deceased into the grave-yard, no access being permitted from the road. Insult was added to injury when one of the Bradshaws began levying ten pence per burial. Three local Catholics took the Rev. Joseph Bradshaw to the High Court in Dublin, which re-instated their right to a free burial.

O'Laverty also speculated that many Catholics either renounced their faith or intermarried with Protestants. In the early nineteenth century the total Catholic community, including women and children, numbered only sixty. In this period Mass was celebrated every month in a farmhouse belonging to Murty Rogan in Ballyreagh, two miles south of Newtownards, by the parish priest of Saintfield, Father William Teggart, and quarterly by the parish priest of Portaferry. They would also gather, a dozen at a time, in a small house in East Street at 'the Clay Holes', near the stream which ran past Anne Street, where Debretta's factory stands today. According to O'Laverty, 'many of them brought with them cans as if coming to the stream for water, being either afraid or ashamed that Protestants should see them going to Mass.'

This situation was remedied in 1811 when Father Patrick Curran, who worked as a tutor to the family of Lord Londonderry, was appointeed first parish priest of Newtownards. In 1812, Father Curran used his influence with Lord Londonderry to obtain the gift of a site in Anne Street, then considered a 'remote part of the town', upon which to build a chapel. The necessary money, about £80, was raised by public subscription, and it is interesting to note that the dissenting congregations were among the largest contributors. The chapel was described as a 'small building of the plainest description... [with] four small windows... two seats and 27 forms.'

The death of Lord Londonderry and the suicide of Castlereagh

The steady advance of the town over this period was due in large measure to the efforts of the first Marquess of Londonderry, who, though many could never forgive him for his role in the suppression of the rebellion, went on to prove himself a generally benign and attentive landlord, who seldom left his estates. His death in 1821, at the age of eighty two, was a real blow to the town. Events then unfurled in macabre and dramatic fashion. The first Marquess's son and heir, Viscount Castlereagh, had had a glittering political career, becoming British Foreign Secretary, and presiding, as every schoolboy and girl knows, at the Congress of Vienna in 1815. But he was to enjoy the title of second Marquess of Londonderry for just one year. He committed suicide in 1822 – the only Cabinet Minister ever to do so. He was succeeded by his brother, Charles, who became the third Marquess.

The Clay Holes, East Street, the area where Catholics worshipped until 1812. Bairdwear currently occupies the site. These adjacent cottages were made of clay and had no back door. (T. Maddock)

The third Marquess had gained a deserved reputation as a fearless soldier in the Napoleonic Wars, and had also had a political and diplomatic career. In 1819 he married Lady Frances Vane-Tempest, the heiress to vast estates in north east England which contained considerable reserves of coal. In addition to these English properties, she had inherited lands from her mother in County Antrim. The Londonderrys became one of the wealthiest couples in the British Isles, with an estimated annual income of well over £100,000, making them wealthier than many European royal families. They chose to live in Durham and London, making only occasional visits to Mount Stewart. It would be unfair to say that the town and parish were neglected after 1822, but there was not the same degree of involvement as there had been, and this distance and relative disinterest was very shortly to take its toll.

10

Disease and dunghills 1830-1848

In 1848, John Andrews JP, the agent for Lord Londonderry's County Down estates from 1839, gave an account of the visit of Sir James Graham, a former British Home Secretary, to the town:

As he approached Newtownards he expressed himself most strongly respecting the town. He said he had found among the adjacent parishes a strong prejudice against Newtownards and from their representations had imbibed the prejudice, but it had completely vanished. He considered it a 'wonderful town'. Were he the proprietor and had he the power to raze the town, he would be sorry to do it. He considered it of great value to the estate and its being the terminus of the railway would very much increase its value and importance.

Graham's effusions had some basis. The population of the town had doubled in the 1830s rising from 4,442 to 8,096. However not everyone was happy about this. The heir to the town, Viscount Castlereagh, who clearly had some sort of environmental conscience, expressed a 'deep regret that the town had been so extended'.

Although Newtownards had become something of a 'boom town' in terms of its economic and population growth, it experienced no corresponding advance towards democracy. In one area there was even a step back – the town lost its right to be represented in Parliament when the Irish Parliament was abolished in 1800. Its powers of self-government remained limited. Ratepayers expected costs to be kept to an absolute minimum, an expectation that was surely fulfilled when, in 1827, the expenditure for the year was only £7.3s.10d. The members of the

The Court House, Regent Street. Courts were held in the 'Old Church' in Court Street until this fine building was erected in 1850. It was thoughtlessy demolished in 1968. (T. Maddock)

Corporation were really only concerned to maintain the peace and impose regulations for fair trading. In order better to fulfil these functions in 1830 it was decided to adapt the old, disused parish church for use as a court house. This Court House was replaced in 1850 by a new one, built in Regent Street.

But in other areas there was almost no progress. The state of affairs whereby a town of 8,000 people, with a self-elected Corporation of only 13, which never met, and whose only function was to convene an annual meeting of 23 persons with power to raise only a minimal sum of money, could not continue for long without ill effects. How were matters affecting environmental health and community welfare, education, lighting, paving, sewage and sanitation, refuse collection, burials, to be dealt with under such a system? Sadly for the people of Newtownards, they were not.

It hardly comes as a surprise therefore, to learn that, according to the Ordnance Survey Memoirs of the 1830s, 'the town inhabitants are in a very sickly state. Fever is very prevalent.' There was no dispensary in the town but one was 'much wanted.' Considering the poor state of the town's sanitation this is not really surprising. Mark Street 'was nearly stopped up with dunghills and requires severe animadversion and active measures of reform.' Mary Street had dirty sewer drains. In East Street the sewers were 'generally filthy and in bad order', and the Mill Yard behind today's Castle Street was described as 'a spectacle of dirt, filth and abomination.' The town was 'neither watched, paved, lighted or cleansed' in the 1830s.

Other infectious and contagious diseases also took their toll. In 1837 the Rev. Mark Cassidy, the town's rector and unofficial 'agent' to the Marquess of Londonderry, reported that there had been an influenza epidemic in the first half of the year 'which has taken off a good number of the inhabitants.' Following this came a devastating outbreak of smallpox. He wrote in July:

I find that it has visited almost every house in the town and neighbourhood... The medical men agree that the number was at the least between 2 and 3,000. The number of deaths was above one in fifty, below one in hundred... Some of the strongest, the healthiest and most temperate farmers on your estate have been marched away in the bloom of youth. My curate, Mr Hill, 26 years of age, one of the most amiable young men I ever knew, who would have been an ornament to the Church... officiated last Sunday in excellent health; he was dead on Saturday.

Cassidy also reported the death of his own family doctor, Alexander McCullough, the son of the minister of the First Presbyterian Church. He had been 'incessant in his attendance on children in fever... This is the fourth medical man we have lost in almost a year – three of them in fever (two in Newtown and one in Comber).' Incidentally, the Rev. McCullough had also now lost five of his six children. Cassidy admitted that:

...the number of deaths was chiefly owing to improper treatment. Where medical men were not called in, the usual treatment was a good quantity of whiskey mixed with pepper and sulphur... and plenty of blankets with a good fire to sweat the patient to bring out the pock. This indeed requires a strong constitution to escape death.

However, with no cure known for small pox or for influenza, and improvements in sanitation an essential for the prevention of 'fever', Poor Law dispensary doctors could have done little to halt the soaring death rate.

When reform of local government finally came in 1840 it was a disappointment. Although the old Corporation of Newtownards was abolished it was not replaced by an elected council. The town was eligible only to have Commissioners. In order to get the services of such Commissioners, twenty householders, each occupying premises having a minimum valuation of £20, had to apply to the Lord Lieutenant of Ireland. The inhabitants of Newtownards, having lost their Corporation, did not waste time in taking up this opportunity, and their application was granted on December 9th, 1841. Fifteen Commissioners were appointed to manage the town. The duties of these Commissioners, however, were confined only to supervision of the lighting and cleaning of the town, and they vowed to act in the most economical way possible:

Resolved, that the Commissioners shall not expend more than £5 per annum in the salary of officers for carrying the Act into execution and it is earnestly hoped that the business may be carried on without any salary whatsoever.

The first rates levied by the new Commissioners came to £100 but expenditure was estimated at £132.12.0d. To make up the deficit they decided to 'pass round the hat' amongst themselves rather than incur debt

A thousand women embroidered linen in the parish in the 1830s. This cottage sat within an old quarry on Scrabo.

or cut back on expenditure; then, true to their resolution, they appointed only one officer – a clerk – at a salary of £2 per annum.

A small first step had been taken towards the establishment of efficient, local government. But the Commissioners were not elected and therefore still not accountable to the residents – only to central government. There was a long way to go.

Economy and commerce: the beginnings of independence

In spite of the general decline of the cotton industry in the province, Newtownards maintained its position as a specialist centre for the weaving of cotton muslin. The Ordnance Survey Memoirs noted that, 'weaving is carried on to a great extent in the town' – but linen, in contrast, was of relatively little importance. Newtownards had no linen market, and in 1837 there were only twenty looms weaving linen, all for domestic use. There were 600 looms weaving cotton muslin. A thousand women were employed in embroidering muslin for Glasgow merchants. It was reckoned that up to four hundred pounds per week was spent on wages for these women, who could earn from 1s.6d to 4s. per day. Contemporary sources remarked on this. The Parliamentary Gazetteer of 1845 noticed that:

...the weaving of muslin employs a large number of the male population [of the Newtownards district] and the embroidering of muslin, for the manufacturers of Glasgow employs many of the female population.

A similar comment is found in the Provincial Directory of 1864. In 1886 six people were listed as agents acting for the handloom weavers in the town.

The quarries at Scrabo also gave employment, as did the lead works at Whitespots. In the Ordnance Survey Memoirs it was said that 'It is a valuable mine. Considerable quantities of lead are extracted from it: some of the veins are so rich as to produce one ton of lead from three tons of the ore.' In the middle of the century wages of £1,000 - £1,200 were paid out monthly, and two thirds of the houses in North Street were occupied by miners. Mr R. Morrow, in an article in *Glimpses of the Ards* , tells us that an Isle of Man company leased the mines from the Marquess of Londonderry, but it would seem that there were problems with flooding in the shafts. To overcome this, the company brought in a steam engine and was able for a while to ship the lead to Bangor where it was sent to Flint for smelting. The mine appears to have employed 'a good number of hands' until the 1860s.

By the second quarter of the nineteenth century the town had its own monied business community. The importance of this can be seen in the 1840s when private enterprise stepped in where, apparently, the Commissioners had feared to tread. On December 13th, 1844 a prospectus was issued, inviting residents to take up shares in a new Gas Light Company, the capital of which was made up of 400 shares at £5 each. The prospectus outlined the the basis of the new Company:

It being determined to light the town of Newtownards with gas, it has been considered more advisable to do so by a Company consisting of the inhabitants of the town, who will have an interest in having gas of good quality and in sufficient quantity than any Contractor who will be a stranger to the town and who would of course merely wish to make the greatest possible profit.

The capital was raised and in 1845 work commenced in Court Street. Over the next twenty years the Company was able to halve the price of gas and more than double the dividend to shareholders.

'The young females dress well but absurdly': the path to the workhouse

When the Ordnance Survey officers arrived in the town in 1833 they found a great deal of building work in progress. 'A considerable number of one-story houses are at present being built,' remarked the surveyor, adding that:

...the houses are generally good. There are about 665 one-storey houses, out of which there are not more than thirty thatched, 469 two-storey houses, 17 three-storey , and 1 four-storey. All slated built of freestone which gives them all a new appearance. The freestone can be procured in the vicinity of the town which, together with the encouragement afforded by the Marquess of Londonderry, has been the means of long rows of generally one storey houses being erected, the Marquess of Londonderry granting leases for 60 years or 3 lives, at the rate of 1s. a foot upon which they can get the house erected at the rate of 1s. per foot... Comfort and cleanliness is attended to.

The good wages that women in the town could earn at 'flowering' work or embroidery was reflected in their dress, to the amusement of the surveyors:

The young females dress well but absurdly. A boa is indispensable, frequently a muff, a small bonnet, shoes with sandals and either white or very bright coloured gown. An umbrella appears to be a necessary appendage, both to males and females.

Men earning a good wage also dressed like dandies, donning 'blue tail coats with bright buttons, corduroy trousers or drab, a showy waistcoat with glass buttons on Sundays and market days. They wear a good hat but when working a very old one, round which there is generally a piece of cord.'If you were in employment in Newtownards in the 1830s then your standard of living would have been comfortable though never luxurious.

Outside the town, in the wider parish, the stronger farmers were doing well, although farm labourers could only expect to earn between 8-10d.

The Gas Works office in Mill Street. (T. Maddock)

117

per day and a rural weaver not much more. Giving evidence to the Devon Commission in 1844, the ever optimistic John Andrews, himself a farmer with several hundred acres near Comber, said that in recent years the position of the small tenantry had improved ' a little', and that the large tenants, renting thirty acres or more, were 'living comparatively like gentlemen; their houses and mode of living testify to it. I have partaken of repasts at their tables as comfortable as I could have prepared at my own.'

Other rural dwellers did not fare so well, as it was impossible to find employment for everyone at a time of such rapid population growth. Andrews reported that in the Newtownards area, 'I am afraid there is an excess of labour even with us; we have too many labourers; no doubt of it.' He went on to say that the position of labourers in the area had worsened in the early 1840s.

This was all the more worrying as there was no state welfare system. Relief of the poor was carried out by charity collections organised by churches and concerned local citizens. Newtownards was one of twelve towns that possessed a House of Industry where the homeless and unemployed were given shelter and work. It is referred to in an account of 1824 as a place where:

...the poor of the parish find an asylum and the means of subsistence; it is supported by subscription and is under the direction of the more wealthy inhabitants of the parish.

The Ordnance Survey Memoirs tells us that it was situated in Pont [? Pound] Street, and was:

...a plain house not built for the purpose it is now used for. The rent is paid by the Marquess of Londonderry, who also contributes £25 a year, formerly £50. It is supported by charitable collection and the greater part of the sums collected in the different places of worship. The number of inmates at present amount to 15; 20 is the average number, some deaths having lately occurred in consequence of the unhealthy state of the town. There are 138 individuals who reside in the town and parish who receive outdoor relief. All persons residing in the parish for the last 7 years and unable to earn a livelihood are entitled to relief. Persons of all denominations are admitted into the house.

The existence of the House of Industry showed Newtownards to have been a relatively progressive and compassionate community by the standards of the time, and it was said to have completely removed the need to beg in the parish.

In 1838 the Poor Law workhouse system was extended to Ireland and arrangements were made on September 3rd, 1839 to replace the House of Industry with a workhouse. This was built on an eight acre site between Church Street and Frederick Street, in the grounds of the present Ards

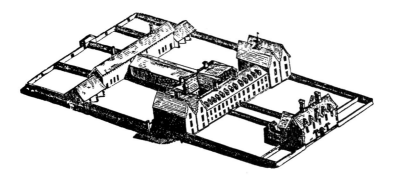

'The poor man's gaol.' Newtownards workhouse was one of 130 which sprang up all over Ireland in the early 1840s.

Hospital. The building was designed to house six hundred paupers, drawn from a wide district, called a Poor Law Union, which in this case stretched to Ballygowan and Moneyreagh in one direction, Kircubbin and Ballyhalbert, and Bangor and Donaghadee in others. The Union covered 94,000 acres and had a population of 54,000; and the first admissions took place on January 4th, 1842. The number of inmates in the workhouse averaged about two hundred, and it cost about two shillings a week to keep each one.

The costs of keeping the paupers were shared equally between the Union landlords and their 18,000 tenants. The workhouse was controlled by a Board of Guardians, eight of whom were ex-officio and twenty-four elected – the first elected representatives in Ireland. Conditions were kept as spartan as possible to ensure that only those who desperately needed help would go in, and to keep costs down. Food was extremely plain. In the minute book of the Newtownards workhouse one reads:

It was resolved that potatoes be given to the paupers [for dinner] for 5 days in the week and rice 2 days in the week, viz. 2 1/2 lbs potatoes and 1/3 quart of buttermilk to each adult for 2 days in the week and 2lbs potatoes and a pint of soup 3 days in the week and 7 ozs. rice and 1/8 quart new milk and 1/2 oz molasses 2 days in the week.

There was usually only one other meal in the day: a breakfast of oatmeal porridge and buttermilk. The Guardians were always seeking to keep costs down. Nevertheless, it is a little surprising to find, amongst the workhouse records, a letter (dated March 19th, 1850) from William Simpson, the Medical Officer, proposing a reduction in the quantity of food for its children:

Gentlemen, I beg leave to suggest that the children under 2 years of age be allowed only 6 oz of white bread and 1 pint of sweet milk per day. My reason for doing so is that the proportion of bread is much too large for the milk. When boiled, the mess is so thick that the children will not take it; and also that Class No. 2, viz. 9 years of age and under 15 be allowed 10 in lieu of 12 ozs. of brown bread on "bread and milk " days and 6 ozs. in lieu of 8 on "soup" days. My reason for suggesting this change is the Master having called my attention to the dinner table on a "soup" day. I found that nearly two thirds of the girls had not eaten the whole of their bread but were taking it out with them.

Had he known the Newtownards workhouse, Charles Dickens would

An Orange parade assembles in Church Street; the workhouse looms over the scene. From an old photograph.

have had a field day! The frugal diet was matched with a dour atmosphere. No tea, alcohol or tobacco were allowed, and meals had to be eaten in strict silence. Families were split up, male and female being housed in separate dormitories. It was called the 'poor man's gaol' and this impression is confirmed by a resolution in the minute book of March 26th, 1850: 'that the Master be directed to order the men at the gates to allow no pauper out without having a pass signed by the Master.' In the Newtownards workhouse children had to have three hours of lessons each morning; on Tuesday and Friday afternoons and evenings they had to sew cotton and on the remaining four days make, mend and wash clothes. Each evening they were taken out for exercise.

This emphasis on education was very contemporary. In 1831 the National system of education was launched in Ireland. Before this, there appear to have been only three schools in the town. Two were Erasmus Smith schools with 120 pupils, and a Classical School with 65 pupils. In the parish there was a school in Ballyblack, and there were Hibernian Schools in Loughries, Drumhirk and Drumawhy, Loughries being the largest with 65 pupils. With the introduction of the new national system, the number of schools in the town increased to six by 1848, with four National Schools joining the the two Erasmus Smith Schools and educating a total of 700 children. Out in the parish there were nine more National Schools, each with an enrolment of about fifty pupils.

'Plain but architectural': three new churches

Like an amoeba splitting, the Presbyterian community kept subdividing into new congregations, and in July 1834 another Presbyterian congregation

Regent Street Presbyterian Church. Its first minister, Thomas Watters, served the congregation for fifty-seven years.

was formed in the town, in Regent Street. According to a contemporary source, 'the circumstance that led to the erecting of this [meeting] house was a division among the congregation relative to the selection of a minister.' The Rev. James McCullough had been minister of First Presbyterian since 1799, during which time the congregation had grown to 1,050 families. On August 28th, 1834 his son, Julius, was ordained as his assistant and successor. This apparent attempt to establish a dynasty gave offence to some members of the congregation, and before the ordination took place, they obtained leave from the Synod of Ulster to establish a new congregation. The new congregation met at first in the Court House until they secured a three life lease from Lord Londonderry for land in Regent Street. The foundation stone of the church was laid by Lord Castlereagh on August 7th, 1834, with the famous Henry Cooke officiating. The first minister, the Rev. Thomas Watters, was ordained in 1835. According to the Ordnance Survey Memoirs the building had:

...a plain but architectural front and may be deemed one of the ornaments of the town. It has cost about £1,000, paid by subscriptions and contributions. Lord Londonderry gave £20 and the ground upon which it stands, Lord Castlereagh contributed £20, the late Lord Dufferin £10... The Rev Mr Watters, the clergyman states that it would accommodate 800... 200 on average attend on Sundays.

In the early 1830s it was estimated that there were 3,481 Presbyterians in the town, 397 members of the Church of Ireland, 198 other dissenters (Methodists and Quakers), and 236 Catholics. In 1838 a chapel was built in Zion Place for a growing congregation of New Connexion Methodists under the ministry of the Rev. Thomas Seymour. The Catholic population rose in company with the population of the town as a whole in the 1830s, to 574, and this necessitated the building of a new chapel, on the site of the old one in Ann Street. It was completed in 1845, when Father William McAlea was parish priest. This picturesque church was used as a place of worship until 1877, and was demolished in 1994.

11

The Famine: Lord Londonderry found wanting?

The Great Hunger

Newtownards did not suffer grievously when the potato crop failed in 1846-7. Its economy was plural (cotton weaving did much to help see the town through), and though the potato was important, local farmers also grew wheat, oats and barley, avoiding the monoculture that proved so disastrous in the west of Ireland.

However the crisis did not leave Newtownards untouched. Admissions to the workhouse more than doubled between October 1846 and January 1847, and by July they had doubled again to 426. (They were not to subside to normal levels until April 1848.) On January 10th, 1847, John Andrews wrote to Lord Londonderry, then living at Wynyard in County Durham, that:

Matters, I lament to say, are getting daily worse. The importation of food, though considerable, does not seem to satisfy demands or prevent the progressive advance of price, and the sufferings of the poor are considerably increasing... Families who have no head to work for them are much distressed. Many such exist everywhere and they are too numerous in Newtownards. After various projects, visiting committees have been appointed and on Tuesday next something will be decided upon, most probably a soup kitchen. The want of potatoes causes an immense consumption of grain by the farmers, which diminishes the quantity available for the market and I regret to say diminishes the resources available for *rent* which I fear will be deficient at May to a larger extent than I had ventured to contemplate. We must however do our best.

His next letter, of January 18th, 1847, sounds a note of increasing alarm:

Since last I addressed your lordship the distress of the poor has been fearfully increasing. The condition of even the fully employed labourer can not now be other than one of straits and difficulty; and it is much to be feared that of the small farmer, who is eating out of his produce, and has little to sell, will become very bad long before harvest. Seed corn must be extracted from our stocks. All this now becomes now truly alarming. Thank God we have not here much pressure

from want of employment. If the weaving should fail, I know not what would become of us. In Newtownards a good subscription has been got up and the soup kitchen will speedily be in operation.

The following month he reported that the soup kitchen was:

...much visited. I lament to say the poor and destitute are pressing on the workhouse beyond its powers of reception... The future is veiled from the most penetrating human eye. No doubt very considerable privation is endured by all from the labouring classes down and exertion through many months will yet be necessary.

The Guardians of the Newtownards workhouse were not confident that they were adequately equipped to discharge their obligations to the poor. They voted by 19 votes to 11 that a petition should be submitted to the House of Commons asking for permission to distribute food to those in need without them having to be admitted to the workhouse. They also petitioned for a change in the methods of assessing the Poor Law rate so that all districts, urban and rural, would pay the same. This would mean a reduction of rates for Newtownards.

Andrews resisted both proposals. In the case of the first he believed that outdoor relief would encourage dependency and pauperism. Regarding the second – an equalisation of rates – he believed it would undermine the relationship between what an area levied in rates and what it paid out in relief: 'the closer responsibility and liability are brought home there will

'Binging' or bedding potatoes, to store them. This practice was routine in the Ards. Potatoes were important but the local economy was mixed, and potato dependency was less commonplace.

be the greater circumspection.' On March 14th, 1847 he was happy to inform Lord Londonderry that, thanks to their soup kitchen, Newtownards had 'no destitution.'

But there was widespread destitution elsewhere in Ireland and the government eventually allowed Poor Law Unions to distribute free food to the needy outside the workhouse for the duration of the crisis. Individual Boards of Guardians could opt out if they felt that their existing arrangements were satisfactory. Newtownards, Belfast and Antrim were the only Unions which did not engage in 'outdoor relief'. By May 14th, 1847 Andrews reported that:

Our [voluntary] Soup Kitchens [in Comber and Newtownards] are so far adequate to relieve the distress which the workhouse cannot meet... and the trading in Newtownards is tolerably brisk so that, on the whole, our situation is comparatively an enviable one. But our workhouse contains 750 in the body of the House and nearly 100 in the Fever Hospital. Very heavy rates are on the point of being again levied, and though suffering much less than others, there is much of gloom in future prospects...

Some found Andrews' attitude unacceptable. In December 1847 one of the Poor Law Guardians, Sharman Crawford, resigned in protest, claiming that there were too many deaths in the workhouse (74 between August and November), and that these were the result of over-crowding, and the fact that people held out too long before resorting to workhouse charity, so that by the time many were admitted they were seriously under-nourished. He claimed that this was 'unjust, uncharitable and unchristian.' This put Andrews under pressure, but he maintained his doctrinaire opposition to giving out free food, insisting that such action must be a matter of *private* charity. This became almost a mania with him. By November 1847 he was arranging for the Poor Law Guardians to rent additional accommodation and extend the workhouse itself by building. 'We will build and build and in the meantime hire and hire but by some means we will protect ourselves against the inundation of outdoor relief.'

It has not been possible to calculate how many people actually starved to death in the Newtownards area during the potato famine, but many of those weakened by under-nourishment, because of the high food prices, died of typhus, relapsing fever, dysentery or scurvy. Not surprisingly a high proportion of the deaths appear to have been in the workhouse. Nor is it clear whether Andrew's approach saved or (more probably) cost lives.

It has been estimated that about 7% of County Down's population died as a result of the Famine. The figure around Newtownards was probably rather less than this, however the number was still sufficient to overload the system. In 1848, the Board of Guardians received complaints from the parish authorities that the parish graveyard was filling up with pauper dead from the workhouse. Consequently, in 1850, the Board bought an acre of ground in the townland of Milecross from Lord Londonderry as a burial ground for the paupers – Bully's Acre.

'He had secured his breeches with one of Chubb's double bolters': the third Marquess condemned

When the famine was at its worst, a great controversy arose about the behaviour of the third Marquess of Londonderry in relation to the suffering. A withering article appeared in the *Londonderry Standard* of January 8th, 1847 entitled 'The Three Marquesses'. Its anonymous author alleged that, when it came to charitable giving, the third Marquess 'had secured his breeches with one of Chubb's double bolters, at least as far as the town of Newtownards is concerned.' He said that Lord Londonery had promised to attend a relief meeting in the town at the beginning of January but, at the last moment, had returned to London leaving:

> ...his agent Mr Andrews, to herald his munificence to the said assemblage. The sum total of his lordship's subscription to the relief fund being no less than £20; and the Marchioness, as if to mesmerise the folk in that quarter with an awestruck feeling of aristocratic charity, actually added £10 to her husband's princely donation.

The article then alleged that Andrews had produced a 'set of resolutions, cut and dry for the occasion', read them out, and that the others present abruptly left the meeting in protest. The writer applauded this protest action: 'the folks there have yet to learn the alphabet of serfism'. The Marquess had made an outstanding 'blunder when he supposed the spirited gentry merchants, and other inhabitants of Newtownards, would tamely allow such conduct to pass without protest,' he asserted, and concluded with a harsh attack on Lord Londonderry's lifestyle:

Let him not wrap himself up in the vain delusion that he was sent into this world merely to revel on the sweat and toil of others, without any care or thought in his part as to how or under what circumstances of pinching economy his revenues are made up. And when the sounds of tabret and harp re-echo through the lofty halls of Holdernesse House, when the feast is spread and lights glare and lackeys bow, and when human greatness seems to forget its mortality, it might be a noble thought for the owner of that magnificent structure to express, namely, that the comforts of his tenantry were at least in equal ratio to the luxury of their lord...

The writer went on to compare Londonderry's contribution with that of the Marquess of Hertford, who, with an income of £80,000 per year, had made a contribution to Lisburn, where 1,600 out of 7,000 were destitute, of only £100. Both these Marquesses contrasted with the Marquess of Downshire who, according to the writer, had reduced the rents by thousands of pounds, offered full employment around Hillsborough, paying good wages and giving out free soup. Two days before Christmas he had two bullocks slaughtered and cut up into 4lb pieces to be given, with a shilling, to poor families.

Andrews replied defending paternalism and Lord Londonderry's approach to the crisis. Lord Londonderry himself had written to the *Downpatrick Recorder* stating that landlords should be free to decide for themselves about rent reductions, adding that 'my scale of rents has been fixed with a due regard to bad seasons as well as good.'

Andrews denied that he had chaired the relief meeting, accused the *Londonderry Standard* of trying to 'disorganise the social relation between Landlord and Tenant', and protested that Lord and Lady Londonderry had visited Ulster to fulfil a promise made by Lady Londonderry to visit her County Antrim tenants, despite the 'inclement season' and alarming rumours of trouble makers. He accepted that the Londonderrys had given £30 towards a soup kitchen but maintained that this was a first instalment.

On January 22nd, the editor replied to Andrews' letter. He defended the paper from the charge of attempting to disorganise landlord-tenant relations, but claimed that Lord Londonderry's threats to violate Tenant Right customs had that effect. The editor questioned whether the famous £30 had ever actually been paid in to the Relief Fund as he had heard that Lord Londonderry, in the past, had not always paid his annual subscription of £25 to the town's former House of Industry. Once again the donation of £30 was scoffed at: considering that he had an income of well over £150,000, 'thirty whole pounds of sterling money, and this out of their hard earned poor pittance, for the relief of the starving poor of Newtownards, was an act of princely munificence!'. He ridiculed Andrews's remarks

An heroic portrait of Charles, third Marquess of Londonderry by Lawrence. 'Fighting Charlie' distinguished himself in the Peninsular War, but less appropriately, applied military methods to the management of his estate.

about Lady Londonderry's resolve to visit her Antrim tenantry as 'superb heroism'. He denied that the weather was inclement, 'and in order to appreciate the martyrdom endured by the noble party it is necessary for our readers only to imagine themselves shut up in a close carriage with velvet cushions and rattling along the road at eight or ten miles an hour!'

Then it was the turn, a week later, of the original 'correspondent' to make his reply to Andrews. He accused Andrews of 'flourishing a pasteboard sword in the now exploded cause of feudalism.' The correspondent noted how merchants of Belfast had donated hundreds of pounds each, Lord Roden had given £500 to his political enemies in Dundalk, and how the Marquess of Downshire had given £10,000. The correspondent said that he had spoken to some residents of Newtownards and they had expressed satisfaction that Londonderry's 'pitiful conduct has been placed on record.'

Meanwhile, as he publicly defended his master, Andrews was privately confiding to Lord Londonderry (February 2nd, 1847) that around Newtownards 'the needy are badly situated'. He went on, 'my plan and object is to press those who are destitute of means to sell and emigrate.' As well, he hoped that an earlier arrangement with 'Dickson, our Newtownards seedsman' to supply the tenantry with good seed would now pay off. Because of Tenant Right 'the poorest tenant feels he has something worth preserving' and would still have an incentive to cultivate corn.

Despite the worsening situation in Newtownards, Andrews maintained his robust public defence of Lord Londonderry's charity and the relief measures taken in the town. The controversy took a new twist when Andrews published another reply, but this time in the rival newspaper, the *Londonderry Sentinel*. In Andrews' letter of February 10th, he maintained that he could prove that he had paid out, on Lord Londonderry's behalf, each year since he had become agent, subscriptions of £25 to the House of Industry.

He also enclosed a letter from Lord Londonderry himself. Londonderry maintained that he had not been asked for rent reductions in County Down. He took advice that there was an 'admirable workhouse in Newtownards' and that the poor were provided for. He pointed out that Lady Londonderry had suggested setting up a soup kitchen and that more money was to be asked for if required. He said 'I am entirely willing to remain in the hands and judgement of my tenantry and my town of Newtownards on this and every other subject.' He declared that he had made a large reduction in the rents on his Londonderry and Donegal estates, and that elsewhere all land under potatoes was completely relieved of rent. He outlined his philosophy on poor relief:

My object has been to increase that reliance on their own energies which our people have always demonstrated, and did not wish to encourage that erroneous system of looking abroad for relief... I decided at an early stage in our distress to adopt and inculcate on those around me, namely, "to help themselves and heaven will help them"... My conscience acquits me of ever having acted wrong[ly] as a proprietor, a landlord or a Christian. Believe me, yours faithfully, VANE LONDONDERRY

The *Standard* claimed that Andrews would not write to them as he did not want readers to see his excuses side by side with their comments. They poked fun at 'Vane Londonderry' calling him 'Vain Londonderry', and referring to 'the title of our maiden city with a weather-cock prefixed to it'. Turning to the contents of Andrews' reply, the paper insisted that Lord Londonderry had not paid his promised subscription to the House of Industry in the years 1824-8, and this information was given to the paper by a member of the committee that ran the institution! The editor alleged that the Lord Londonderry had a system of fines which had to be paid on the renewal of leases in County Down, and that this was only abolished after his son's intervention. The editor also alleged that Lord Londonderry had tried to undermine Tenant Right.

Turning to Lord Londonderry's letter, the editor claimed that Lord

The famine controversy was played out in the pages of the Londonderry Standard, later the Derry Standard. The rival Londonderry Sentinel was Conservative in politics and the natural platform for Lord Londonderry's counterblast.

Londonderry had received no applications for rent reductions because, a few months before, he had published a statement saying that he had decided not to make any rent reductions despite the onset of the famine. The editor again compared the amount of Lord Londonderry's donation with that of 'three or four insignificant muslin manufactures [of Newtownards?] who beat your Lordship and Lady Londonderry hollow in the way of liberality to your own starving people.' Finally, the editor mocked Lord Londonderry's claim to have never 'acted wrong[ly] as a... Christian': 'His Lordship is then in a most enviable state of inward blessedness for we imagine that some of the Apostles themselves could scarcely have made such a declaration!'

Perhaps the plight of the poor in Newtownards could have been made easier had negotiations between Andrews, on behalf of Lord Londonderry, and the Belfast and County Down Railway Company for the sale of land for the new line been concluded earlier. Negotiations to purchase land began on January 18th, 1848 when the famine was at its worst. Naturally, Andrews was asking for as much as possible. He admitted privately that he was asking for sums that 'were higher than I have yet known to be paid.' Negotiations dragged on for weeks as 'they cannot be pressed without weakening our position.' By mid-May they were concluded and the railway company began work, employing 'the labourers whom the farmers from want of money and dearth of food have been throwing off.' If these negotiations had been concluded earlier, and the poor employed, their suffering would undoubtedly have been lessened.

In defence of Lord Londonderry, it must be said that he did increase his contribution to the soup kitchen considerably when asked. The family distributed clothes. Also, his share of the Poor Law rates, which supported the workhouse, was almost £500 a year. He set up links between his estates and his collieries in Durham, which provided jobs for some of the unemployed. He made money available for drainage schemes. But he could also be extremely insensitive. In 1848 the family made 'extensive additions', costing £15,000, to their mansion at Mount Stewart. This created work, and may have been an attempt at relief, but it appeared to most as conspicuous consumption at a time of general want, an impression that can hardly have been dispelled by its lavish opening in late November of that year. As the *Downpatrick Recorder* reported from Mount Stewart:

On Monday evening the splendid suite of spacious apartments were thrown open to the reception of the nobility and gentry of the county who began to arrive soon after 9 o'clock. The band of the 13th regiment was in attendance and about 10 o'clock, dancing commenced which was kept up with spirit and animation till 1

Mount Stewart, which was enlarged at the time of the Famine.

o'clock when at the supper table, extending the entire length of the new dining room prepared for the reception of 100 guests at the centre table with tables adjoining the *coup d'oeil* exhibited a display of beauty and fashion seldom surpassed in the County of Down.

Perhaps the most important consideration, and one not appreciated by contemporaries, was that Lord Londonderry did not have access to his entire annual income of £200,000. About £175,000 was his wife's, and this was tied up in a Trust which he could not touch. He had to make his Irish estates self-sufficient. Although his gross rental from the County Down estates was £23,000, and from Londonderry and Donegal, £2,000, yet when salaries, subscriptions, arrears and interest payments were deducted, he ended up with a loss of £2,000 per annum. In June 1847 the Belfast Banking Company asked him to pay his debts of £2,500 or they would make Andrews liable for them.

'The multitude are proverbially fickle': popular reactions

Inevitably, news of the war of words over the extent of Lord Londonderry's charity reached the people of Newtownards. Hostility was vented towards Londonderry at a meeting in the town. This hurt the third Marquess and Andrews wrote seeking to console him:

I greatly lament that your lordship should be so wounded... and I think your lordship ought not to estimate the tenants generally by the indications of a meeting of the town of Newtownards where haughty spirits may have felt a gratification in exhibiting their independence. After all, my lord, we must not expect too much from weak and fallible and selfish men. Gratitude, it has been too truly said, has more regard to future expectation than to past favours and the multitude are proverbially fickle and unstable; but from my soul I do not believe that there is at present any default of affection or good feeling to your lordship. It has been the selfish few who may be disappointed that their rents were not now reduced.

Lord Londonderry's popularity fell while that of his son, the Viscount Castlereagh, rose. On February 15th, 1847, Lord Londonderry wrote to Andrews bemoaning the:

...attempt to raise the popularity of the son at the expense of the father. All may, and do, worship the rising sun and 'the evil that men do live after them but the good that they do is often interred with their bones' so do I think it will be with me with my Irish estates.

Lord Londonderry's view would seem to be borne out by the fact that a dinner was held in the Market House on Thursday August 19th, 1847 to honour Viscount Castlereagh. On his arrival in the town 'bonfires were lit on the hills around the Lough and presented a brilliant spectacle, and beer, at Lord Castlereagh's expense, was distributed at the bonfires.' Speeches referred not only to the demonstration of the townsmen's own 'energy, industry and independence during the late trying season [as shown] by our charity to the poor' but also to the fact that they were 'generously assisted by his lordship [Viscount Castlereagh] and his noble parent'.

Nevertheless it is clear that there was immense discontent in the town during the famine. The obituary in the *Newtownards Chronicle* in 1893, of David McKean, refers to the danger of rioting. At the time of the famine, McKean was a highly respected agent in the town for Messrs. Brown, sewed muslin manufacturers of Glasgow, who contracted work out to local people. He eventually became assistant to Lord Londonderry's agents from 1862-87, and was an elder of Second Presbyterian Church. The obituary throws light on the mood of the town during the famine:

At the time of the potato blight, great distress prevailing here, as indeed everywhere throughout the country, threats of bread riots were heard. The late Mr John Andrews, the agent of the estate, dreading bad consequences from the assembling of the masses and the temper they manifested, solicited the intervention of Mr McKean as the most likely person to bring them to reason, which happily he succeeded in doing.

Nationalist Newtownards?

The year 1848 was a time of revolutions and attempted *coups* all over Europe. In Ireland, as might be expected, the political temperature was particularly high. Here, the Young Irelanders, 'on behalf of the people of Ireland', sought a repeal of the Act of Union. The government responded by arresting the movement's leaders and soliciting statements of loyalty to counteract their claims. In April 1848 Andrews suggested that Lord Londonderry prepare two, one each for the parishes of Newtownards and Comber, after which 'the principal inhabitants could then be invited to attach their signatures which are procured without the risk of inviting a public meeting.'

Towards the end of April a private meeting took place of 'the most influential inhabitants of Newtownards' with this in mind. But Newtownards' nationalists, led by John McKittrick (a Guardian of the workhouse and draper in Conway Square), and the parish priest, had already seized the initiative and had submitted a petition declaring that Newtownards sought the repeal of the Act of Union. The meeting decided that a counter petition should be sent but, as Andrews said to Lord Londonderry, 'they desired me to request that your lordship would forego a public meeting which they feared might be disturbed as such meetings often been by the adverse party however small'. Finally, on May 9th, 1848, a larger meeting did take place. It renounced McKittrick's petition and declared its support for the Union:

This meeting conceives it absolutely necessary to repudiate on behalf of the great body of the population of the town and neighbourhood, the sentiments contained in a petition for Repeal of the Act of Union... which has emanated from a small and inconsiderable section of the inhabitants and to remove the impression which that petition may have had upon the Legislature that public opinion in this district is any degree favourable to the repeal of the Act of Union.

12

The Tenant Right War: The End of Deference?

The real issue in Newtownards at the end of the 1840s, however, was not repeal but Tenant Right, also known as the 'Ulster Custom'. Landlords were usually happy to grant the Tenant Right as it brought them advantages too. Andrews testified before the Devon Commission in 1844 that evictions were rare in Newtownards because farmers knew they must either pay their rents or lose their Tenant Right. But he also admitted that it was the best way of improving the estates, and he confessed privately to Lord Londonderry that granting it secured his place in the affections of the tenantry.

Many landlords, however, were unhappy with the idea of Tenant Right as a 'right' held by the tenant, preferring to see it as a privilege they conferred. So when Sharman Crawford of Crawfordsburn, a liberal landlord, introduced a Bill to legalise the Custom in the House of Commons in 1847, the landlord interest combined to defeat it. (Viscount Castlereagh, who approved of Tenant Right as a concession, but not as a statutory right, spoke against Crawford's Bill). But the issue did not go away. In 1850 tenants in Ulster went on the offensive and formed a Tenant League, which demanded fair rents and a legalisation of the Custom.

A lively branch of the Tenant Right Association was set up in Newtownards with Guy Stone Esq. JP of Barnhill, Comber as its chairman, and the Rev.Julius McCullough, minister of First Presbyterian Church, and the nationalist John McKittrick as joint secretaries. Both Catholic and Protestant tenant farmers supported the Association as all could see the benefits that would come if Tenant Right was made a statutory requirement. The tenantry in Newtownards believed it to be a right which dated back to the plantation, but after Viscount Castlereagh's equivocal speech, they felt that an element of uncertainty had crept in.

On March 6th, 1850, Lord Londonderry issued a statement to his tenantry, expressing his disapproval that 'my hitherto peaceable and excellent farmers had unhappily caught the insidious mania of the discontented and designing disturbers of the tranquillity of Down.' He referred to Presbyterian ministers 'lending their places of worship for

Facing ruin: thirty-three evictions took place at the Quarter Sessions in Newtownards in the summer of 1851.

declamations on temporal discontents', mentioning the Rev. Hugh Moore, the Non-Subscribing Presbyterian minister and the Rev. Julius McCullough by name. He promised that 'if prices become lower I will then attend to what is just between us', but concluded with what must be seen as a thinly veiled threat :

You must receive this Tenant Right as a boon, and God forbid that any circumstances should ever arise between us to make the holding of it from any of you. But the late violent language and proceedings in Ulster render it absolutely necessary that there should be no mistake between us on this most important subject.

Like his father, Lord Londonderry believed that the way to deal with discontent was with firmness. Thirty-three evictions took place at the Quarter Sessions in Newtownards in the summer of 1851. He also dismissed those of his staff who were not made of stone, 'for inefficiency in not collecting arrears'. A new era was defined in landlord-tenant relations in Newtownards. From now on:

Tenants paying in rents or arrears must understand their first duty is to the landlord on whose soil they exist, and from whom their livelihood comes and they [must] pay no debt until the remaining gale and arrears to the Office are made good. Should they attempt to do this, or abstract or have any part of rent abstracted from them for other and such purposes they will never receive a lease from Lord Londonderry and they will have notice to quit if they dare disobey these directions.

In September 1851 he stopped or reduced his public subscriptions to local good causes:

Acting as they have done why am I so indulgent? The arrears ruin me. £20,000 is now due me. Why am I so much worse off than others? If tenants pay me, all my subscriptions shall be restored. Till they do I shall cut down everything to the lowest possible rate in every way I can.

He cancelled his subscriptions to the:

Watching and Lighting of Newtownards	£30.0.0
Farming Society	£23.1.6
Royal Agricultural Society	£10.10.0
Chemico Agricultural Society	£10.10.0
Flax Improvement Society	£5.0.0
Deaf and Dumb Institute	£5.0.0

He also reduced by up to half his subscriptions to the Mount Stewart School Master's and Mistress's, and Comber School Mistress's Sunday allowances, Miss Hoey's Infant School and Clothing Society, his contribution to the cost of fuel, repairs and requisites for schools in Mount Stewart, Newtownards and Comber, and even the fees for the organist of St. Mark's Parish Church.

The tenants hardened their attitudes too. There was great unrest: haystacks were set on fire in Killarn, Ballyrogan and Craigantlet. Tenants began to organise. Two farmers from each townland were appointed to parish committees to work for rent reductions. They argued that reductions would benefit the landlords too. John Moore of Milecross said, 'Sir, if rack rents are to be kept up until our poor fellow-countrymen are brought to the workhouse or grave, what will my Lord Vane [Londonderry was the Earl Vane in the British peerage] do with his impoverished and desolate Newtownards and Comber.' A 'Great Baronial Tenant Right Meeting' was held in Newtownards in October 1851. The poster advertising it proclaimed:

Let the Sycophant and the Slave who prefer poverty and degradation to comfort, and the chain of tyranny and oppression to the liberty of freemen, 'at home by their fireside stay,' but let the HONEST MEN OF DOWN, who love their wives, their children and their brethren COME ONE AND ALL.

Lord Londonderry was outraged. He tried to stop the meeting, threatening to confiscate the Tenant Right of anyone who attended. Twenty extra constables were drafted in to the town but, though the meeting was well attended, all remained calm, despite the presence of several 'bailiff looking persons', who were said to be trying to stir up trouble. After the meeting, the following order appeared in the Agent's Book:

Lord Londonderry orders that not one of the thirty men who attended the Tenant Right meeting on the 21st inst. shall ever dispose of their farms by private negotiations and settlement and have the Tenant Right so called, and hitherto granted by me...

Lord Londonderry carried out his threat. At a stroke, he had effectively ruined thirty families. In November, Londonderry tightened the screw still further. On the 3rd of the month the Agent's Order Book noted:

The tenant farmers are to be generally and individually informed that unless their arrears of rent are paid up to March '50 during this month and by the 25th inst. – they will receive no considerations for any new valuation that is making nor will the old leases have any renewals – Indulgences must have limits – and all rents and arrears due to May 1851 will be expected peremptorily to be paid into the office in December and January 1852. A copy of this order was handed to each one of the bailiffs with orders to inform the tenants individually.

'They will sting him if they can': the 1852 election

The General Election of 1852 offered both sides the opportunity to demonstrate their strength. Sharman Crawford decided to stand as a candidate for County Down. Normally, Lord Londonderry would expect to control one of the two seats for the county, the other going to the representative of the Marquess of Downshire, the other great County Down proprietor. Since 1826 a seat had been held by Lord Londonderry's heir, Frederick, Viscount Castlereagh, and under normal circumstances he might have been expected to stand again. But these were not normal times. Castlereagh had shown liberal tendencies and was known to be sympathetic to the cause of Tenant Right. In short, he had become an embarrassment to his father.

Could Lord Londonderry control his tenants and direct them to vote only for his new candidate, or would they vote for the Tenant Right champion, Crawford, against their landlord's wishes? The election raised important questions, questions about the influence of the aristocracy in mid-nineteenth century politics, and the extent to which they were still deferred to:

...it is patent to all observers of passing events that the Noble Marquess himself, by his overbearing manner, actually swelled the ranks of the Tenant Leaguers in his own towns of Newtownards and Comber. He gave the wasps' nests the vitality they possess, and it is not surprising that they will sting him if they can.

Lord Londonderry initially asked his tenants to vote for his nephew, David Ker of Portavo and Montalto, but the two men quarrelled, so Londonderry instructed his tenants to vote only for Lord Edwin Hill, who was the representative of the Downshire family. (Ker fought on, in spite of losing Londonderry's endorsement.) 'Plumping' for Hill would mean that they would only be able to cast one of their two votes. At this time, there was no secret ballot and those who voted against their landlord's wishes took a risk of incurring his displeasure. 495 of his tenants had the franchise. Would they vote for Hill or Crawford?

Crawford came to speak in Newtownards on June 26th. Guy Stone presided at the meeting, and the *Northern Whig* reported that when Crawford rose to speak, the 'immense assemblage', greeted him with 'the most enthusiastic cheering which continued for several minutes'. Crawford spoke out in favour of the independence of labour, an end to high rents, justice to the tenantry and non-sectarian politics.

John Andrews was present at the meeting and was suitably dismissive, describing the speeches as 'harangues'. It was, he said, 'held on a piece of ground held in perpetuity by one of the League gentleman', implying that, had it been rented from Lord Londonderry, the meeting would never have been allowed. He estimated the number of voters present to have been about a hundred, (out of about eighty-five voters in the town and less than two hundred in the rest of the parish), along with 'twice as many Newtownards idlers, women and children.'

The Londonderry camp was reasonably confident that the tenants would vote as they were told to. Lord Londonderry engaged his Belfast solicitor, Robert Kelly, to visit the tenantry in the weeks preceding the election

Waiting for the bailiff? Lord Londonderry threatened to evict seventy families in the wake of the bitterly contested 1852 election. Farmer's cottage, Ballyskeagh.

informing them of his wishes. Kelly reported back that:

Many of them are afraid to conform to your lordship's wish for fear of their neighbours but I am happy to say that this is not general; it merely exists in some parts of the estate... The majority are still disposed to stick by your lordship through thick and thin and the electors in one townland (the largest in the estate) are going in a body to carry out your lordship's wish and plump for Lord Edwin.

Londonderry seems to have been surrounded by people determined to tell him what he wanted to hear. In every townland, a majority had said in the canvass that they would vote for Hill. The results were a great shock to Londonderry. In nearly all the townlands in the parish of Newtownards, Crawford topped the poll. In the parish as a whole the results were Crawford: 179 votes, Hill: 133, Ker: 55.

It was a significant rebellion, and a notable local victory. As the *Northern Whig* said 'we must pay tribute to the gallant men who, at the Newtownards polling booths, redeemed the pledge they had made at County meetings [of the Tenant Right Association].' However it was still not enough to secure the return of Crawford for the county. Hill topped the poll, Ker came second, and Crawford third, with a third of his vote coming from the Newtownards polling station. The townlands of Ballyrogan, Ballymagreehan, Ballyalton, Ballyskeagh Low, Ballyhaft, Ballyblack Little, Drumawhy, Cunningburn, Tullynagardy, Ballyharry, Ballywatticock, and Cronstown, and the town of Newtownards all turned in outright Crawford majorities.

Retaliation followed swiftly. The following entry appears in the Agent's Order Book on September 13th, 1852:

In looking over the reports of the Tenant Farmers he finds on a number of 315 or 320 persons who have exercised their independence [in the recent election] which

William Sharman Crawford, of Crawfordsburn, the darling of the tenant farmers, seen as a traitor by his fellow landlords. From an old newspaper cutting.

they have a perfect right to do so. SEVENTY individuals of the number are indebted on the books in no less a sum than upwards of £2000, ranging from £20 to £30, £50 and £100. It will hardly be argued that if men choose to be independent they are at liberty to remain in debt. Can there be justice in men acting independently of their landlord in not paying him for the soil they possess? Lord Londonderry desires no favour from any one, but he is in a position to peremptorily to insist upon these *seventy* individuals, of whom he has sent a list to the office, to pay up all their arrears of rent. To those who have crops, stock and cattle on the grounds and are apparently solvent, no difficulty need impede. To those who have not the immediate means, Bills at one or two months may be taken by the agent. Surely no honest tenant would owe his landlord, and at the same moment think himself justified in disobeying him by boasting and acting upon his own independence? Let every farmer honestly pay, and let him do whatever he likes. But skulking from paying for his holding, while he goes to meetings for subscriptions, tea parties, dinners, is the conduct of a knave and dishonest man.

Lord Londonderry therefore sends these express orders to his Agents to inform the *Seventy* men alluded to of his fixed determination: if all rents do not immediately come *in this month and the next,* distresses are forthwith to be issued and ejectments at the Sessions, as Lord Londonderry is not afraid of letting his lands to Scotchmen or let them lie waste. [This] is the same if no rents are got. And a sufficient number of Bailiffs are to be employed and the Constabulary to be called in if necessary.

Tower, Scrabo Hill

Londonderry still had tremendous power over his tenants, and under this pressure, the local Tenant Right Movement crumbled, never to recover. The prosperity of the 1850s masked the issue, and when the Tenant Right movement became more established in the south of Ireland, the sight of Catholic farmers marching on Protestant landlords stirred mixed emotions, and the Presbyterian farmers of Newtownards never again fully put their weight behind the movement. In the election of 1857 two Conservative landlord candidates were again returned, and held the seats continuously through to 1874.

Scrabo Tower

The third Marquess died in 1854, and in July of that year, a group of his admirers met in the Newtownards Rectory to discuss building a memorial to him in the square. He had been the proprietor of the town and parish since 1822 – a period which had seen many changes, and it was thought fitting that some permanent memorial should be made to him. In 1855, however, it was decided that the memorial should instead be erected on Scrabo, and that the design should be the subject of a competition, with the cost of the work not to exceed £2,000. The eventual designer of the Tower, Charles Lanyon, came fourth, but had his proposal adopted because it came within the price range. In the end, however, the 135 feet high monument actually cost £3,010.

The foundation stone was laid in a ceremony on March 6th, 1857. A special train was laid on from Belfast which stopped at the foot of the hill. Long lines of pedestrians made their way up from all directions. The marquee erected at the crest of the hill was not needed as it was a beautiful day; beside it, a flag pole and a platform were also in place. The new Marquess and Marchioness of Londonderry arrived just after two o'clock. A procession was formed and the distinguished party, which included the Bishop of Down and many of the county's gentry, made their way to the top of the hill, preceded by the Marquess's Highland piper. A jar containing an inscribed scroll to the late Marquess, copies of the national and local newspapers of the day, an Ordnance Survey map of County Down, the coins of the realm, and a list of the names of subscribers was cemented into the foundations. The Union Jack was then hoisted as a signal for the firing of a *feu de joie* from a nearby battery of guns. The band of the Royal North Down Rifles then struck up the National Anthem followed by 'Partant pour la Syrie' and the 'Royal North Down Quickstep'. The account of the proceedings in the *Illustrated London News* of March 28th, 1857 concluded with the band entering Newtownards:

...playing popular airs. The day being fine, and it being weekly market day, the town was crowded with the farmers of the surrounding district, whose respectable

appearance indicated the prosperity enjoyed by the inhabitants of this populous portion of the country, the Yorkshire of Ireland.

It has been said that the inspiration of the monument was the gratitude the tenantry felt for the concern shown to them by the third Marquess during the famine, and indeed 450 of the 600 subscribers were connected with the estate. However, there were about 1,200 tenant farmers on the estate and an urban population of many thousands in Newtownards and Comber, so that 450 was not a large proportion of the whole tenantry. In fact, given the hostility to the third Marquess in these years, it would probably be a misrepresentation to claim that the Tower was erected by a grateful tenantry. Two thirds of the cost was raised by 98 individuals (the list headed by the Emperor Napoleon III of France), most of whom were fellow gentry from Antrim and Down, and personal friends of the Marquess. One must wonder if the inspiration for the monument did not owe more to his victory in the recent Tenant Right 'war', than to the character of the man himself. If the Tower is a symbol of anything, it is surely a symbol of landlord power. Whether he was working on his farm or travelling through the parish, whenever the tenant farmer looked up, the Tower would be there, a gracious but stoney reminder of who was in charge.

But it would be an exaggeration to maintain that landlord-tenant relations in Newtownards were bad throughout the nineteenth century or that the third Marquess of Londonderry was hated. As with 1798, the situation

'Whenever the tenant farmer looked up, the Tower would be there, a gracious but stoney reminder of who was in charge.'

141

was more complex than that. The Londonderry family were generally respected within the parish. The family usually abided by their motto of 'Live and let live'. They tacitly accepted Tenant Right, and Andrews' management of the estate was accepted by most as efficient and, in normal circumstances, humane.

The accession of the new Marquess (the former Viscount Castlereagh) did much to renew good relations between tenantry and landlord. Castlereagh had always been popular, and in November 1854, he held a reconciling dinner for William Sharman Crawford in the Assembly Room of the Market House. The new Marquess was much more in tune with the feelings of his tenantry than his father. He was very much aware of past difficulties and keen to build bridges. As the *Northern Whig* of February 21st, 1857 noted:

His lordship [the fourth Marquess] says he admits to its full extent the principle of security to the tenant his *bone fide* outlay and improvements, not only as a matter of justice to the occupier, but also an encouragement to future exertions.

Given the fourth Marquess's willingness to address the concerns of his tenantry, there seemed to be was every prospect of a renewal of the harmonious landlord-tenant relations customarily enjoyed in Newtownards.

13

A 'First Rate' Business Town 1855-1885

Stagnation and revival: economics

For the first ten years of this period there was prosperity. Farmers were able to get good prices for their produce. Wages rose and people had more money to spend. The population increased, reaching 9,547 in 1861.

But it was not to last. Depression struck in the mid 1860s and lasted until the late 1870s. The American Civil War of 1863-67 cut off supplies of raw cotton, and the hand loom weavers' situation became precarious. A Commissioner for the National Board of Education described Newtownards in 1868 as 'a poor town'.

The railway, which had seemed such a boon when it opened on May 6th, 1850, proved to be a mixed blessing. It ran from Belfast to Comber, then swept north to Newtownards around the foot of Scrabo Hill. The station was originally beside the present Strangford Arms Hotel, but when the line from Belfast was extended to Donaghadee in 1861, a new station was opened on the site of what is today the Technical College. A long embankment was built to bring the line up the hill to the station, and away in the direction of Conlig and thence to Donaghadee. Five trains a day were running to Belfast by 1857. No line was ever laid from Newtownards

NEWTOWNARDS

Newtownards Railway Station. The station stood on the site of what is today the Further Education College.

SCRABO. STRANGFORD LOUGH 3817. W.L.

Single-roomed cottage by
the shores of Strangford.

to Bangor but there were several plans to build a railway to Portaferry, none of which came to fruition.

The railway helped to destroy local, small scale industries which could not compete with cheap imported goods brought in from outside the town. A world-wide industrial boom had ended in 1874, and with overseas demand falling, English firms looked to Ireland as a market and their mass-produced goods flooded Irish provincial towns in the mid 1870s. Thus, brewers, tanners, bakers, tailors, glovers, and chandlers suffered.

In the late 1870s the handloom weavers, hitherto the economic backbone of the town, met in Conway Square to highlight their plight. In 1877, 208 weavers were unemployed and a further 400 were working fourteen hours a day for half wages. Anne Street, Thomas Street, Shuttlefield, James Street, Wallace's Street and Greenwell Street were the worst affected areas. The town's clergy and business owners organised a collection of money and public works. A path was laid from the old Comber Road to the top of Scrabo Hill where flowers and shrubs were planted. Unfortunately, within five years, the plants had all been eaten by cattle! The distribution of money did not proceed so well: some weavers complained that the money was finding its way to poor labourers and not to handloom weavers. In January-February 1881, the coldest winter of the century, a Coal and Relief Fund was set up for which public subscriptions were solicited and a fund-raising concert of songs and readings was held.

Hard on the heels of the industrial crisis came an agricultural crisis. Four bad harvests between 1877-1882, together with a fall in grain prices due to cheap imports from the North American prairies, caused a down turn in farming. In a gesture of goodwill towards his hard-pressed tenants, the fifth Marquess of Londonderry reduced the rents in 1878 and 1882.

The coincidence of these two economic crises does much to explain the fall in population during the 1870s and the early 1880s. The 1881 census reported a ten year drop of 871. This was the first time that the population of the town had fallen since the crisis of the mid seventeenth century. Most towns, except Belfast, had the same experience. The number of inmates in the workhouse in the 1870s rose to over four hundred, and the number receiving outdoor relief jumped from only one person in 1861 to over four hundred.

In order to recover, it was essential for local industries to mass produce and diversify. The editor of the town's new newspaper, the *Newtownards Chronicle*, founded in 1873, was critical of local men with capital who tended to hoard it or 'devote it to the erection of imposing ecclesiastical structures.' He considered that in the early 1870s 'the second town in the County is in a state of manufacturing stagnation.' However, not all the town's money went into the pockets of local capitalists or was spent on grandiose churches. Some began to be reinvested in the new factory-based textile industries.

This process had begun a few years earlier, in 1865, when George Walker opened a spinning mill at Castle Gardens. A year later James Apperson began to manufacture shirtings using handloom weavers, and by 1874 was giving employment to several hundred. In 1884 he moved to a large factory at the top of Thomas Street and Mark Street using gas powered weaving looms and he was able to employ about one hundred handloom weavers in their own homes in the 'busy season'. In 1873 William Dobbin opened a factory in South Street bringing a hundred handloom weavers under one roof.

The establishment of textile factories really took off in the decade after 1874. In that year William Sibbald Johnston, a thirty-eight year old Scot who had started a linen business in Belfast in 1866, built a factory in Kiltonga to bleach linen on the four acre site upon which the Bradshaws had once had their linen bleach green. By 1886, he was employing ninety workers continuing the tradition of Kiltonga as a site for industry which continues to this day. Another bleaching business was revived near Movilla by Messrs. Woods of Leeds in 1878. In 1882, J.R. Sefton & Co.

The Ards Weaving Company. In 1886 Bassett wrote of it that, 'A more delightful or healthful situation could not be found.' The site, on the Crawfordburn Road, is presently occupied by a car showroom.

started a new weaving factory in William Street, which, within a few months was employing 'hundreds'. Not long afterwards Samuel Greer & Co. started a knitting factory in Court Street. The Ards Weaving Company was established in 1882 on the Crawfordsburn Road. It had 250 looms powered by a steam engine and employed 220 in 1886. In 1884, Stevenson, Ledgerwood, & Co. of Regent Street began producing hosiery and skirts on the site of the old brewery. At the time it was the only steam powered hosiery factory in Ireland. By 1890 it was employing two hundred.

Some of the development was due to local capital and enterprise. Newtownards had pulled itself up by its own bootstraps. Lord Londonderry had also played his part by issuing very long leases or fee-farm grants to the new factories. It was a generous gesture, and Stevenson the industrialist reckoned at the time that 'this was the starting point of the prosperity of Newtownards.' By the early 1880s Newtownards was finding its way out of recession. In 1886 Bassett's County Guide said, 'From a business point of view, Newtownards is a first rate town.'

'Let them rant and sing': regular and radical religion

The town's churches went from strength to strength in this period. Regent Street Methodist moved to a new building in 1854, and its old premises at the corner of Regent Street and Lower Mary Street were taken over by the Reformed Presbyterian Church. A Fourth Presbyterian congregation started in 1854 in Court Street, moving to South Street in 1859.

1859 saw a further impetus to the spiritual life of the town. A local school teacher, M. Harbinson, had a burden to see the 1859 Revival extend to Newtownards. He began a weekly united prayer meeting, along with open-air and cottage gatherings. In May, the headmaster of the Model School in Ballymena, and a Scripture Reader, William McIlwrath, were invited to the town to relate the story of the revival to a meeting in First Newtownards. Great interest was shown and on June 20th, 1859 Mr McIlwrath was appointed agent of the Town Mission and became the leader of the major revival which swept the town in that year. This revival started at a meeting conducted by McIlwrath in Ballyblack on the last Sunday in June. The first week-night prayer meeting was held in the Reformed Presbyterian Church in Anne Street with two hundred present. Numbers so increased that the meetings had to move into larger churches. According to Harbinson, 'in no part of the province, so far as I can learn, has there been a more genuine work of grace than in the town of Newtownards.' The Rev.W.D.Weir's history of Greenwell Street Presbyterian Church quotes an account of August 20th, 1859:

A wonderful change transformed the town, and the Sabbath... is now so strictly observed that the stillness of the streets is seldom broken, except by the crowds that flock to the several churches. Districts of the town that on Saturday evenings used to be so turbulent that the very police were timid... are now perfectly quiet and peaceful.

The spirit of revival was most conspicuous at the time of the annual Harvest Fair at the end of September. At this great gathering, usually renowned for drunkenness and disturbance, a great public prayer meeting was held from 2-6pm:

It was... interesting in the extreme to see a large body of people kneeling down in prayer in the public market place of a populous town, many of whom had never bent the knee for that purpose in any place. Such a scene, it is admitted, was never previously witnessed in Newtownards.

The ministers of every denomination were kept busy in counselling. Church membership increased. For example, the number of families in Regent Street Presbyterian Church increased from two to three hundred. Two new Presbyterian Churches were created within ten years of the revival.

The first of these was Strean Presbyterian Church, which opened in 1866. As with the establishment of Regent Street Presbyterian Church in 1834, Strean's inception was the result of a disagreement in First Presbyterian Church over the appointment of a minister. By 1865 the Rev. Julius McCullough was aged, and desired that a minister be appointed who would be both his assistant and his successor. Some members of the congregation disagreed and left. Thomas Strean, a wealthy member, held a meeting of dissidents in a solicitor's office to discuss the setting up of a new congregation. They decided to go ahead. Meetings were held in the Market House, and the Comber Presbytery was asked to provide preachers.

Strean Presbyterian Church, founded by Thomas Strean in 1866. Strean had left a large share of his money to his solicitor rather than to his relatives. The family went to the law over this, and when they returned victorious from the hearings in Dublin, they were met at Bradshaw's Brae by a crowd of several hundred, with flaming torches and fireworks, who cheered them all the way down to the town.

The General Assembly received the new congregation in 1866. Thomas Strean gave £5,000 towards building the church and another £8,000 towards purchasing land at Brooklands. The preacher at the Dedication of the new church in 1867 was the famous hymn writer Horatius Bonar. and its first minister was the Rev. Dr. William Todd Martin, formerly of First Newry. By 1869 its congregation had risen to 114 families.

The second of the new churches was Greenwell Street Presbyterian. This grew out of the ministry of William McIlwrath. McIlwrath married a local lady, Eleanor Wallace, in 1860, and established a meeting place in a store at the rear of his father-in-law's house in 27 High Street. He continued to hold meetings there while he completed his theological studies. He found that many in the poor eastern district of the town did not attend any place of worship and in 1869 he decided to start a church in Greenwell Street, his wife donating £750 for the building. The congregation grew to five hundred, and in 1877 the building was enlarged to take another two hundred.

The Catholic community also continued to expand, and in 1875 the foundation stone for a new church was laid by the Bishop of Down and Connor, 'at the head of North Street in a commanding position convenient to the railway station.' The Catholic parish benefitted by the the conversion of Lady Londonderry to Catholicism in 1855. With her own money, she not only paid for the extensive site but also for the construction and the fitting of the church, which was opened in 1877. The *Newtownards Chronicle* reported that the Dedication was attended by the Marchioness and 'a great number of the Protestants of this town and district.'

Relations between Protestants and Catholics were usually good. One notable exception, however, was the ongoing battle between successive parish priests and the Board of Guardians of the workhouse. In the autumn of 1875 for example, Father Patrick McConvey, complained that the Board of Guardians had placed a sickly thirteen year old Catholic boy into the care of a Protestant tailor in Greyabbey, who, as well as giving the boy an apprenticeship, was intent on converting him to Protestantism. He also complained that tracts were being distributed to Catholics. The Guardians replied that their policy was to place pauper apprentices to masters of their own religion, but that, owing to a shortage of Catholic masters, this was not always possible. They maintained that tracts were not being given out, but that a Catholic boy had 'found one' and had kept it.

In July 1884, Thomas Sexton, the Nationalist MP for West Belfast, raised questions in the House of Commons concerning discrimination against Catholic inmates in Newtownards workhouse. He was told in reply that there was no Catholic on the Board of Guardians because none had stood for election; that the salary of the Catholic chaplain was less because the number of Catholic children was considerably smaller; and that only eight Catholic children had been sent out to apprenticeship and of these only about four were thought to have converted to Protestantism, and that this did not deserve the charge of proselytising.

But this conflict was untypical. Even with the establishment of the Protestant Institute in 1882, which was 'zealous for the maintenance of sound Protestant principles and the promotion of union among the Protestant communities of Newtownards', the preacher at its opening, the Rev. Hugh Hanna, insisted that 'the voice of sectarian rancour will not be heard.'

Interestingly enough, the major incidence of religious strife in this period was not between Protestant and Catholic at all. An editorial in the *Newtownards Chronicle* on August 7th, 1880 tells the story:

Within the last few weeks our tranquil and respectable borough has been invaded and taken possession of by "the Salvation Army" as they call themselves – a body of militant males and females who have made The Good Templar Hall their Headquarters and the streets of the town their recruiting districts. What may be the precise object of this visitation we confess we have no means of ascertaining. Who invited them, what they want, or what they expect by their fantastic exhibition in our midst nobody seems to know; but this at least is certain, that their presence among us, in the way in which it manifests itself is not likely to affect much good and is only calculated to bring ridicule on religion. One would have thought that

R. C. Church, Newtownards   Co. Down

St. Patrick's Catholic Church. Thought to have been built on the choicest location in the town, this impressive building was the result of Lady Londonderry's patronage.

if there was one town in Ireland more abundantly supplied than any other with religious privileges in the shape of places of worship and zealous ministers it were Newtownards... Their intentions we have no doubt are honest enough and if they would only have the good sense to confine their exertions within four walls none would probably object or interfere with them. But it is intolerable to have them day after day and night after night parading through our thoroughfares with hideously unmusical noises and escorted by the choicest ragamuffins in town and we must indignantly protest against its continuance. The thing is distasteful to every religious denomination and is especially unbecoming in a set of people who boast in their supreme holiness and regard the rest of the world as miserable sinners. Let them rant and sing as much as ever they like in the Templar Hall and if they do any good there so much the better; but we most decidedly object to their making a mockery of religion as they are now doing and exhibiting themselves as a laughing stock to be gazed and sneered at wherever they show their faces abroad.

In an attempt to be fair-minded the proprietor printed a letter against his own views the following week. David Hutchinson, a native of Newtownards, reminded the readership that other zealous ministers in Newtownards had experienced ridicule. Could the sounds of the Salvation Army be worse than the drunken blasphemies that were often heard on the streets of Newtownards?

But the criticism of the Salvationists did not stop, and indeed was stepped up throughout August and September 1880, until it became akin to persecution. Mocking sketches in the form of military despatches were regularly printed on the Army's activities. Attacks were resumed in April 1881when the paper complained of their:

...discordant noises, unearthly yells and other unseemly doings, all for the 'love of God'. It is disgraceful and ought not to be tolerated in a law-abiding community like Newtownards. Whilst they are parading in force they are doing nothing else but obstructing the thoroughfares and turning our otherwise peaceable Sabbath day into a common bear-garden. Petticoat organisation of this class – under the garb of religion – is the most demoralising of all cants... The preaching of the Gospel should not be undertaken by dismissed ballet girls and questionable musicians of the tin-whistle variety.

It must be appreciated that it was then generally felt that preaching normally should only be undertaken by men who were theologically trained and ordained in a recognised denomination, and the town's nine Presbyterian churches would have insisted that music should be confined to the singing of psalms without instrumental accompaniment. Also, these early Salvationists did not help their cause by the violence with which it was said they threatened their critics. It was their practice, too, to have a person walk through the streets of Newtownards on Sunday mornings between 5-7 a.m. ringing a hand bell!

Feelings ran so high that violence did occur. On October 9th, 1881 about thirty members of the First Battalion of the Royal Irish Rifles kicked at the door of the Good Templar Hall in North Street where the Salvationists were meeting, and smashed the windows on either side of the door, the fanlight and some upstairs windows with the buckles of their belts.

Within a few years, however, the town had accepted the Salvation Army. The *Newtownards Chronicle* wished them every success in a Festival which was organised in February 1888 in their hall in Frances Street. It was reported that the festival had a ' very respectable audience... everything was conducted decently and in order.' One of the speakers stressed that it was only justice to say that the paper had spoken of them very favourably, and that they wished that other newspapers would follow the example of the *Newtownards Chronicle*, as when they got a footing in the town they could not be put out of it.'

'Knitting, darning and cooking': education

The influence of the churches was exercised far beyond the walls of their church buildings. Very soon after the National system of elementary education had been established, schools became denominational in character throughout Ireland, as each denomination came to manage its own schools, though children did not have to attend any religious instruction of which their parents disapproved. Three schools were Presbyterian controlled (No. 2 East Street, Mill Street and Greenwell Street), another was Non-Subscribing (No.1 East Street), and another was Methodist (Zion Place).

By degrees most of the town's schools came into the National system, and though their names are familiar to us – Londonderry, Castle Gardens, and the Model – the education they provided was very different. In 1885 the Erasmus Smith Boys and Girls Schools amalgamated to become the Regent Street National Schools, controlled by the Church of Ireland. They were known as 'the Londonderry Schools'.

The Walker Mill School, set up in 1869 in Castle Gardens, also joined

'The Londonderry Schools.' These schools were supported by successive Lords Londonderry, and were controlled by the Church of Ireland. The site, on Regent Street, latterly the Town and County Hotel, is currently occupied by Health and Social Service administrators.

the National system in 1884 in an impressive ceremony presided over by the Bishop of Down and Connor with the rector, Dr. Pooler, in attendance. The Bishop hoped that the school would focus on knitting, darning and cooking, rather than on anything more academic. Dr. Pooler approved of the fact that the 'half timers' could receive an education while continuing to bring money into their homes. The 'quality' then proceeded to Regent House, the home of the school's founder and benefactor, George Walker, where lunch was provided.

The new Castle Gardens National School immediately fell foul of Nationalists, who objected to the fact that a hymn had been sung at the school's opening, an act which provoked a rather cheap attack in Parliament by Francis Joseph Biggar, the Belfast merchant and antiquarian, and Nationalist MP for Cavan. It also fell foul of the the Ards Presbytery a few months later when it accused the school of proselytising Presbyterian children by having them examined in the Apostles' Creed and having to listen to Episcopalian children being drilled in their catechism. The school claimed that the matter was an administrative error, and Walker maintained that he had no desire to proselytise and indeed the reason why he had turned the school over to the National Board was so that the Presbyterian children could be taught one hour per week by a Presbyterian clergyman. The matter was amicably resolved.

The town's two educational showpieces were the Model School and the Intermediate. The Model School was set up in 1862, and it was much larger than any other school in the town. Model Schools were part of an ambitious plan on the part of the government to 'model' non-denominational secular instruction with the provision for separate religious instruction. After 1870 Model Schools were phased out, but the Newtownards school retained its name and it succeeded as a 'model' school by its own efforts, under the National School scheme. E.A.M. Hanna, in his study of 'the Model', has concluded that its attempts to attract, through a three-tiered scale of fees, pupils from all social classes, and from a wide geographical area, were largely successful. The school declined in numbers in the 1870s and 1880s because of the depression, and it declined further after 1892, when compulsory free education was introduced, because it was a fee-taking institution. But the main hindrance to the evolution of the

Model School was the creation of the Intermediate School in 1878.

In 1878 the government took an initiative aimed at encouraging secondary education, and leading figures in Newtownards were quick to seize the opportunity it provided. The middle classes felt that, while the sons of the gentry had their private education and the universities, and the labouring poor had the National Schools, they were rather neglected. 'We have no intermediate education', said the Rev. Joseph Bradshaw, 'where respectable farmers and shopkeepers and merchants' sons can get an education.'

A meeting of half a dozen clergy, who represented all the denominations in the town, and fifteen professional and business men, was held on Thursday September 19th, 1878. Money was pledged for a headmaster's salary. At the second meeting it was decided to pay the principal £200 per annum, plus two thirds of the results' fees, the remaining third to be distributed among the assistant teachers. At the next meeting a week later, the fees were set, enrolment was arranged for the following Saturday, and the clergy started teaching in Strean Hall on Monday October 14th with twenty-one pupils – less than four weeks after the initial meeting! This is what the burghers of Newtownards were capable of, when they put their minds to it.

The 1880s were a period of great success for the Intermediate School. The staff was increased to four and the results in the national Intermediate examinations were excellent. In Ireland the average pass rate for these schools was 60%; in Newtownards it was 85%. The school's success affected the Model School. The latter sought to keep pupils until they were fifteen but because the Intermediate School enrolled twelve year olds, it creamed off the older, middle class pupils. Some of its pupils from these years went on to achieve prominence: for example, William McFadden Orr became Professor of Applied Mathematics and Mechanics

Model School, Newtownards

The Model School may have been one of the largest buildings in the town when it was built in 1862.

in the Royal College of Science in Dublin, and Sir William Maxwell became Director of Posts and Telegraphs in India.

'The majority present preferred giving orders to working': municipal affairs

Newtownards was then governed by fifteen Town Commissioners. Each was elected for three years, and five were to retire in rotation annually but were eligible for re-election. Only about five hundred individuals out of a total town population of about 9,000 were eligible to vote for them. The Commission was composed of local businessmen and proprietors. For example, its chairmen in the 1870s and 1880s were Andrew Menown, chairman of the local Gas Company, and Robert Caughey, owner of a printing, painting and decorating and funeral undertaking business in Frances Street. Other Commissioners in this period included John McVane, a sewed muslin agent of Regent Street; George Dickson, the nursery owner; William Mayne, grocer and grain merchant of High Street; William Dobbin, factory owner in South Street; James Brown, draper in High Street; James Jeffrey, auctioneer and hotelier; John Gray, a landowner, living in Frances Street; James McDowell, a farmer from Ballycullen; John Brown, baker in Frances Street; John Copeland, wine and spirit merchant and owner of a post and livery stable, mineral water manufacturer and wholesale bottler of West Street and Conway Square; Edward McCall, haberdasher in High Street; John Ramsay, sewing agent of Frances Street; Robert Dunn, coal merchant of Regent Street; John McClement, chemist of Castle Street; Samuel Kelly, grocer of Frances Street; John Ramsay, pawnbroker and sewing agent of Frances Street; and Horatio Doggart, a handloom weaving agent of Court Street.

Although there were supposed to be annual elections for five of the Commissionerships, candidates were returned unopposed until, in October 1877, the owner of the *Newtownards Chronicle*, the then liberal William Henry, decided to stand for election. A contest, he said, was a 'phenomenon which is rarely witnessed hereabouts.' Henry spoke of his own 'gallant resolve to break down the barriers of local exclusiveness', and how 'the Commissioners exerted themselves to keep him out of the charmed circle and maintain the representation as a sort of family party.' He was elected and his victory was felt to be a triumph for the ordinary man. Tar barrels were lit outside his home and he was carried on the shoulders of a large crowd through Regent Street, Conway Square, High Street, Mill Street and over to the offices of his paper in Frances Street, where fireworks were let off.

Passionate exchanges were not uncommon at the monthly meetings, with Commissioners insulting one another and storming out! In general, though, they were conducted amicably with a genuine desire to act together for the welfare of the town. The business of the Town Commissioners was reported in the *Newtownards Chronicle*, and their activities attracted regular correspondence, maintaining accountability of a kind.

The main business of the Town Commissioners concerned gas and water. In 1867 the Commissioners got into a dispute with the Gas Light Company over the cost of street lighting. Both sides issued circulars explaining their position, and for almost two years the streets were not lit at all. In 1870 a new company called the Gas Consumers' Company was formed. It had its works in Mill Street and many of the Town Commissioners became shareholders. Perhaps not surprisingly, this new company won the contract for street lighting. In 1873, after three years of competition, the two companies merged. In 1884 it was decided that the Town Commissioners should buy the Gas Consumers' Company on behalf of the town and operate it as a public utility. It was purchased for £9,386.10.0.

Sanitation was also a problem. Because the town was low-lying it was liable to flooding, and when this occurred sewage found its way in to the town's drinking water, which was pumped from wells at various locations in the town. In 1877 a Royal Commission concluded that these problems:

...led to the frequent occurrence of typhoid fever and scarlatina which is more liable to spread more rapidly here than in many other places due to large number of mill hands in the town and the total absence of any precaution to prevent them carrying infection into the crowded workroom whenever a case of fever arises in their houses.

The report did little for the town's popular reputation as a healthy place in which to live. Because the town was well sheltered from the north winds by its hills, it was said that 'people coming here with chest complaints

Newtownards Railway Station, when in use, from an old photograph.

soon recover'. These claims could hardly have been made by the end of the century because, by then, the hopes of the editor of the *Chronicle* in 1873 – 'to see our surrounding townparks studded with tall chimneys, even should it take somewhat from the salubrity of our healthy atmosphere,' – had been fulfilled.

The town had no fire fighting arrangements until 1877. The subject came to the fore when a family of seven was burned to death in South Street. In the wake of the tragedy, Captain Hamilton, of the local militia, the Royal North Down Rifles, suggested that some of his men act as a fire brigade. His idea was taken up and twenty three were employed on a retainer of 10s. a year each plus 5s. per fire. The Fire Brigade was not very efficient at first. At a fire at the new gas works in Mill Street, the hose of the town engine would not work, and 'the water carts and buckets of the Town Commissioners were also brought into requistion but little good was effected for some time as the majority present preferred giving orders to working.' On another occasion, the town engine could not be brought out because the key of the shed could not be found! Soon the Town Commissioners took over the running of the fire service, with one of their number serving as captain.

The town was considered to be generally peaceful and orderly, needing only eight policemen to keep it under control. Normally there was very little trouble, and what there was was usually of a prankish nature. For example, at the Harvest Fair of 1873, a crowd took over the railway station in 'plebeian playfulness', and had the town at their mercy for a couple of hours. The principal threat to the quiet of the town came from occasional skirmishes between the militia and the residents.

'Bad feeling existed': the Royal North Down Rifles

In 1854 the Royal North Down Rifles moved into a military camp of twelve acres on the Comber Road, where they developed a rifle range, reputed to be the best in Ireland, even though half of the camp was liable to flood in periods of wet weather. The Royal North Downs were a militia unit which provided basic military training for several weeks each year for volunteers. Also, when required, it would sent levies of partially trained soldiers to the regular battalions of the Royal Irish Rifles. The provisioning of the camp by local businesses, helped the town's economy. The Royal North Downs had been called up during the Peninsular War, and were not stood down until the after the occupation of Paris in 1814. They were also recalled between 1855-59 for the Crimean War and the Indian Mutiny.

The military authorities believed that 'the people of Newtownards were not anxious for them and that bad feeling existed between the townspeople and the men of the regiment' because there was from time to time trouble between the town and the militia. One summer's evening, in June 1877, three young officers of the local militia threw vinegar and pepper on the heads of passers by from the windows of the Assembly Room of the Market House. A crowd gathered outside which was about to storm the building and was only with great difficulty restrained! To avoid further friction, the militia was transferred to Kinnegar in Holywood in 1885 as an experiment, a move that was seen as a serious set-back for the town in terms of its status and the loss of business involved.

The town had other links with the British Army. Contemporaries believed that few towns in Ireland had given as many recruits to the different regiments as Newtownards had. From 1861, the camp on the Comber Road was used to accommodate soldiers from other regiments who came to Newtownards for their annual musketry course. There were occasionally incidents between the townspeople and the regulars. Much depended on the character of the regiment. For instance the relations with the Stirlingshire regiment (75th Foot) stationed in the town in November 1875 were atrocious. There were brawls on two evenings in that month and the number of policemen was raised to twelve. Again, in October 1877, three soldiers fought with locals in Conway Square, but in general the relationship between the town and the visiting regiments was excellent.

'Crowds paraded the streets cheering for Lord Castlereagh': the decline of liberal Newtownards

The period up to 1886 was a time of intense political activity: between 1868 and 1875 Newtownards voters went to the polls every other year! Voting by secret ballot was introduced in 1872 and the general election of

Left holding the baby. The women were the main earners in many households. Flowering in the townland of Loughries.

1874 gave voters their first opportunity to exercise their franchise completely free of the influence of Lord Londonderry. The fourth Marquess died in 1872, and ownership of the town and parish passed to his half-brother, George Henry. The fifth Marquess preferred to live quietly on his wife's Welsh estate, so links between the locality and the owner became less intimate than before. In the 1874 election, James Sharman Crawford stood as a Tenant Right Liberal. Crawford was described by his opponents as 'the nominee of a few Belfast Radicals and a clique of county agitators.' At first, the voters of Newtownards thought that Crawford, as a Tenant Right candidate, had the support of the new Marquess. But they were wrong. Lord Londonderry had a notice published informing the local electorate that he wished to give this:

...mendacious report a most unqualified denial. On the contrary it is the earnest wish of Lord Londonderry that Lord Edwin Hill-Trevor and Colonel Forde should be returned as members of this county.

This did not seem to make any difference. Crawford was elected with 4,814 votes, and had the Newtownards voters to thank. Newtownards was the largest polling district in the County with 756 eligible voters, and 560 voted. It was reckoned that they voted 10:1 for Crawford. The news of his victory was 'mysteriously delayed', but when it finally reached the town, Joseph Gibson, a solicitor, and principal supporter of Crawford, announced the news to a crowd waiting outside the Post Office. It was apparently Conservative supporters who gathered for, as the *Chronicle*, which backed the Liberal cause, reported:

...he was met by derisive cries and booed by a crowd of roughs and amongst whom we don't think there was a respectable Protestant, although they cheered loudly for 'Hill and Forde', and shouted ' No Chronicle'.

But within a few years the same voters were beginning to think that their interests might be better served by the British Conservatives. They were not happy with the Liberal leader, Gladstone's, willingness to accede to the demands of Irish nationalist politicians. The next election, in 1878, showed a shift of support in the area away from Liberalism to Conservatism. Perhaps Crawford could have stayed this drift but he had died, and in the interval Viscount Castlereagh, son and heir of the fifth Marquess of Londonderry, contested the second seat as a Conservative.

This young man, then aged twenty-six, rose to the position of Lord Lieutenant of Ireland and also held Cabinet posts. But what made the difference in 1878 was the fact that he was 'a fast friend of Tenant Right'. On this occasion there was no need to look beyond the 'natural' leader. Castlereagh, although a Conservative, campaigned on a 'liberal' platform, seeking Grand Jury reform (a long running demand by the people of

Newtownards, who much disliked paying the county cess), Intermediate education, and to bring the Sabbatarians with him, Sunday closing.

On May 18th crowds gathered around the Post Office to hear the results announced. On hearing of Lord Castlereagh's success, they moved to the *Chronicle* offices where they were addressed by William Henry, whose paper this time had done so much to promote the Conservative cause. The following description, from the *Newtownards Chronicle*, vividly portrays the extent of Conservative feeling in the town:

Flags were hoisted from the Londonderry Arms Hotel, the Old Cross, the Estate Office, the Temperance Hotel, the Assembly Rooms, etc. and large crowds paraded the streets cheering for Lord Castlereagh and groaning opposite the houses of Mr Andrews' [the Liberal candidate] supporters. Two of the oldest voters in the district, the Messrs. Crawford of Ballyharry were borne in triumph through the leading thoroughfares while Mr Henry of the Chronicle and the other members of the local Committee received a perfect ovation whenever they appeared. Some thirty or forty extra police were drafted into the town... but so far as we can learn no occasion arose for their interference and there was not a single prisoner in the lockup on Sunday morning. When darkness set in dozens of tar barrels were lighted in the Square, Frances Street, Court Street, Regent Street, Mary Street, Mill Street, Greenwell Street etc and large bonfires blazed for the greater part of the night on Scrabo, the Cairn, Tullynagardy, Whitespots, Drumawhy, Loughries, Movilla and on all the hills in the vicinity of the town... There was also a pyrotechnic exhibition on an extensive scale in the Square.

On Monday evening the rejoicings were continued, tar barrels being lighted in William Street, at Movilla, Scrabo, Tullynagardy and the hillside at Cowie's Craig. As 9 o'clock approached, large numbers wended their way to the Glen quarries, recently opened by Messrs Russell and Co., where some experiments with dynamite were performed by Mr James Carson of Court Street. There is a profusion of furze in the district which when ignited lent a brilliant but weird aspect to the deep glen, around which hundreds of people had assembled and whose cheers for the popular candidate rent the air until the night was far advanced.

Dr.William Todd Martin, of Strean, was typical of many Presbyterian ministers who put their weight behind the Liberal party because it championed the interests and values of Non-conformity.

This election marked the turning of the tide. Later that year, in July 1878, the fifth Marquess invited all 1,200 of his tenantry to a dinner served in two great marquees on the lawns of Mount Stewart. Eight hundred turned up and there were many expressions of harmony between landlord and tenantry.

But how secure was the Conservatives' hold of the county's two seats? The Newtownards small farmer was traditionally a Liberal. For many families in the district, Conservatism was a new allegiance, and it seemed that the new found Conservatism in Newtownards might be tested in the election of 1885 when the franchise was extended to all males over the age of twenty one. In addition, the county was divided into four single-member constituencies. The electorate in Newtownards jumped from about 800 to 2,000 out of a total electorate for the new North Down constituency of 9,000. On the surface this appeared to favour the Liberals, and a meeting of the Ards Liberal Club was held in Pound Street to consider how best to mobilise the workers' vote. A large number of the newly enfranchised working men were in attendance. The leading Liberals were two former chairmen of the Town Commissioners, Robert Caughey and Andrew Menown, and two Pesbyterian clergymen, the Rev. William Wright, minister of First Newtownards, and the Rev. Dr.William Todd Martin, minister of Strean. However, the issue of Home Rule, and the coming together of the Conservatives, the Anglican Church and the Orange Order wrested the initiative from the Liberals.

Political opinion hardened. William Wright's invitation to address the annual Twelfth demonstration in 1885 was withdrawn on July 8th – because he was a Liberal. At one Liberal meeting a voice shouted in exasperation, 'Whoever intends to stand should at once get himself made an Orangeman, get introduced into the Lodges and try and convert the members of that body to Radical Orange principles.'

Meanwhile, the local Conservatives had chosen Colonel Waring of Waringstown to be the Conservative candidate, primarily because he was the County Down Deputy Grand Master of the Orange Order. The leading local Conservatives were James Brownlow of Killynether House, and Andrews' successor as Lord Londonderry's agent, William Henry, George Walker, Thomas Mayne and the Rev. William McIlwrath of Greenwell Street, traditionally a conservative congregation. The presence of Mr McIlwrath, a Presbyterian minister, was seen as a great coup for the Conservative cause.

In the event, contrary to the hopes of the Liberals, most of the new electors voted Conservative. Colonel Waring, an old-fashioned Tory, was returned for North Down. The electorate moved from a Liberal to a soft conservative, then a traditional Tory position. The Protestant community was reorienting and perhaps even splitting along denominational lines. The Presbyterian clergy were largely Liberal, while the Conservatives continued as an episcopal party with a large popular following. This period was one of those rare eras when the division of political feeling was along British party lines. But it was not to last.

14

Unionists and Home Rulers 1886-1900

'The stronghold of Unionism'

When Gladstone embraced Home Rule he re-aligned politics in Ulster. Liberal Unionists now found common ground with the Conservatives in the maintenance of the Union with Britain.

In February 1886, a Unionist meeting took place in the Assembly Room of the Market House. People from all parts of the old political spectrum, who had been attacking one another just three months earlier, now shared a platform, expressing their support for the Union. The Rev. William Wright, the Liberal, commented that people in the town were wondering had he turned his coat. He said that he had always been a Liberal, but there were some questions which were above party politics. As the *Newtownards Chronicle* put it:

We rejoice that Newtownards has come well to the fore in this matter and at this great crisis in our country's history Liberals and Conservatives have been able to forget old differences... preventing the dismemberment of this great Empire and the handing over the wealth and prosperous classes of the country to the tender mercies of the National League [the Land League organisation] with its allies the moonlighters, the midnight marauders and the dynamitards. So far as the Ards is concerned the cry has gone forth that we will not have these men to rule over us.

When the news of the first Home Rule Bill's defeat was announced there were rapturous celebrations. The town's two bands paraded. No less than eight bonfires were lit on Scrabo Hill, which were seen for many miles. At a meeting in the Assembly Room of the Market House, the sixth Marquess of Londonderry described the Ards as 'the stronghold of Unionism (Applause)' and encouraged Ards men to proselytise:

In this district, we are, I may say, almost unanimous in our views with regard to the Government of Ireland. Because you have no opposition in this district you have the power and the will to devote yourselves to securing Unionist members for those seats in Ulster that are at present represented by Home Rulers.

The Liberals won the General Election of 1892, and in the following

William Ewart Gladstone, author of the first Home Rule Bill. Many local farmers admired his championing of tenant ownership, but feared his advocacy of Home Rule. This unsympathetic cartoon shows him as the tool of the Land Leaguers.

year Gladstone introduced a second Home Rule Bill. On the eve of its introduction, a meeting was held at the Protestant Institute in Mary Street. The hall was packed to overflowing. Charles Brownlow, Lord Londonderry's agent since 1887, and himself an Orangeman, chaired the meeting. In language that seemed strange coming from a representative of the establishment, he said that now was the time for every Unionist to come forward and:

...if necessary when constitutional means fails to take other measures for the preservation of our lives and liberties. I hope it will never come to this; but God only knows what we might be called upon to do and now is the time to prepare.

William Sibbald Johnston proposed the formation of a Unionist Club in the town. When the Rev. William Wright came forward to speak he was loudly cheered, and there was a voice from the audience, 'You are on the right side now. (laughter)'. In language echoing that of his Volunteer forebearers in the 1790s, Mr Wright declared:

I hope the time will never come when we will have to take any other measures than those peaceable but we will never submit to have our lives and liberties handed over to men whose actions show that they have not the smallest conception of what true liberty means (Applause).

A thousand were enrolled in the club in a week. To all intents and purposes the Newtownards district really was a 'stronghold of Unionism'. But was it unanimously so?

'Sturdy Presbyterians... sturdy Home Rulers': Nationalism in Newtownards

Unionists themselves estimated that out of the constituency of 9,306 electors in North Down (the seat of which Newtownards was considered 'the capital'), there were perhaps 1,500 Home Rulers, for Home Rule feeling was strong among Presbyterian tenant farmers. These men were accustomed to thinking of Conservatism as indistinguishable from landlordism, and therefore anathema.   Some of them believed that a proper solution to the vexed land problem could never be found by an Imperial parliament full of landlords, but only by a local parliament which more faithfully represented the tenant farming interest.

Newtownards' tenant families were facing hard times. The price of labour was rising. Locally, labourers' wages had doubled from about seven shillings a week to fourteen between 1878-1886. (This of course was good news for the labourers, and admissions to the local workhouse halved over the period). But rents had not fallen to match the rising labour costs and falling farm prices. Many farmers' leases on the Londonderry estate had been renewed in 1859 when the price of wheat was twice what was in 1886. A number of farmers had used their capital in order to pay the rent and some maintained that if they were to sell their entire stock it would not raise enough .

At the end of 1886 Lord Londonderry offered a 10% reduction in rents on the 1859 leases, but none on any lease that had had its rent reduced by a land court. The farmers thought that 30% rather than 10% would have been more realistic. A delegation went to Mount Stewart, where they were hospitably given lunch. Lord Londonderry listened to them for forty minutes, then read a prepared reply offering a 15% reduction and an additional five months to pay. He maintained that rents had increased on

Smallholding beside Strangford. Note the boat. Many small shoreside farmers supplemented their income with a little fishing.

Strangford Lough and Scrabo Hill, Newtownards.

average by only 4% since 1852, and he noted that only 109 tenants out of 1,260 had sought rent reductions through a Land Court.

The situation had not improved by the following year, when the farmers' representative association, the Newtownards Tenant Farmers Association, invited Colonel Waring, their MP for North Down, and Michael McCartan, a Castlewellan solicitor and Nationalist MP for South Down, to address the tenants on the workings of the recent Land Act, 'to show that there was no political feeling on the matter'. Colonel Waring, a substantial landowner, declined to attend – and he missed an exciting evening! Halfway through the meeting, the Rev. William Wright marched up to the platform and, without permission from the chairman, called on the meeting to 'disapprove of the invitation being given to Colonel Waring and Mr McCartan and refuse to hear Mr McCartan.' This met with both loud applause and considerable dissent. The chairman tried to keep order, and when William Gibson JP of Ballywalter, tried to intervene there were shouts of 'Go home, you Home Ruler!' Eventually the meeting had to be abandoned and the organisers reconvened a smaller meeting of their own where Michael McCartan was able to be heard.

The meeting must have done some good. Lord Londonderry announced a 20% reduction in rents and shocked the locality in February 1888 when, 'much against his inclination', he made a public offer to sell his estate to his tenants if they paid the equivalent of their rents, less 20%, for the next 49 years. The offer had a mixed reception. The Newtownards Tenant Farmers Association recommended that it be rejected. Although purchasing would mean a 20% reduction, this left them no better than at present and the present was intolerable, not to mention the taxes they would have to pay as newly created landowners. They maintained that 'very few' took up the offer but Lord Londonderry, on the other hand, declared that 'many' had bought out.

The Unionists of the area looked askance at these goings on. They were sure that the Newtownards Tenant Farmers Association was a cover for Home Rule activities. They seemed to have proof of this in an episode which took place on the evening of Friday April 27th, 1888. A meeting of the Association was to take place in the Ulster Hotel, Regent Street – its usual venue. The meeting was not publicly advertised, and the local police got word that the guest speaker was to be no less than John Dillon, MP for East Mayo, the deputy leader of the Home Rule party. At 7 o'clock, an hour before the meeting was to start, the police went to the hotel and informed its proprietor, Mrs McKee, of what they knew.

She was mortified, and maintained that she would not have allowed such a meeting had she known who was to speak at it. At 8 o'clock, Dillon and McCartan arrived at the hotel (together with a detective who was shadowing Dillon, for he was out of prison on bail). They were met by the

John Dillon, leading Nationalist politician, who made a controversial visit to Newtownards in the 1880s.

organisers of the meeting, Robert Caughey, William Gibson and David McMaster. Mrs McKee and her assembled relatives refused them admittance, and the party was forced to move across the street to John Murray's drapery, where they were ushered through the shop into a shed in his yard, while constables 'stared at every person entering'! The meeting took place, with the organisers claiming that 'all the forces of landlordism were set at work but the plans of the clique were circumvented.' Dillon attacked landlordism, and appealed to both Protestant and Catholic tenants to resist their oppressors.

The local paper poked fun at the meeting 'in the Coal Hole', and claimed that out of fifty-two present there were less than twenty who were actual tenant farmers. But the matter did not end there. The Cabinet Minister for Ireland was asked twice in the House of Commons about the events of that evening in Newtownards. The episode gained prominence and embarrassment value because it had occurred on the Lord Lieutenant's estate.

Meanwhile, the tenant farmers on Lord Londonderry's estates who had decided to force rent reductions through the Land Courts were experiencing

165

delay in having their cases heard. It was tempting to conclude that, as Lord Londonderry was the head of the Irish government, he had used his influence to have the cases delayed. The Solicitor-General denied this in the House of Commons. Moreover, as they waited, they were being asked to pay the old unreduced rent, and threatened with legal proceedings when they offered to pay the reduced rent that Lord Londonderry had offered to the rest of his tenantry. Their frustration helped to strengthen their Home Rule convictions. The Newtownards Tenant Farmers Association passed a resolution on July 2nd, 1888:

That this association whose membership is composed almost exclusively of Presbyterian farmers, consider the imprisonment of Mr John Dillon MP as a most arbitrary act on the part of the Irish government.

Hugh Ferguson, David McMaster and R.B. Caughey travelled to Kilkeel where they voted for a resolution expressing 'the fond hope that Providence may spare [Gladstone] to see restored to Ireland her native Parliament in College Green.'

The Land Court did not hear the cases on Lord Londonderry's estates until May 1890. Rents were reduced by almost 25%, and Lord Londonderry appealed thirty of the decisions. His preferred option was to sell his lands, indeed he believed that owner-occupancy was the key to the solution of the whole 'Irish Question'. By the end of 1892, two hundred tenants had purchased their farms, while others sought rent reductions of 50%.

In March 1893 the Ulster farmers sent a delegation to London; two of its members being R.B. Caughey and Hugh Ferguson. They were interviewed by the *Westminster Gazette*, which was sympathetic to the Liberal Government. As the newspaper reported:

Staunch Presbyterians by faith and extraction, solid successful farmers by profession, men of substance and local influence, no men could afford a greater contrast than they to the ignorant, lazy lack-land, priest-ridden fiction which Unionists invent as the type of the Irish nationalist... They are large farmers in Ulster and they want a Bill for a revision of rents made on prices alone. Reckless Unionists speak and write of the Land agitation as if it were blackgaurdism. One wishes that such persons could be brought face to face with these sturdy Presbyterian farmers. Mr Ferguson is a tenant of Lord Londonderry and was refused any reduction of his rents pending the hearing of his application for a judicial rent in the land court. He won his point however and Lord Londonderry's demands were made very short work of by the judges. 'And yet,' says Mr Ferguson, 'Lord Londonderry is called one of the best landlords in Ireland.' 'And so he was once,' says Mr Caughey. And how, we enquire, that he isn't so any longer? 'He had a different agent once,' explains Mr Ferguson.

Sturdy Presbyterians, our visitors were no less sturdy Home Rulers. The whole structure of Orangeism is to their minds nothing but a branch of Landlordism. The landlords plant Orange lodges and enrol as many labourers as they can to counteract the farmers' votes. As for 'Roman Catholic tyranny', these stout

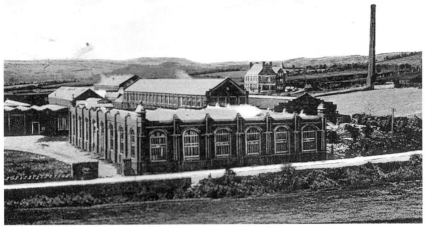

The Glen Print Works, Crawfordsburn Road, from an old postcard. The textile industry was booming in this period. The Territorial Army currently occupies the site.

Presbyterian farmers laugh the scare to scorn. 'I know Ireland well', says Mr Caughey. 'Cork, Waterford and other parts as well almost as Ulster; and this I can positively say – and I say not without shame – that only in one quarter of the country is religious bigotry to be found - and that is in Protestant Belfast.'

In spite of these professions, however, Home Rule sentiment in Newtownards was on the wane. By 1894 half of Lord Londonderry's Down estate had been sold to tenants. Land grievances had been the engine which drove their politics, and as these disappeared, the farmers' Home Rule sentiment moderated. At a Unionist rally in 1894 the Rev. William Wright reported a remark which had been made to him by a large tenant farmer: 'Mr Wright, we will take Home Rule for two or three years until the Land Question is settled and then we will let it go again.'

The process of land purchase continued steadily, so that by 1914 it was said that Lord Londonderry had very few agricultural tenants left. There was so little to do that in 1901 his agent resigned to work for Colonel Nugent of Portaferry, and was not replaced. (Lord Londonderry was represented by his agent in England and any remaining work in the area was handled by William Ditty, as sub-agent.) As the land issue receded so too did Home Rule politics, but it is interesting to note that Home Rule had significant Presbyterian support within this heartland of Unionism until almost the end of the century.

Jobs, houses and sports

While the small farmers had it tough, the textile industry was booming. By 1900 almost five hundred were employed in Walker's Castle Gardens mill, and almost three hundred in Stevenson's in Regent Street. The Glen Printing and Finishing employed three hundred. Thomas Lavery set up his Hemstitching Company in Ann Street at the end of the 1870s and was employing two hundred girls by 1900. Messrs. Freeland and Iveston were in West Street; Messrs. Corry and Company were on the Shore Road, and William Grant's Movilla Weaving Factory employed over sixty. The consumption of gas in the town rose from 8 million cubic feet in 1886 to 21 million cubic feet in 1906.

North Street NEWTOWNARDS

North Street, below the Railway Station. This would have been many visitors' first view of the town. Great efforts were made to decorate the street to give celebrity visitors a good first impression.

The 1891 Census revealed Newtownards to be one of the few towns in Ulster that had experienced a growth in population (from 8,176 to 9,339) in the decade since 1881. This was a source of great pride at the time. The town was expanding northwards and westwards. The sod-cutting ceremony for Victoria Avenue took place in April 1887. It had been intended that the street should be called Railway Avenue until one of the Town Commissioners patriotically suggested Victoria Avenue, as it was the Queen's Jubilee Year. In 1891, houses and villas there were going up 'faster even than was anticipated,' meeting a demand from the town's expanding professional and merchant families, and the Avenue quickly became one of the town's most fashionable addresses. Balfour Street was begun in the early 1890s. New houses were being built in James Street and William Street. In 1895, houses began to be built on the 'North Street hill'.

The occasion of the Queen's Golden Jubilee was celebrated by the loyal citizens of Newtownards. June 21st, 1887 was marked by the nation as 'Jubilee Day' and the Town Commissioners recommended that shops and factories close. They organised a Sports Day at the militia's new camp at Milecross, to music provided by the workhouse band. Also one hundred tar barrels were lit on Scrabo Hill and its mighty pyre could be seen as far away as Belfast and Downpatrick. Ten years later, in 1897, the Diamond Jubilee was similarily celebrated. No-one could accuse the people of Newtownards of not knowing how to enjoy themselves!

The period also witnessed the flourishing of many social, sporting and cultural activities. One wonders where people found the time or the energy. Until 1893, shop workers worked from 8 a.m.-7.30 p.m. Monday to Friday, and to 11p.m. on Saturdays which must have contributed greatly to the bustle of Saturday nights. An early closing movement began in 1893 to have shops close for a half day – at 4 p.m. – on Thursday, and at 9 p.m. on Saturdays.

Newtownards' oldest recreational society was probably the Horticultural and Horse Jumping Association, which was founded in 1854, horse jumping

being added in 1876. Its annual show in Dickson's Nursery grounds, on the present site of the Ards Shopping Centre, was a important occasion, bringing many visitors to the town. Bassett described it as 'one of the most successful of its kind in Ireland.' There was a successful lacrosse team, the first in Ireland, and five of the Irish team were from the local club. There were several soccer teams – Kiltonga Rangers, Castle Gardens Wanderers, and the Ards Harriers and Athletic Football Club. There was a rifle club, a cricket club, a cycling club, the Kiltonga Curling Club, and for the less energetic there was a literary and debating Society, the Young Men's Mutual Improvement Society, a YMCA and YWCA, a choral society and two elocution classes. The Good Templars and the Masonic Order also had lodges in the town. The most ambitious project was the Ards Recreation Society. In December 1891, a group of local businessmen began to develop tracks for horse racing and trotting, and pitches for lacrosse, soccer, cricket and lawn tennis on a twenty acre site on the Comber Road.

Nursery Lane. On the left is Dickson's office, now the goods entrance of the Ards Shopping Centre; ahead is Church Street. (T. Maddock)

Celebrity visitors

During the 1890s the town basked in the reflected glory of the Londonderry family. The sixth Marquess entertained many important guests, including royalty, at Mount Stewart. On each occasion the leading citizens of the town were anxious to meet and honour these visitors as they passed through. On Tuesday April 4th, 1893 Arthur James Balfour, the leader of

Arthur Balfour, a leading Conservative and Unionist politician, who visited the town in 1893. Many townspeople hoped he could contain the demand for Home Rule.

the Conservative party, and later Prime Minister was so honoured. Flags flew from most buildings and the whole town was decorated with banners and bunting, 'the like of which the oldest inhabitant of Newtownards had never seen before.' A crowd of 8,000 filled the Square to hear Balfour speak. A street was named in his honour. On Tuesday May 27th, 1893 it was the turn of the Marquesss of Salisbury. His was the first visit of a serving Prime Minister to the town.

The first royal visit came on Saturday September 4th, 1897, when the Duke and Duchess of York passed through the town on their way to Mount Stewart. They were met at the station by their host the Marquess. Forty dragoons were drawn up outside. North Street was one great continuous scene of gilt-headed, crimson clothed masts, arches of evergreens, flags, banners, streamers, scarlet and gold drapings and messages of welcome. The entrance to the street had a floral arch, flanked by pedestalled and crown surmounted masts. As the cortege passed into Frances Street, the entire length of Church Street, Regent Street and Frances Street, nearly a mile in length, was said to be one mass of bunting: 'Thousands of flags and streamers formed a kaleidoscopic canopy over the whole space.' High Street was, according to the *Chronicle*, 'like an enlarged scene from a fairy opera, or, of what one reads of a Venetian carnival.' There were several floral arches with messages of goodwill and each shop and house was elaborately decorated with flags. As the party entered the Square, there were great roars from the assembled crowd of several thousand. After an address of welcome and reply, proceedings were brought to close by the singing of the National Anthem by upwards of one thousand children dressed in red, white and blue sashes. As darkness fell most houses were illuminated with coloured candles and Chinese lanterns. It was a day to remember.

'Put in by herring cadgers and loafers': the 1898 riots

When Colonel Waring died in 1898, a by-election was called. The Conservatives were in power with a comfortable majority. There was no fear of Home Rule, and the Conservatives were expected to win the 1900 General Election. In these secure conditions, two Unionists vied for the seat.

No election caused so much interest since the famous contest of 1852. Mr John Blakiston-Houston of Orangefield was an elderly, well respected, local landlord, and had the support of the Conservative elite, the Orange Order, and of many older voters. His opponent was a young, energetic, Scottish Presbyterian called Thomas Lorimer Corbett, who had the support of the Presbyterian clergy, and might be called the 'popular' or the 'Presbyterian' Unionist candidate. There was a strong feeling that Presbyterians in Ulster were under-represented within Unionism. Corbett stood for the middling commercial and farming interests and the industrial working man.

Blakiston-Houston won narrowly, thanks to nationalists' votes. Newtownards voted for Corbett, who more accurately represented the majority Presbyterian opinion in the town, while Houston represented the minority Episcopalian and Catholic communities. Feelings in the town ran high, and on the night that the result was declared, supporters of Blakiston-Houston called at the homes of Town Commissioners and asked if they could light a bonfire in the Square. No Commissioner would give his assent, but the supporters went ahead and lit a bonfire to the accompaniment of drums. When the fire was almost burned out, a procession with lighted torches began to walk through the principal streets. A Corbett crowd, with a band, took this as a challenge and began to shout, 'Corbett for ever' and bore down on them, seizing their torches and tossing them into the crowd. A little girl's hair and pinafore were burned, and another woman lost a tooth. A policeman was struck on the face and his tunic set alight. Another crowd of Corbett followers arrived with a banner which said 'Houston – put in by herring cadgers and loafers' (a reference to the Portaferry vote!) The banner was speedily thrown in the flames and tramped in the mud by their opponents.

For the remainder of the evening the streets were in the possession of the Corbett crowd, and the police charged them several times. The mob then seized the water cart and barrel of a contractor who was paving the west side of Conway Square, and put out the remains of the offending bonfire. Then they marched round the Square smashing windows in the Town Hall and the Rev. William McIlwrath's manse. The police, by now reinforced, again charged the rioters who ran up Frances Street then turned and threw stones, severely injuring some of the policemen. Eventually the rain, which had been falling lightly all evening, began to

The Rev.William McIlwrath, who, unusually for a Presbyterian minister, consistently supported the Conservative party. He had his windows broken in the 1898 riots.

get heavier and this proved more effective than the police in dispersing the crowd.

A few weeks later three thousand turned out to hear the defeated candidate in the grounds of the Ards Recreation Society. He was feted at the Railway Station, where four bands led the procession to the Comber Road. All along the route were cheering crowds, with ladies waving handkerchiefs. After speeches at the grounds, the crowds made their way up South Street where all the inhabitants had illuminated their houses. Corbett was idolised in the area. In the succeeding months babies were being baptised with the name Corbett!

But Corbett's time would come, just two years later. In the election of 1900 he won decisively. To prevent a recurrence of the riots of 1898, eighty extra police were drafted in, bringing the numbers up to one hundred. The Council banned all torchlights, bands and bonfires and, perhaps most effective of all, public houses were closed from 2pm on Saturday, through to Monday. Thomas Corbett represented the constituency faithfully until his sudden death in 1910.

'Kitchener found it more advanced in Khartoum': municipal matters

The old century finished in a forward-looking manner, with the acquisition of a new Town Hall and a fully democratically elected Urban District Council. Lord Londonderry gave the Market House to the Town Commissioners as a gift. Far from being delighted with the thought of acquiring such a splendid building, the Commissioners were thrown into a dilemma. They had struck one of the lowest rates in Ireland; and maintaining the building would place an extra £60 pounds a year on the rates. At present, it was possible to have the use of the building for nothing by simply writing to the agent. The shrewd Commissioners immediately saw that it was not necessarily a good deal. On the other

The Square and High Street from an old postcard.

hand, the building was used frequently, and it was undoubtedly a prestigious asset, even if costly. The gift was accepted. The town received the building for 999 years for the rent of an ear of corn, commonly called a peppercorn, on the condition that Lord Londonderry could have use of the rooms at twenty-four hours notice. The presentation of the Market House took place in September 1897. It was to be called the Town Hall, but to many residents, for years to come, it would still be the 'Market House'. The Commissioners were canny enough to charge for its use, so it operated at a slight profit for them.

In 1899, following new legislation, the town became subject to an Urban District Council, while the district around was to be administered by Newtownards Rural District Council. The franchise was extended too. All who were entitled to vote at parliamentary elections could also now vote in council elections. This brought the number of voters from about six hundred to 2,125 of whom 593 were women. The Councillors now had to take the views of the skilled working class into consideration, as this very illuminating letter to the *Newtownards Chronicle* from 'A poor weaver' shows:

I am one of a large number of voters in back streets such as East Street, Greenwell Street and Movilla Street who derive no benefit, or next to none, from Commissioners at all, good bad or indifferent. Some of them I do not know, except that I usually see their names in your paper when I have a penny to spare, and I do not expect people who live in Victoria Avenue, High Street or Regent Street to know much about us or our surroundings. Still, we are now enroled as voters and have a voice in the election, everyone of us who has a house, large or small, and I would impress upon everyone as such, who sees and knows the utter neglected state of the districts I allude to, and other districts as well, to refuse their votes to any candidate who does not in the face of the public pledge himself to take some steps to remedy the present state of things. The lighting of the back streets is miserable. There are cow-houses and pig-styes in the town cleaner and better paved than some of the footpaths. There are whole rows of houses without any sanitary accommodation whatever... Talk of civilisation and the progress of the age. I will venture to say that Kitchener found it more advanced in Khartoum than in some of the back streets of Newtownards.

(The editor was so impressed by this letter that he asked its author to stand in the forthcoming elections!)

Conditions in the poor quarter had improved little since the 1830s, and perhaps even since Wesley's visits. In 1899 the burning issue for most residents was the question of obtaining a proper water supply. Newtownards was the only town of its size whose water supply was obtained from pumps drawing up sub-surface water; and it had no proper sewerage system. Sewage was discharged into open drains and carried out by 'the canal' to the floodgates, with the danger that contamination could seep into the drinking water. This problem put off business: it was a saying at the time that 'Newtownards had nothing to offer the businessman but a bit of cheap land and no water.' The new Council came into being in 1899. Nearly half the Commissioners were replaced, unable to win the confidence of the new electorate, defeated largely on their stance on the 'water problem'. This was the most sweeping change ever to effect the local body . And so, with this election, the Town Commissioners were swept into history, and democratically accountable local government was born.

15

'The Most Loyal Town in Her Majesty's Dominions' 1900-1918

On the morning of Tuesday February 28th, 1900 news arrived in the town of the first defeat of the Boers in their own territory. Crowds gathered. Factories sounded their horns. Work stopped and there were tremendous scenes of celebration. On the next afternoon, there was a rumour that Ladysmith had been relieved. Again the work places emptied. No town in the province, it was said, celebrated the victory with as much enthusiasm. On May 25th, word of the relief of Mafeking arrived. Though

The Royal visit of 1903, from an old photograph.

it came at night when many were in their beds, the news was announced by the sounding of factory horns and the ringing of church bells (being a Newtownards patriot was a twenty-four hour occupation!). This led to a week of almost constant festivities. At the victory parade which followed the fall of Pretoria, to loud cheers, the Council Chairman described Newtownards as 'the most loyal town in Her Majesty's dominions'.

The loyal residents had their reward three years later when the new king, Edward VII, and Queen Alexandra passed through on their way to see the Londonderrys at Mount Stewart. This was the first visit of a reigning monarch to the town. The celebrations surpassed even those marking the visit of the Duke and Duchess of York six years before. The only hiccup involved the entrepreneurial decision to erect a large stand along the entire front of the Town Hall as a grandstand where seats were offered at the cost of one pound. Despite their loyalty, very few were prepared to pay for the seats at that price, and up until the last minute the stand was almost empty. However, just before the royal party appeared, a huge crowd broke through the barriers and charged for the grandstand, filling the empty seats, much to the chagrin of the élite of the town, already settled in the front row.

The birth of motor transport

On Saturday February 3rd, 1900, a motor car was seen for the first time on the streets of Newtownards. The twentieth century had arrived! Although most areas in Northern Ireland did not have motor bus transport until the early 1920s, the first scheduled commercial public bus service in Ireland began at least thirteen years earlier, between Newtownards and Portaferry. In October 1907, a sixteen horse-power green Albion charabanc owned by the Irish Motor Transport Company of Edinburgh set off from Newtownards to Portaferry with a company of distinguished passengers, and completed the twenty mile trip in an hour and twenty minutes. It was intended to offer two return trips each day, but the service folded.

Happily, in 1908, the Newtownards-Portaferry twice daily service was resumed by the Reliance Motor Service and within a few weeks was joined on the route by a competitor: J. B. Ferguson, the owner of a garage in Chichester Street, Belfast, joined up with Hugh Graham, who ran a posting establishment in North Street, to put a double-decker Milnes Daimler bus on the road. It carried passengers and the Royal Mail between Belfast and Portaferry, making one return journey each day.

In June 1914, James O'Brien of Portavogie entered the fray with a thirty seater double-decker bus which he called *Pride of Ulster*. It was the first passenger bus in the British Isles that could be heated during the winter, and an Englishman was brought over to drive it since it was thought that no local man could handle such a large vehicle. So by 1914

Londonderry, Carson and Walter Long. This Unionist triumvirate visited the town on Easter Monday, 1912.

there were three services operating from Newtownards down the Peninsula. In addition, and in the other direction, in December 1907 a thrice daily bus service was launched between Newtownards and Bangor.

The Home Rule Crisis

The introduction of the third Home Rule Bill in 1912 precipitated another constitutional crisis. As one might expect, given the strong pro-Union feeling in Newtownards, few townspeople saw merit in the Bill, and a concerted effort was made to resist it.

The local campaign was organised jointly by four organisations: the Orange Order, the North Down Unionist Association, the Newtownards Unionist Club (which was the most active and carried the most clout), and a new group, the Newtownards branch of the North Down Womens' Unionist Association.[1] Its role was to assist with fund raising and, as the crisis deepened, it developed nursing and hospital arrangements in readiness for the anticipated conflict. It welcomed all classes and within two years a staggering 1,797 women had joined the Newtownards branch – about a third of all the women in the town.

On Easter Monday 1912, these organisations received the leaders of British Unionism, Bonar Law, Sir Edward Carson, Walter Long and the Marquess of Londonderry. It was a hectic gathering. Bonar Law, himself of Ulster Presbyterian stock, later told the *Pall Mall Gazette* that, 'At Newtownards I was surrounded by people grasping my hand and saying, "You are like us. You are one of ourselves." ' He was deeply impressed by their commitment to the Union. The following day, travelling by train, coach, cart and on foot, over 1,100 Newtownards people led by 'Lord Londonderry's Own' Flute Band, attended the monster rally of 100,000 Unionists at Balmoral.

The campaign of 1912 climaxed with Ulster Day Rallies all over the province on Saturday September 28th, and the signing of the Solemn League and Covenant. To prepare for this, Newtownards held a rally two days before Ulster Day, on the evening of Thursday 26th September.

The factories of the town closed early at 5 p.m. to enable their workers to attend. Almost every house in the town was decorated with flags. There was a mood of excitement and anticipation. The Town Hall was festooned with Union Jacks, and on the west gable wall was a huge scroll stretching from corner to corner on which was written 'ULSTER IS RIGHT'. The Guild Hall of the First Presbyterian Church was decorated with a large poster proclaiming 'NO HOME RULE'. The speakers, who arrived in Captain James Craig's car, were greeted with enthusiastic cheering and escorted to the Guild Hall by 'Lord Londonderry's Own' Flute band, two dozen torch bearers, and a large crowd of spectators.

The Guild Hall was soon filled and an overflow meeting had to be held in the Town Hall. When it too overflowed, an open air meeting took place in Conway Square. As Lord Londonderry and the special guests, including Colonel Sharman Crawford, entered the Guild Hall the audience rose en masse and cheered for several minutes. The Rev. W.P. Moran, the Methodist minister, introduced the first hymn, 'O God, our help in ages past'. Lord Londonderry began with an apology from Sir Edward Carson who regretted being unable to address the meeting in 'the Unionist stronghold in the Ards'. To ringing applause Lord Londonderry said he did not think that Sir Edward was right in saying that Newtownards was only the stronghold of Unionism in the Ards – it was the stronghold of Unionism in Ulster . He was glad to think that the town regarded him as a friend and neighbour, because the interest of Newtownards was as dear to him as any one. He went on to say that the prosperity in Ulster was dependent on maintaining the Union, and that he would return to assure Sir Edward Carson that the whole of Newtownards was at his back.

The signing of the Covenant

On Ulster Day, Saturday September 28th, 1912, the town solemnly displayed its attachment to the Union. Signing the Covenant was not something that one did lightly. To emphasise the point, services were held in First Presbyterian and the parish church an hour before the signing. The service in the former was jointly taken by the ministers of the Methodist Church, First, Second, Strean and Regent Street Presbyterian Churches, with the Rev.Dr. Wright being the speaker. He outlined the dangers of Home Rule under which all power would be in the hands of one party, and invoked the spectre of the Catholic Church, which was then going through a bellicose, proselytising phase – the *Ne Temere* decree, anulling marriages between Protestant and Catholics unless they had taken place in a Catholic church, had been issued just four years earlier. He referred to the Scottish

The Rev. William Wright, minister of First Presbyterian Church from 1879-1919 (Doctor of Divinity after 1912), popularly known as 'the bishop of Newtownards.'

Covenants and the role of covenants in the Bible and in history and urged his congregation to stand firm in the defence of their rights, religion and liberties. Both churches were full and in each service the speaker read out the text of the Solemn League and Covenant. Religion and politics were deliberately fused. The cause acquired the character of a crusade.

The signing of the Covenant took place in the Guild Hall from 4-5 p.m. and in the Town Hall from 4-10 p.m. About 2,000 men signed it, and about 2,000 women signed a similar Declaration. The Covenant and Declaration were available at specified times in the Town Hall each day for the next two weeks. In total 5,392 signed (2,474 men and 2,918 women), pledging themselves to resist Home Rule 'using all means which may be found necessary.'

On Thursday January 16th, 1913, a wet, miserable evening, the Home Rule Bill was debated in the House of Commons. In Newtownards, 'huge crowds' led by bands met at the Orange Hall and then marched through the town centre to Conway Square, avoiding Mr Edward McCall's house in High Street. He was a prominent and highly respected Catholic who regularly had won the votes of Protestants in elections to the Town Commission, in spite of his Nationalist views, and his wife had recently died. 'Thousands' had already gathered in the Square. A tar barrel was lit in the centre. Thomas Lavery read and commented upon extracts from the Bill, then, to loud cheers, he attached it to a pole and set it alight from the blazing barrel. He waved the burning document aloft and the band struck up the National Anthem, at which point the crowd removed their hats and joined heartily. Large numbers then moved round to the *Chronicle* offices to hear the result of the division in the Commons as it came through by telegraph. The passage of the Bill was greeted with loud boos and angry declamations.

The Ulster Volunteer Force

The existence of the Ulster Volunteer Force was first publicly acknowledged at a social organised by the local Unionist Club a few weeks later, on February 26th, 1913. Political actions alone would not preserve the Union. Colonel Sharman Crawford told the meeting that there was going

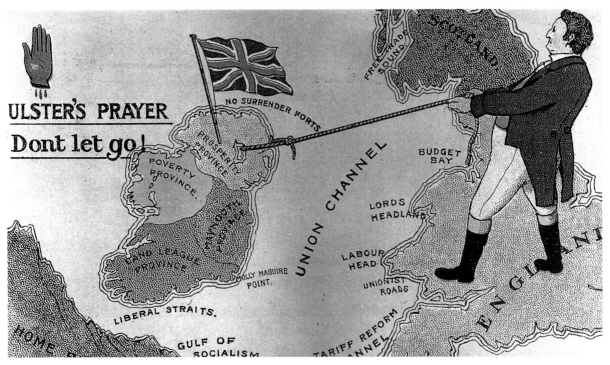

ULSTER'S PRAYER
Dont let go!

Contemporary pro-Union propaganda postcard.

to be a new 'mobile force which would operate on the frontier line. Big things will probably happen in the autumn,' he continued, 'and I want the men of Newtownards to prepare during the summer months.'

At first, Newtownards people were slow to join the UVF. By June only a 'fair' number had enlisted and, of these, a number had not turned up for drill, held every Tuesday night in the Orange Hall. However, it is worth noting that the average working week was six thirteen-hour days and perhaps it is not surprising that men did not turn out for drill in the evenings! This depressed Dr. Wright. William James Ferguson, the Council Chairman and a major local employer, however, was optimistic:

I am convinced that the men of Newtownards will be 'there' when the time comes. They were 'there' at Balmoral and when the time comes to handle the rifles which the Government have not seized – and there are plenty in the country – they will be 'there'.

Ferguson was right. Morale was undoubtedly boosted by an impressive muster of 2,500 UVF men at the Six-Road-Ends on Thursday July 24th, 1913, who met to hear speeches from Carson, Craig and Sharman Crawford. The cottages which lined the routes displayed Union Jacks to encourage the streams of people as they made their way to the venue. The Newtownards contingent carried rifles and were led by 'Lord Londonderry's Own' Flute Band, and some buglers. Another 3,500 spectators turned up to witness the spectacle and hear the speeches. Having been inspired, many more joined.

By the end of 1913 the men of the Newtownards District of the UVF had been welded into a fairly cohesive force and were ready for their first official inspection. It took place in a field behind the Castle Gardens spinning mill on a wet Saturday in December. Despite the continuous fall of heavy sleet, seven hundred men mustered, representing the seven companies of the Ards Peninsula, including two from Newtownards

Recruitment was brisk over Christmas. By the end of January 1914 the seven hundred had become one thousand, with much of the growth coming from the town of Newtownards whose companies doubled from two to four: 'A' Company commanded by Montserrat Walker, 'B' Company commanded by James Blow, 'C' Company commanded by Wright's son Matthew, and 'D' Company commanded by W.H. Webb. With growth came reorganisation. The companies from Newtownards, Comber, Donaghadee, Greyabbey, Ballywalter, Mount Stewart, Kirkcubbin and Portaferry were made into the 2nd Battalion of the North Down Regiment.

The local Volunteers trained with a view to resisting the authorities who might impose Home Rule upon them. For example, in field manoeuvres in February 1914, 130 Newtownards men defended the railway line from 'attacks' by Comber Volunteers. It was thought that 'drill should be combined with prayer' and in March 1914 a series of weekly prayer meetings was launched.

The major spring training took place on Easter weekend on the Clandeboye estate with the same ingredients of drill, manoeuvres and prayer. The four Newtownards Companies marched over to Clandeboye on Easter Sunday to attend a drumhead service. They marched over again on the Monday, with transport and ambulance wagons at the rear, and companies from the First Battalion engaged companies from the Second in war games on the demesne

Gun running

But prayer and drilling do not win wars. The UVF needed arms. They got them on the night of April 24th, 1914, when 25,000 rifles and three million rounds of ammunition were landed at Larne, Bangor and Donaghadee. It was the job of the Newtownards men to collect the guns at Donaghadee.

The local Volunteers had drilled that Friday night as usual but before they were dismissed they were told to re-assemble at 10.00 p.m. and bring rations for twelve hours. They had no idea where they were going, or what they had to do. Between five hundred and a thousand turned up. They speculated as they set out, some suggesting Portaferry, others Mount Stewart, others Ballywalter. When they were led up to the Movilla Road the men guessed their destination must be Donaghadee or Millisle. As they marched on towards the coast, whispers began to pass along the lines that it was a gun-running operation. The Newtownards men marched directly to the harbour and cordoned it off. The coastguards had already been detained. By this stage, few were still asleep in Donaghadee, but no

Dawn at Donaghadee. The steam crane moves the guns to waiting cars.

one was allowed near the harbour without a pass.

The boat was expected at 2.00 a.m. A small force of police arrived at 2.30, but being greatly outnumbered, were unable to do anything. At 3.00 a.m. motorcycle despatch riders arrived with news that weapons had been successfully landed at Larne and Bangor. The men could not refrain from cheering, but as dawn broke there was still no sign of their expected boat. Men were marched off in squads to a local café where they were supplied with coffee. Finally at 5.30 a.m. the *Innismurray* arrived. A steam crane got the boxes of guns ashore, where motor cars, drawn up along the quay, were filled up and driven off to Newtownards and the surrounding countryside, where the arms were concealed for a few days before further distribution. Over seventy tons had been landed and distributed in under two hours.

There was only one fatality – Herbert Painter of Donaghadee. He was a coastguard, and when the officers in Donaghadee had first realised that something was afoot, he had been sent posthaste to the Divisional Officer at Ballywilliam but he had dropped dead from over-exertion en route.

The 'industrial capital of Down.' Newtownards at the turn of the century.

'The industrial capital of Down'

We should not let Newtownards' enthusiasm for the Union distort our picture of the Edwardian town. In the years before the war, Newtownards was a bustling, peaceable country town more renowned for flowers, fairs, and textile manufacturing than guns. As the *Chronicle* said in 1914, 'if the average school boy was asked what our town was best known for, he would in all probability reply, "Dickson's roses".' Dickson's had been started by Alexander Dickson, a Scotsman, who had opened a seed merchant's shop in High Street in 1836. In time, the business expanded and moved to the corner of Frederick Place and Church Street and the area across from it became known as 'the Nursery'. By the early 1900s the business employed seventy men. In 1907 the Royal Horticultural Society awarded the firm its Victorian Medal of Honour. In 1912 the *Gardener's Magazine* of London said that Newtownards had:

...attained to a high position as a great centre of rose growing and rose raising so that it has become a household word wherever roses are grown and appreciated, or, in other words, throughout the civilised world.

1912 also saw the building of another textile factory, the Ulster Print Works, on the site of the Flush Hall farm, now just behind the Scrabo

Flush Hall, the site of the Ulster Print Works. Now under and adjacent the Scrabo estate.

MAY this
GOOD LUCK
that some
Folks have
brought to
their doors,
BE
nought to
compare,
OR
A PATCH UPON YOURS.

At Newtownards

A postcard sent from Newtownards in 1911, highlighting its reputation as a textile centre.

estate. The Ulster Print Works was important in two respects: firstly, all the capital was raised from local business men; secondly, it gave work to men at a time when much of the town's factory workforce was female. Women were the breadwinners in many homes. The driving force and managing director was William James Ferguson, the owner of a hemstitching business in West Street.

Pre-war Newtownards was a force to be reckoned with. In November 1912 the *Belfast News Letter* called the town 'the industrial capital of Down':

Few towns in Ireland of its size can boast of so many or so great variety of industries within its borders. A casual walk through its comparatively quiet streets gives little indication to the observer of the amount of work that goes on daily in its many busy hives of industry. Only at meal times or after working hours can any conception be had of the numbers employed in this seemingly quiet town within six miles of Belfast city boundary. A large trade is done in the factories. Damasks and linens are manufactured extensively and a large wholesale trade is carried on in woollen shirtings and skirtings, while flax spinning affords employment to many, supplying linen yarns for weaving and thread manufacturing purposes and making a large selection of hempen twines which are greatly appreciated in the finishing industry. Other important industrial enterprises include printing and finishing works and laundries. The town can boast of being the first to introduce the manufacture of hosiery by machinery into the North of Ireland thirty years ago and at the present time still claims to have the largest factory of this kind in Ireland, its manufacture being accepted as standard articles throughout the world. Hemstitching of handkerchiefs gives employment to the female portion of the population. Reference to Newtownards from an industrial point of view would not be complete without mention of the famous nurseries which create employment for a large amount of male labour while the success of the firm may be appreciated by the fact that they hold the appointment of rosarians to His Majesty the King. In the spring of the present year large print works were opened and equipped with the latest and most up to date machinery, this undertaking representing an investment of local capital amounting to about £40,000. Carriage and van building is carried on extensively and road metal quarries are worked on the outskirts of the town while the manufacture of mineral waters is a growing industry.

The article also commended the town's Regency street plan:

Few provincial towns can boast of such fine thoroughfares. If many of the buildings are typical of a bygone time, the streets and footpaths are worthy of imitation by many towns which perhaps lay claim to more progressive methods. Granolithic and tar macadam enter largely into the composition of the footpaths which evoke favourable comment from all visitors.

The author praised the Urban Council as a 'progressive' body and described how the town had been provided with a public water supply at a cost of £20,000 in 1907. Service pipes, valves and hydrants had been laid down in the streets so that the water, taken from tunnels and reservoirs on Scrabo Hill, could be piped to houses, and, as if to show the town's pride in its new water system, a large number of street fountains had been erected. Over one thousand houses, half of all the houses in the town, had piped water by 1914, enjoying 'an ample supply of the finest spring water'. The town's new sewage system also won plaudits:

In 1910 they also embarked on an entirely new sewerage scheme, discarding all old sewers. The main system has been completed and the work of new house connections is increasing rapidly. This scheme is also estimated to cost £20,000 The gas undertaking is owned municipally and was purchased twenty nine years ago. The town claims to supply the cheapest gas of any inland town in Ireland. A Technical School was established under municipal auspices in 1903 and is still managed by its first principal Mr Philip Cole. A new race course was inaugurated in the spring of this year and its first meeting was held in the new grounds in May. A Golf Club was established in 1907 and comprises a membership of about 100. The present population of the town is 9587 which represents a 5% increase in the last decade.

The First World War
Britain declared war on Germany on Tuesday August 4th, 1914. That evening, royal proclamations calling out the Army reservists were posted around the town. Excited huddles formed around the notices and when bugles sounded 'The Assembly' in various parts of the town, large crowds – family friends, the patriotic, the curious – made their way to the Bridewell

to watch the members of the local militia, the 4th Battalion of the Royal Irish Rifles (the Royal North Downs), report for duty. The reservists were medically examined and given uniform, clothing and equipment. That evening an additional thirty young men enlisted, and a further eighty-six joined over the next few weeks.

For the next two days reservists arrived on every train and by Thursday the mobilisation was complete: four hundred men assembled at the grounds of the Ards Recreation Society on the Comber Road. When they left for Holywood they were accompanied for part of the way by the local companies of the Ulster Volunteer Force, who cheered them heartily when the time came to part company.

Not only men but horses were needed for the Army. The September race meeting of the Ards Recreational Society was cancelled and the government started buying up horses in the area, with local people pleased with the prices they were getting!

The first scare of the war involved a German who lived quietly at the lead mines at Whitespots. Paul Wentzel was an engineer who had arrived in the area in 1910 along with other Germans who were investigating the possibility of re-opening the mine. The project was abandoned and everyone except Wentzel returned to Germany in 1912. Following the outbreak of war, Wentzel's home was raided. Sketches of fortifications, what appeared to be codes, maps of Belfast Lough and Aldershot Barracks, and a photograph of naval vessels off Bangor were found in his home, along with a camera, flashlight, rifles and ammunition. He was promptly arrested as a spy. But Wentzel denied this, and claimed that, as he had once been a captain in the German army, he had an interest in military material. It could not be proved that he had been spying, but as he was a German, he was detained for the duration of the war. Some local people could not contain their curiosity and there were break-ins to Wentzel's house while he was in custody. Some 'souvenirs' were taken and those guilty were arrested and sentenced at the local court.

Meanwhile, the fate of hundreds of local members of the UVF had still to be decided. At the end of August, Carson and the government struck a deal. Home Rule would not be implemented until after the War and there would be some special accommodation for Ulster. The Ulster Volunteer Force would be kept together as the the 36th (Ulster) Division, and the men would be enrolled in territorial units formed out of local Volunteer regiments and trained initially in Ulster.

Both of north Down's Volunteer regiments were grouped together as the 13th Battalion, part of the 108th Brigade of the Royal Irish Rifles, 36th (Ulster) Division. Enrolment from the UVF in Newtownards commenced on the evening of Monday September 7th. 'A' and 'B' Companies assembled at Walker's Mill Yard. Lord Dunleath took the chair and called on Dr.

Wright to address the Volunteers. He explained the welfare arrangements for their wives, families and dependents and made an earnest appeal for them to defend the Empire. 'C' and 'D' Companies met in the Orange Hall where Colonel Sharman Crawford delivered a similar message. Altogether 130 men came forward from the four Newtownards Companies of the UVF on that first evening, with Hugh Brown of Greenwell Street being the first Newtownards Volunteer to enlist. 119 were passed as medically fit. As each man came forward to be measured for his uniform, a Boy Scout handed him a bar of McClinton's Hibernia Shaving soap and a card printed in gold, gifts from John McClement JP. The card read:

> I would be True for there are those who trust me,
> I would be Pure for there those who care,
> I would be Strong for there is much to suffer,
> I would be Brave for there is much to dare,
> I would be a Friend to all, the foe, the friendless,
> I would be always Giving and forget the gift,
> I would be Humble for I know my weakness,
> I would Look up and laugh and love and lift.
>
> Will you make this your personal pledge?
>   May God bless and keep you
> Your friend
JOHN McCLEMENT
>
> Newtownards
> September 17th 1914

On Friday September 18th, the enlisted men marched through the town for the last time as Volunteers, led by a fife band and followed by a large group of residents, mostly women. Although the men were cheered, there was a noticeable absence of euphoria. They then marched to their camp at Clandeboye. These were their first steps on a journey which would take them to the Somme and for many of them that journey would be one way only. By the end of September a total of 387 Newtownards men were serving in the Army and Navy. By November 1914 the number had risen to 418.

In the meantime the Council set up a Newtownards Relief Fund and collections were organised in the factories throughout the town. A Soldiers and Sailors Families Association was established and Newtownards ladies were asked to knit socks, Balaclava helmets, woollen waistcoats, gloves and mittens, and donate chocolate, peppermint sweets, lead pencils, briar pipes, tobacco packed in thick tin foil, cigarettes, tins of Vaseline and boracic ointment. The Newtownards Girl Guides sold badges to raise money so that every local ex-Volunteer training at Clandeboye (140 by November) could be given a pipe.

At the end of September, the Ards Recreation Grounds were taken over by the military as a training camp and and about a thousand soldiers from mid-Antrim were stationed there. Boredom was a problem and so in December 1914 the Council made the Assembly Room available to the soldiers as a recreation room, supplying newspapers and books, sets of dominoes, draughts and chess. In May and June 1915 mission services were held for the soldiers at 'the camp' and an average of seventy came along each evening.

Meanwhile, training continued at Clandeboye. This involved long marches over rough ground, carrying heavy loads of stones in a haversack, bayonet fighting which included stabbing at stuffed figures, and practice at throwing hand grenades. In the spring of 1915 training was extended to include 'entraining' – how to board and disembark from a train in an orderly fashion – using rows of seats in an open field. Because the Newtownards men were stationed so close to their homes they would often 'go home' unofficially on a Sunday. In early July the Division was moved to Seaford on the Sussex coast, then enjoying warm weather. The Division then completed its training on the rifle ranges at Bordon and Bramshott in a balmy holiday atmosphere, before being moved to France in October 1915, to the Somme sector in Picardy.

At home recruitment proceeded. The town's most persistent recruiting sergeant was probably the *Newtownards Chronicle*, which regularly published patriotic verses designed to urge and shame 'laggards' into enlisting:

> A hundred years ago your fathers fought
> As you must fight for liberty today.
> Beside that heritage all else was naught,
> And shall you prove yourself less staunch than they?
> The hour has struck, and Britain asks your vow
> Of loyal and ungrudging service – now!

By the middle of 1916, 850 Newtownards men were serving in the Army and Navy. The town was the third largest supplier of recruits in Ulster, after Belfast and Lurgan.

The first local casualty was Lance Corporal David ('Big Davy') Smyth, son of Samuel Smyth, a coal merchant of Mill Street. Big Davy was wounded by a bullet at Cipley at the end of August 1914. He was in the Royal Irish Rifles, which had been part of the British Expeditionary Force. He was reported as vowing, 'I hope it won't be long until I get a chance of getting my own back.' The first man killed was Andrew Russell, of 18 Mark Street, a reservist with the Cameron Highlanders. He died after being hit by a bullet in the chest in September 1914, leaving a wife of nine months who had, the day after his death, given birth to a baby daughter.

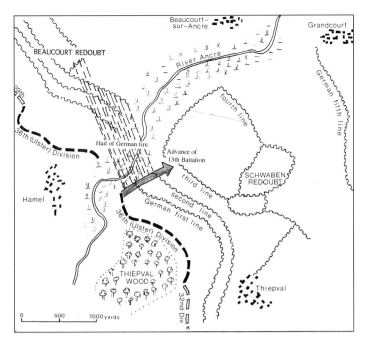

The first day of the Battle of the Somme. (after Michael Hall)

The dead man's mother, Mrs Russell, had all five of her sons in the Services. A steady stream of Newtownards casualties followed.

But the stream became a flood after the battle of the Somme in July 1916. The Ulster Division was to attack from Thiepval Wood. The 108th Brigade was to attack German positions astride the Ancre river, with the 13th Rifles – the County Down men – to attack south of the river. Robert Doggart from Newtownards described the battle as 'a nightmare come true'. William Brown, from Movilla Street, who like many others had 'forced his age' to get enlisted, found himself in charge of four Vickers water-cooled machine guns at the battle. He recalled drawing water for the guns from craters in which dead soldiers lay, and even, when there were shortages, having to drink this water himself. As one officer, Brigadier Broadhurst, observed:

At first south of the Ancre everything went well and 108th Brigade moved over the first German trenches with little loss. Scarcely were they across, however, when the German batteries opened a barrage on "No man's land". Simultaneously the skilful German machine gunners, who had remained safe from bombardment... raked our men from the flank and the rear, thinning the khaki waves. Officers went down and men went on alone... The 13th Irish Rifles... lost nearly all its officers even before it reached the enemy trenches.

Robert Doggart's duties included carrying the wounded back from the front: 'we did not stop for three days,' he recalled, the casualties were so heavy. It was thought that only one in ten of the 13th Battalion survived the first few days of the battle of the Somme. News of the deaths did not reach Newtownards until July 8th, and then the town received only news of officers. Traditionally, junior officers led their units from the front, stepping out with the polished blackthorn stick of the Irish Regiments or a revolver, but because the preliminary bombardment had failed to silence

189

Newtownards funeral of the period.

the German machine-guns, casualties in these ranks were particularly heavy. The first Newtownards fatality to be announced was Dr. Wright's son, Matthew. By July 15th there was still no offical casualty list for Newtownards. Rumours abounded and 'much anxiety' was expressed in the town over loved ones.

The little that there was to go on was extrememly alarming. Captain Elliot Johnston, son of Samuel Johnston, owner of the Glen Print Works, was killed on that first day. A few days earlier, he had led three fellow officers and one hundred men in a daring pre-battle raid on German lines, bringing back thirteen German prisoners. Another officer casualty was Lieutenent J. L. Peacock, the Town Surveyor. Captain G.W. Webb of the Royal Flying Corps, brother of W.H.Webb, the owner of Ards Weaving Company was missing, shot down over the battlefield.

By September 1916, the full extent of the catastrophe was becoming clearer. Norman Nevin, then a seven year old living in Court Street, remembers people at their half-doors watching with dread as the postman made his progress up the street. Where would he stop? Would he deliver a soldier's letter, letting the family know all was well, or an official communication, 'the wee brown envelope'? Neighbours warned one another of the postman's approach: this was something you had to steel yourself for. When a woman got a letter from a son, brother or husband she would come out and share the news and there would be a collective sigh of relief; in other houses there was grief and silence.

The *Chronicle* calculated unofficially that 63 had been killed in the campaign, 34 were 'missing', 100 were wounded and eight were prisoners of war. About one in nine of the Newtownards people who were then serving might therefore have been killed in the Somme campaign. The final death toll for the whole war was over 300 out of a total of 1,400 servicemen and women, a reminder that, terrible and concentrated though they were, Somme deaths accounted for a minority of total casualties. Also, many more were injured, physically and psychologically, and came back to the town to find themselves objects of pity to adults, and objects of ridicule to uncomprehending children.

1   The list of the office bearers in these four organisations includes some of the most prominent people in the town. The District Master of the Orange Order was T.R. Lavery, the owner of the Ann Street Hemstitching Works, a JP and a former Council chairman; its Deputy District Master was David O'Prey, a Councillor and the owner of a painting and decorating business; and its chaplains were Rev. William Wright and the Rev. William Whatham of St. Mark's Parish Church. The president of the Newtownards branch of the North Down Unionist Association was the Rev.W. Wright. The Honorary Patron of the Newtownards Unionist Club was the sixth Marquess of Londonderry and Honorary Vice-Presidents were W. Mitchell-Thompson, MP for North Down, W. Sibbald Johnson, owner of the Kiltonga Bleach Works, Alexander Dickson, of the horticulture business and County Councillor, Samuel Johnston JP, owner of the Glen Print Works, R.R. Webb, owner of Ards Weaving Company and Captain J.S. Henry, owner of The Newtownards Chronicle. Its chairman was W.H. Webb, Managing Director of Ards Weaving Company and the Secretary was Montserrat Walker, son of George Walker of Castle Gardens Mill. The Treasurer was William Ditty, sub-agent to the Marquess of Londonderry. The president of the local Women's Unionist Association was the Marchioness of Londonderry and the Chairwoman was Mrs Dunbar-Buller of Woburn, Millisle. The Vice-Presidents were Mrs Whatham, Mrs W. Wright and Mrs H. Johnston, the Treasurer was Mrs T.R. Lavery and the Secretaries were Miss Ferguson and Miss Iveston.

16
Quieter Times 1918 to the present

After the crisis of Home Rule, and the greater trauma of the First World War, the town settled down to quieter times. Its mood had changed. In the aftermath of the 'the war to end all wars', there was in Newtownards a turning away from the hitherto uncritical adulation of the 'Empire' and the boundless optimism about its future. No longer would its citizens get up in the middle of the night to celebrate imperial victories in far flung corners of the Empire as they had done in 1900. The loyalty was still there of course, but it was viewed with more sober realism, with the increased realisation of what that loyalty had cost.

But it was cost of a different nature that ex-servicemen now had to deal with. This new mood became apparent when the Council could not agree to spend the money on a war memorial to the three hundred men from the district who had lost their lives. In the 1920s, frustrated ex-servicemen made their own out of snow, with the inscription 'LEST WE FORGET', in the square in front of the Priory. Their motive was to shame the Council into action but the only action that was taken was against themselves. The police were called and each man was fined a shilling for loitering. The Council did not get round to building a War Memorial until 1934. In the meantime, ex-servicemen built their own of wood in the grounds of their premises in Victoria Avenue.

The veterans had returned not to 'a land fit for heroes' but to unemployment and hardship. Jobs were difficult to come by even in a thriving manufacturing centre like Newtownards. At this point Lady Londonderry intervened, announcing plans to build an elaborate series of gardens at Mount Stewart. These renowned gardens were built with ex-service labour, and the fantastic stone figures that adorn them were worked by local craftsmen. The work and the gardens, a throwback to the age of benevolent paternalism, provided many, much-needed local jobs.

The rise and fall of Ards Airport

One of the few positive features to emerge from the War was air travel. Aviation technology had advanced to the point where passenger flights

A message in snow. This snow memorial inscribed 'Lest we forget' was built by veterans on the green in the 1920s in order to shame the Council into building a memorial to honour the fallen.

were possible, and in 1924 Belfast Corporation opened an airfield at Malone, but soon afterwards it had to be abandoned due to flooding. Northern Ireland ugently needed an aerodrome. In 1933 the seventh Marquess of Londonderry, who was an enthusiastic aviator, announced his intention to build an aerodrome on some of his land at Newtownards. In 1934 the Governor of Northern Ireland, the Duke of Abercorn, officially opened Ards Airport, Northern Ireland's first civil airport.

The airport became an important conduit. Over six hundred passengers passed through it in the first five weeks and there were enough thereafter to run the services at a profit. The skies over the town were busy each day with planes flying to all the major cities in the British Isles. Many airline companies operated out of Ards in the mid 1930s: Blackpool and West Coast, Isle of Man Air Services, Northern and Scottish Airways, Olley Air Services and Railway Air Services. The Royal Mail was also brought in to Ards.

John Corlett's *Aviation in Ulster* relates how passengers travelling from Belfast to London were collected at the Midland Hotel at York Road at

The famous Dodo Terrace, at Mount Stewart. The gardens were built by local veterans, the figures made by local artisans.

8 a.m., and chauffeured to Ards in a Daimler. On arrival at 8.45 a.m. passengers and their luggage were weighed and tickets issued or validated. The ticket clerk then ushered them to the airplane, and the flight began at 9 a.m. sharp. There was a fifteen minute stop at Liverpool where passengers could get out. At noon the plane landed at Croydon, and from there the passengers were driven to Victoria Station, where they arrived at 12.45 p.m.

Because Ards Airport was situated at the head of Strangford Lough and the runway was a mere eighteen feet above sea level, landings could take place in thick fog. On reaching Strangford Lough, the wireless operator would wind out a hundred feet of copper wire with lead beads on the end. When the beads were felt to touch the water the captain knew that he was one hundred feet above sea level! There was then a carefully timed rate of descent as the wire was wound up. When grass instead of sea could be seen through the fog then the plane was at the airfield. If it was stormy a 'catching party' was requested. This consisted of the ground staff of three, who would pounce on the airplane, two grabbing the wings and the third the tail to hold the plane down, with all three racing along holding it down until it came to a standstill!

By 1938 the Ards Airport was flourishing, and was rated the seventh busiest in the British Isles. But with the opening of the Belfast Harbour Airport in 1938 business collapsed. All the airlines immediately transferred their flights to Sydenham and Ards went extremely quiet. The airport never really recovered from this disaster. It was left with the activities of the Northern Ireland Flying Club, which gave instruction and took passengers on pleasure trips, and the private planes of Lord Londonderry and his family, and a few others.

The airport's most celebrated visitor was probably Hitler's ambassador to Britain, and later Foreign Minister, Joachim von Ribbentrop who touched down in 1937, on the way to visit the Londonderrys at Mount Stewart.

'An amazing number of buses': public transport

The majority of people in Newtownards, while they might enjoy watching the planes, were unlikely to be able to afford to use them. They had to fall back on the less spectacular, but affordable and regular public bus service. There were an amazing number of buses to choose from. By the mid 1920s there were three companies operating on routes down the Peninsula, six to Belfast and two to Bangor.

The principal operator on the Peninsula was the Ards Motor Transport Company. This was a merger formed in September 1916 from the Reliance Motor Service, James O'Brien and a service provided by the mill owners David Hutchinson and Thomas Somerset.

The Ards Motor Transport Company ran from Newtownards to Portaferry via Kircubbin and Portavogie and from Newtownards to Donaghadee via Bangor, though the Bangor-Donaghadee leg was dropped in the early 1920s. Its buses were primrose yellow with solid tyres and had an entrance platform at the rear from which an outside stair led to the roof. The roof had side boards to carry luggage and market produce and young male passengers would often climb up and sit on them. To carry more, particularly on market days, the mudguards were replaced with metal shelves.

The company did not always have the monopoly on the Peninsula. In 1919 Robert McGivern of Carrowdore ran three round trips each day between Newtownards and Carrowdore. In 1920 A. J. Moss of Newtownards brought a former London bus, which he had painted maroon, on to the road. By 1926 he had a whole fleet of buses in operation: two green charabancs, a 32 seater Leyland with pneumatic tyres and two small Lancia buses. Also in this period, Robert and James Lawther ran a service between Ballywalter, Carrowdore and Newtownards.

In the mid 1920s no less than six companies ran services between the town and Belfast: the Ards Motor Transport Company; the Pioneer Motor Service run by James McCartney of Newtownards from 1924; the Imperial Bus Service owned by Messrs. Crawford, Weir and Baird which ran from Belfast to Donaghadee via Newtownards from 1925 using yellow buses with a black roof, later changed to yellow and brown; the Lancia Bus Service owned by Eadie and Tornie from 1925 who sold out to the Moss Line in 1926; and finally the Kane Brothers of Millisle who ran from 1926 four maroon and cream buses each called the 'Millisle Queen', eight round trips per day from Belfast to Millisle via Newtownards. Competition was so intense that the fare was reduced to 6d. (9d. return) but patrons

A charabanc pulls up in the Square en route to Belfast. This old, grainy photograph captures Newtownards between the era of the horse and the age of motor transport.

tended to be very loyal to one company and would wait patiently for it to arrive, ignoring the others.

The Ards Motor Transport Company, which had a finger in every pie, also ran a service from Newtownards to Bangor via Conlig from 1916. Matthew Morrow's Enterprise company from Bangor competed with it between 1919 and 1925.

The situation became rather less complicated in 1927, when six of the largest proprietors in Northern Ireland merged to form the Belfast Omnibus Company. Many other local bus companies joined forces with this conglomerate: the Ards Motor Transport Company and the Moss Line both joined it and consequently the B.O.C. had a near monopoly on the Peninsula and Bangor routes. In 1935 the Northern Ireland Road Transport Board bought up all existing bus companies and so the era of unfettered competition, which is still seen by some as a golden age, came to an end.

'Mr Calder always got his own way': the Ards Hospital

By the twentieth century the Infirmary wing and the Fever Block of the workhouse were being used for the treatment of any sick poor of the area and not solely for sick inmates. New legislation allowed workhouse infirmaries to be converted into district hospitals, thus removing the stigma of the workhouse from the institution. The Medical Officer of the Poor Law Union, Dr. Parke, urged that advantage should be taken of this concession and the Infirmary wing be converted into a district hospital. Local ratepayers objected. However resistance softened when a child died in the Infirmary as a result of a cross-infection of diphtheria from the Fever Block. Preparations were made to found a district hospital.

In January 1932 the new Board of Governors agreed that the Medical

Officer in Charge must be a Fellow of the Royal College of Surgeons and should live in Newtownards. They would pay him £500 per annum. The 28-year-old Alexander Calder was appointed. Calder was an Edinburgh man who had gained his FRCS in 1930. He took over a hospital of 84 patients, with a nursing staff of one matron, three ward sisters, a night sister, six assistant and four probationer nurses. In the first six months 757 patients were admitted. To help him Calder had only one medical assistant, who was was in charge of the Fever Hospital, the medical and maternity patients, anaesthetics, dispensing and a clinic for venereal diseases. Mr H. W. Gallagher records that at Mr Calder's first meeting with the Board of Governors he presented them with a list of apparatus required for the wards and theatres at an estimated cost of £5,000. The Governors were horrified and the Chairman said, '£500 yes, but £5,000 is out of the question .'

Mr Calder expecting such a reply also had his written resignation ready and presented it to the Chairman and left the meeting. The Governors soon changed their mind and sent the Clerk, Mr John Warden, to bring Mr Calder back. From that time onwards Mr Calder always got his own way... and guided the hospital until his death in 1965, by which time Ards Hospital was reckoned to be one of the best... provincial hospitals in the Province.

The decade before the Second World War witnessed tremendous expansion in the hospital service. In the second six months of the hospital's existence there were 493 operations, so that it became necessary to take on a house surgeon to assist Mr Calder. In the following year, 1934-5, 2,433 patients were admitted (236 to the infirm [geriatric] hospital, 513 to the fever hospital and 306 medical, 108 maternity and 1270 surgical cases to the general hospital. More medical help was essential to cope with these soaring numbers, and an anaesthetist and obstetrician were appointed in 1935. An Eye, Ear Nose and Throat surgeon and a pharmacist also joined the staff in these early years and another physician was appointed in 1937, when the Fever Hospital passed to the control of GPs. In 1937 land was purchased for a maternity block. Ards was the first hospital outside Belfast to have a laboratory, to which a bio-chemist was appointed in 1939. A separate children's unit was also started.

From the outset a strong bond between hospital and community was created. Naturally, the community was appreciative of the medical expertise now available, but the hospital itself was grateful for help given by the community. Money was donated for modern X-Ray equipment which was the first of its kind in the United Kingdom, and in 1933 the Ards Summer Football League were the first subscribers to the Radium Fund. The hospital has continued to be well supported through the decades, notably from the mid 1950s by the Ards Hospital Ladies Committee.

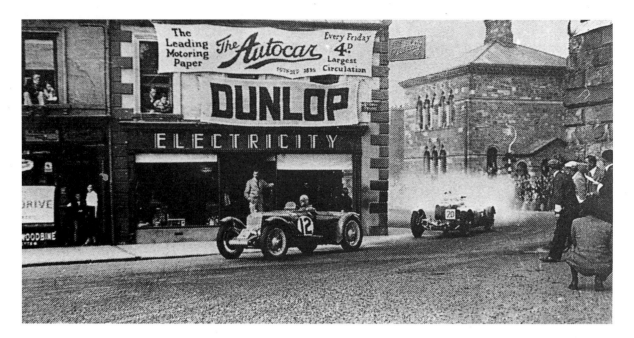

The Ards Tourist Trophy Race

The Ards T.T. race was a hugely popular annual event. Crowds of up to half a million came each year to watch the six hour race over the thirteen mile Dundonald-Newtownards-Comber circuit. Starting from Quarry Corner, outside Dundonald, the cars approached Newtownards from Bradshaw's Brae, the steep descent providing the smaller cars with their fastest part of the course. They approached the railway bridge at speed and entered the town at Church Street, passed along Regent Street and then turned sharp right into Conway Square – if they could – for many often went too fast and either hit the sand-bagged Town Hall or chose to pass behind it at the last minute. The best European drivers could take the corner expertly by placing their nearside front wheel within a foot of the corner kerb. The cars then crossed the Square, negotiated another small entrance into South Street, which was also sand-bagged, and so on to Comber.

Motor racing is a dangerous sport and there were fatalities on the circuit over the years – but not amongst the spectators until, in 1936, local driver Jack Chambers lost control of his Riley as he negotiated the railway bridge at Church Street. As he came out from under the bridge he skidded down the street, just past the Strangford Arms Hotel, and, about two hundred yards from the hospital, hit a lamp post. As he did so, he clipped a long line of spectators. Eight were killed and forty were injured. The tragedy, understandably, greatly disturbed the local authorities. There was widespread concern, especially over the question of who was responsible for compensating the victims and any others that might be killed or injured in future. The Council organised a plebiscite of residents in the streets directly affected by the race and a majority agreed that it would be best to discontinue it. The T.T. races were never held on the Ards circuit again .

Urban District Council to Municipal Borough

The population of the town rose only slightly between the wars, but its growth continued, albeit at a steadier rate than before. In the late 1920s the Council swept away a lot of the town's poorer eighteenth and early nineteenth housing stock, replacing it with neat new dwellings. It also built new houses in Upper Movilla Street, Greenwell Street and Corry Street, and offered local builders a subsidy to erect private houses. This growth is partly reflected in the increased income from rates etc. (in 1926 annual revenue was £17,500, in 1936 £26,000, and in 1946 £35,000) and the corresponding expenditure of the Urban District Council on services and facilities such as the drilling of boreholes in Ballycullen to ensure an unlimited supply of pure water.

In the late 1920s and early 1930s electric street lighting was introduced but some old gas lamps remained in use until the Second World War, lit and extinguished every evening by the lamplighter. The Council continued to produce gas for the town at very reasonable rates. The annual output of gas rose from 44 million cubic feet in 1916 to 95 million cubic feet in 1946. Town gas was available for cooking (gas cookers, if not bought outright, were available for hire from the Council for five shillings per annum), water heating, space heating and refrigeration.

In 1936 the local firm of Alexander Dickson and Sons celebrated its centenary. To mark the occasion, the head of the family Chevalier Dickson (or Chev-a-lier as he was known) presented the town council with a chain of office fashioned out of gold from medals won by Dickson's own roses. On the reverse of a pendant, which attached to the chain, was inscribed:

This gold chain of office was presented to the Municipal Authority of Newtownards by a family named Dickson with thankfulness to God for one hundred years successful work in horticulture.

Plenty of parking spaces! The west side of Conway Square during the 1930s.

A great day out. The 'crocodile' of children heads out to Milecross. Tom McIlwrath's outings on the last Saturday in June were, next to Christmas, the highlight of the children's year. (S. Mawhinney)

The Council welcomed the gift enthusiastically but felt that it would be more appropriate if the chain were a mayoral chain and petitioned the Governor asking to be elevated to the status of a municipal borough. This was achieved in May 1938: the chain had found its mayor.

Social life between the Wars

In the inter-war years much of the social life in Newtownards still centred on traditional activities. An afternoon or evening stroll in the company of friends remained a popular pastime. Children walked to the afternoon Sunday Schools in the school houses at Tullynagardy and their elders enjoyed Sunday evening walks after church from Kerlin's Lane to the Flood Gates and back. Many young people did this even on winter's evenings. Another favourite was up the Bangor Road to the lead mines. The more energetic went along the old Shore Road, up Finlay's Road, and back home by the Bowtown Road or, alternatively, up through Kiltonga and around the back of Scrabo.

Young men would take dogs up into the fields to hunt for rabbits, or greyhounds to catch hare. All kills were eaten. Easter Monday and Easter Tuesday were marked by rolling hard-boiled eggs down Scrabo Hill.

Organised events were part of the social calendar too. For example, the Greenwell Street Sunday School Fetes were held on the last Saturday in June. These were called 'Tom McIlwrath's outings' after the Rev. Thomas McIlwrath, the minister of Greenwell Street Presbyterian Church from 1900-1947, who always led the procession from the Church to Milecross. The Fete was officially for the children of the Church's Sunday School but almost 2,000 children of all denominations regularly took part! Members of the Church would make collections in the days leading up to the Fete, and free film was provided to those with cameras. For those without cameras, photographs of the event could be purchased from local chemists on the Saturday evening. Different town bands took it in turn to lead the procession – the Scouts, Newtownards Silver, 1st Ards B.B. and 'Lord Londonderry's Own' Flute. Understandably the huge procession virtually took over the town, and when the parade reached Milecross the children had tea, ran races and played games.

Plays put on by St. Patrick's Amateur Dramatic Society were another great treat. It was formed in 1906 and performed to packed and appreciative houses right through to 1939. It produced such plays as 'The Shaughraun', 'East Lynne' and 'The Colleen Bawn'. There were two cinemas – the Regent and the Ritz.

The Ards Lacrosse Club catered for bowls, hockey, cricket and tennis. There were two football clubs, a Senior and an Intermediate, and the Newtownards Swimming Club. There were four bands in the 1930s: the Dr. Wright Memorial Pipe Band, the Field Marshal Sir Henry Wilson Memorial Flute Band, the First Newtownards Old Boys' Silver Band and the Newtownards Amateur Pipe Band.

Education

In 1933 the town and parish district had thirteen primary schools: Ballyrogan with 92 pupils, Castle Gardens Junior (300), Drumhirk (33), The Londonderry Boys and Girls, amalgamated 1929 (380), Loughries (65), Loughriscouse (36), Movilla Senior (476) and Movilla Junior (330), Newtownards No.1 and No.2, Greenwell Street, Newtownards Model (527), and St. Finnian's (88).

Secondary education had had its 'ups and downs' since the founding of the Intermediate School in 1878. It closed in 1895 partly due to competition from Campbell College but also because not enough residents were willing, or able, to pay for an academic education for their children. However a

But who's going to clear up afterwards? Picnic time at Milecross from an old photograph. (S. Mawhinney)

Ladies' School which had opened in 1893 in Alexandra Terrace in Victoria Avenue proved successful.

In 1903 a Technical School had been established and in the 1930s it offered courses in Commercial Subjects, Building and Engineering trades, Domestic Economy and Art.

In 1918 a group of local figures – the Rev.R. Maxwell King, the Rev.W. R.Sloan, Captain J.S.Henry, Messrs. F.C.Glasgow, H.Savage, S.Grant, R. Edgar and James Holmes – sought to resurrect the Intermediate School but could not persuade Dublin or the Council to let them use the Technical School premises in South Street when they were not in use during the day. The following year they decided to press ahead anyway and opened a school for boys in in Strean Hall. Mr John Rodgers BA of The Academy, Cookstown was appointed master. The School opened in September 1919 with 34 pupils and an assistant for Mr Rodgers, Miss E. M. Crouch. By 1924, when the number of pupils had grown to 89, the school's name was changed to Newtownards Academy and it amalgamated with the Ladies School, whose principal was Miss Brown, bringing the numbers to 129. In the mid 1920s the new co-educational school was spread over three sites – Strean Hall, the corner of High Street and Conway Square with domestic science taught at South Street. In 1928 the school governors bought Regent House, which had been commandeered during the War by the War Office, and the school, by now consisting of 155 pupils, moved in. The premises were found to be inadequate and in 1962 the school moved to its present site on the Circular Road. Secondary education was expanded after the 1939-45 War when the Movilla and Scrabo High Schools were established.

The Second World War

When the Second World War broke out, Newtownards people once again volunteered to serve their country in a variety of ways. About eight hundred joined the Armed forces. In contrast to the 1914-18 War when the great majority had joined the Army and fought in France in one battalion, men and women were distributed throughout the three services and fought on different fronts. This dispersion minimised the casualties but makes it virtually impossible to record all their exploits. However one son of Newtownards deserves particular mention. Lieutenant Colonel Robert Blair Mayne, is considered to have been one of the six co-founders of the Special Air Service Regiment and was one of the most highly decorated soldiers of the war with four Distinguished Service Orders and the French Legion d'Honneur and Croix de Geurre.

Mayne earned his first DSO while he held the rank of lieutenant; it was unusual for this distinction to be awarded to a junior officer. The raid on Tamet in the Libyan desert on December 14th, 1941 was the first joint

Blair Mayne.

operation of the recently formed SAS with the Long Range Desert Group, and the twelve-man party had driven six days from their base, three hundred miles away, into enemy-occupied territory. Mayne and another five of the party left the others and drove an additional thirty miles to the Tamet airfield. There Mayne burst into the Mess and fired fifty rounds into a group of thirty German and Italian pilots. Over the next fifteen minutes, twenty-four planes and a petrol dump were destroyed. Philip Warner said:

A memorable feature of this raid was Mayne's destruction of a plane with his bare hands. The panel lights were on, and Mayne thinking it was empty, approached it stealthily. It was empty, so he pulled out the instrument panel – for a souvenir, as he put it. Mayne's enormous physical strength was well known both on and off the rugby field, but this was more than anyone could have expected.

Mayne's biographers, Roy Bradford and Martin Dillon, describe this raid as 'the bench-mark against which future levels of achievement [of the SAS] would be measured, the brilliant opening night that inspired confidence in future performances – and a long run.'

People at home were also very active in support of the war effort. Many served as ARP wardens, joined the Red Cross, the St. John Ambulance Brigade or the Women's Voluntary Service. The ARP control room was in the Town Hall and had two 'out' stations. One was in a hut belonging to Greenwell Street Presbyterian Church, where the Red Cross were stationed; the other was in buildings in the Regent Street markets, where the Queen's Hall now stands, and the St. John Ambulance were stationed there. An Auxiliary Fire Service, consisting of two manned cars which pulled water pumps mounted on trailers, supplemented the local fire service.

The Council organised the collection of scrap metal, waste paper and books. In the case of the latter, an unusual 'Mile of Books' was organised. A literal mile of books was collected and laid out along Regent Street. Rest and Welfare Centres were set up in Regent House, Movilla and the Technical Schools. These centres were used as temporary accommodation for evacuees from Belfast.

On the night of the major air attack on Belfast, Easter Tuesday 1941, Newtownards aerodrome was hit by explosives and incendiaries. It was a public holiday and many people had been at the town's two cinemas. The blackout had been in force since 9 p.m., and at 11 p.m. the air raid siren sounded. Within a few minutes the distinctive sound of German planes could be heard, and indeed they flew so low that their markings and crew were clearly visible. As a preliminary to the bombing, the Luftwaffe dropped incendiaries on Scrabo Hill and set it ablaze. These, together with the parachute flares which were dropped, lit up the whole town.

Some think that the Luftwaffe, as they flew up Strangford Lough, believed that they were flying over Belfast Lough and mistook Newtownards for Belfast. Alternatively, it is possible that they chose to strike at targets that lay near their flight path and, as the airport was being used by the Services, it was deliberately targeted. This view is supported by the fact that a few weeks before, a lone German reconnaissance plane had flown over the area. It had been broad daylight and the plane, although very high in the sky, was clearly visible to people in the town. Some of the planes that bombed the airfield came from the direction of Belfast and appeared to be a detachment from the main raid there. The suggestion has been made that the planes followed the 10.30 p.m. train from Belfast, though given the great differences in the speed of aircraft and trains, this seems rather fanciful!

Ards Airport was the only specifically military target outside Belfast. In 1940 the Airport had been taken over by 231 Squadron of the RAF as a reserve for Sydenham which was overcrowded because of training exercises. Two tarmac runways were constructed for Westland Lysanders,

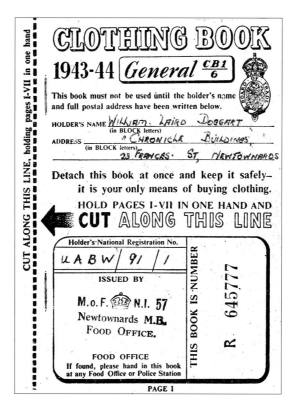

'Detach this book at once and keep it safely – it is your only means of buying clothing.' World War Two clothing ration book – with twenty four unclaimed coupons still inside!

which were used for dawn and dusk anti-invasion patrols, and for patrolling the border with Eire.

On that fateful Easter Tuesday evening seven large explosions were heard. Bombs fell on the Green Road, on Scrabo Hill, two on the Comber Road and the remainder on either side of the Comber Road at the airfield. One Nissen hut, which contained teenagers from the Young Soldiers Battalion of the Inniskilling Fusiliers, who were too young for active service, but deployed as guards, took a direct hit. A number of young people were killed. An official casualty list for the raid on Ards Airport has never been found and so accounts vary as to the number of fatalities. Local sources have it that thirteen died. The Auxiliary Fire Service, a group from the Greenwell Street ARP, and RAF personnel were soon at the scene, and the wounded were taken by the latter to Ards Hospital, where the Regent Street St. John Ambulance unit was waiting to assist. Local fire, ambulance and rescue services were at full stretch that night, with some units being rushed to Belfast to assist their hard-pressed city colleagues.

The Easter Tuesday raid had one beneficial side effect. The Belfast plane maker, Short and Harland, anxious to avoid further attacks, dispersed as many of its operations as possible. A machine shop was set up in what had been the Glen Print Works, with a large fabrication area where aircraft details and small sub-assemblies were produced. Sheet-metal presses and large shaped panels were made at a new factory at Hawlmark where the 'half acre', used by Ards United, was taken over to build a new factory which has been a place of employment ever since. Webb and Company was taken over by Lee Guinness.

But the war years were not all work and no play. Although the former Catholic Church in Ann Street was taken over briefly for the war effort, it was soon back in action as a dance hall used by Jimmy Heaney's Band and the inimitable Portaferry Hawaiian Band. In 1942 concerts and dancing were introduced on Sunday evenings. In 1944 the St. Patrick's Players re-formed and continued to produce plays until 1957, apart from an interlude in 1948-1949 when they broadened their repertoire to include choral productions.

The treatment of veterans at the end of the Second World War contrasted sharply with the shabby treatment afforded those of the First World War. Ten thousand pounds were collected locally for a Peace Celebrations and Welcome Home Fund to enable over five hundred servicemen to be given money at a ceremony in the Guild Hall. VE and VJ days were celebrated by open-air dancing for several evenings in Conway Square.

After the War

In the early post-war years, Newtownards could claim more diversification of industry than any other town in the province, with the exception of Belfast. There was official optimism that Newtownards industries could be maintained and extended and new enterprises introduced. The town's industries participated in the province's postwar boom. For a brief period it was hoped that it could become a centre of aircraft manufacture. Shorts retained its factory and Miles Aircraft of Woodley, Reading, built a factory beside the original hangar built by Lord Londonderry in 1934, in which they produced the Miles Messenger, a small single-engined communications aircraft which had been ordered by the government. The company persuaded the government to assist with building a factory. Miles Aircraft (NI.) Ltd. began operations in April 1946. But the parent company collapsed, production ceased, and the factory was subsequently bought by the Crepe Weavers Ltd.

Good old double deckers. The bus depot, early 1960s.

It then seemed as if the aerodrome was fated to become a race circuit for cars and motor cycles, but it was rescued by the opening of the Ulster

Flying Club in May 1953. The new club was supported by Short and Harland and had the Ministry of Civil Aviation's approval for private pilot licence courses.

The airport's fortunes appeared to revive in April 1955, when Silver City Airways announced that they would be running a daily air car-ferry service from Newtownards to Stranraer (Castle Kennedy). This novel idea had worked well for the Company in services between the south of England and the Continent. Mobile ramps were positioned beside the airplanes and cars drove on and off just like the sea ferry. However its initial success proved to be short-lived. The enterprise was crippled by fuel shortages following the Suez Crisis, and the fast developing sea ferries moved in to take all the business.

In 1958 Queen Elizabeth the Queen Mother laid the foundation stone of a new Civic Hall, to be known as 'The Queen's Hall', in Regent Street. The new building contained a library, reading room, a minor recreation hall and a main hall for concerts, conferences and dances. It held theatrical performances by St. Patrick's Choral and Dramatic Society from 1961 to 1966.

Long established textile businesses endured through the 1960s. George Walker & Co., Webb & Co., the Ulster Print Works, James Mairs Ltd., S. Corry & Co. carried through to the 1970s. They had been joined by newer companies such as Crepe Weavers, Ards Manufacturing Co., the Ards Swiss Embroidery Co. and the Lewinters of Vienna. The traditional firms associated with the town – Dicksons and the Glen Laundry, established in 1896 – were also in operation.

In the late 1960s as political tensions in the province increased and

Programme for the Regent Street cinema, February-March 1955 when the main attraction was 'MARTIN LUTHER, The Man who Changed the World Forever!'

violence erupted, a section of Newtownards opinion became highly critical of the government's law and order policies. On Tuesday January 29th, 1969 a hostile crowd in Newtownards greeted the Northern Ireland premier, Captain Terence O'Neill, with cries of 'Protestants go to prison and thugs go free', a reference to the three month prison sentences recently handed out to the Rev. Ian Paisley and Major Ronald Bunting. Later that year, in October, 110 members of the Ulster Special Constabulary in the Newtownards district resigned together, in protest at the Hunt Report's recommendation that the force be disbanded. In the early 1970s the Rev. Ian Paisley and William Craig told Newtownards audiences that if security did not improve they might have to defend themselves.

Local Unionists' anxiety about security never developed along the lines suggested by Paisley and Craig, but concern about Northern Ireland's constitutional position did bring some Newtownards people on to the streets. Tensions were high in May 1974 when the Ulster Workers' Council organised province-wide strikes in protest against the Sunningdale Agreement and the power-sharing executive. In Newtownards, the Ulster Workers Council operated seven road blocks of cars and lorries which were manned by local young men from Monday 20th to Thursday 23rd May, making it the only town in Northern Ireland to have been continuously road-checked without interruption. Traffic was reduced to a minimum and work at local factories, shops and farms was greatly disrupted, with queues at the employment exchange which almost continually stretched for over one hundred yards. As food supplies dwindled, local farmers, who were sympathetic to the stoppage, were reported to have been supplying strikers with milk, vegetables and chickens.

The province's relationship with Dublin was of interest to Newtownards loyalists. In 1981, Margaret Thatcher visited Charles Haughey in Dublin and agreed to search for possible 'new institutional structures'. In response, the Rev. Ian Paisley organised a 'Carson Trail' which was modelled on the 1912-14 campaign of covenant-signing and mobilisation. A subsequent rally was centred on the Orange Hall in Mary Street and its organisers, erroneously, claimed that it was the biggest demonstration ever to have been held in the town. A quasi-paramilitary organisation, Paisley's 'Third Force', was mustered in the Square in Newtownards.

More creatively, in the wake of the 1985 Anglo-Irish Agreement, two Newtownards brothers, Chris and Michael McGimpsey, challenged the legality of the Irish Republic's territorial claim over Northern Ireland in the Republic's highest court. Their arguments were rejected, but their initiative provided one of the few indications that life stirred within Unionism in the late 1980s, a particularly moribund period for that cause.

Since the 'Troubles' began, the town and district has also suffered directly from terrorism. A supermarket and the town's remaining cinema in Regent Street, and bars in Castle and Frances Streets, were damaged or destroyed by fire. On Monday July 5th, 1993 a massive car bomb devastated Regent Street. Several people have been murdered, victims of terrorist violence.

Old Newtownards gradually faded away in the 1970s. The railway closed in 1950, a victim of spread of more flexible bus services and the increase in motor car ownership. Most of the mills and factories were gone by the 1970s, unable to compete with the man-made chemical fibres such as rayon, nylon and terylene which were introduced in the 1950s.

On the other hand, some changes were for the better. Slum dwellings were pulled down as the town was able to benefit from the subsidies which were given to local councils to build new houses. These projects were usually on a small scale. Large scale building was undertaken by the Northern Ireland Housing Trust which was set up by the Stormont Government at this time. One of its first projects was the Scrabo Estate which was built in the late 1940s.

In 1973 the municipal borough ceased to exist and Ards Borough Council came into being as part of local government reorganisation in Northern Ireland. For the first time since 1613 the town was without its own government, but it became the administrative centre of an area of 143 square miles, taking in Comber, Donaghadee and the peninsula with a population of about 70,000.

The gathering of the 'Third Force' in the Square, Newtownards, November 1981. (Pacemaker)

Candy apples 15p.
Newtownards, market town.

Ards Shopping Centre, or 'Woolco' as it is more popularly called, was one of the first enclosed shopping malls to be established in Northern Ireland. It opened in June 1976 on one of Dickson's rose fields, which had brought the town such fame, and the site on which the once renowned Horticultural and Horse jumping Society's annual show had been held.

The seventeenth century Plantation created the Scottish town of Newtownards. In 1965 another 'plantation' was planned for the area when the Wilson Plan recommended that Newtownards become one of several new 'growth centres' around Belfast, to absorb its surplus population. The historian Jonathan Bardon has said that not since the Ulster plantation of the seventeenth century was so much thought given to planning Ulster's future. The 'plantation' was well under way in the 1970s, accelerated by violence and the threat of violence in Belfast in the early 1970s. Fewer people were employed locally and Newtownards became a dormitory town for Belfast. To accommodate the growing number of commuters a dual carriageway was built in the early 1980s between Newtownards and the city.

To facilitate the expanding population, which increased from 14,000 to 24,000 during the 1970s and 1980s, new public sector housing was built – the Glen Estate in the early 1960s, and the West Winds Estate in the late 1960s. Both were to a significant extent peopled by newcomers from Belfast. Substantial private sector housing was added in the 1970s in the Rosehill area and in the 1980s along the Bangor, Donaghadee, and Movilla Roads. The amphitheatre of hills which has for centuries overlooked the town is now covered with houses and a part of it.

Not only has there been a change in extent and population but, assisted by the advent of television, there is even a different accent in Newtownards. A newspaper editorial of 1897 observed that Newtownards 'is as much a part of Scotland by customs and accent, and the immigration of Scotchmen, as places which are, geographically, more entitled to the name'. Newtownards people liked to think that they were closer to Scotland than they were to other parts of Ireland. The Scots dialect and colloquialisms were still a pronounced feature of the Newtownards accent until after the Second World War. However the expansion since the 1970s – the new 'plantation' – has helped to change this. At the beginning it was noted that Newtownards has had many 'lives': it has recently entered into a new one.

Bibliography

A. Primary sources

Seventeenth century (chapters 5-7)

Hill,G. (ed.) *The Montgomery Manuscripts* (Belfast, 1869)

Eighteenth century (chapters 7-8)

Crawford,W.H. Trainor,B. (eds.) *Aspects of Irish Social History 1750-1850* (Belfast, 1969)

Harris,W. *The Antient and Present State of the County of Down* (Dublin, 1744)

Londonderry Papers: D. 654, D.3030, D 3099, T.1536, T.2281, The Public Record Office of Northern Ireland (hereafter PRONI)

PRONI, *The Penal Laws* (Belfast, 1971)

PRONI, *18th Century Emigration* (Belfast, 1972)

PRONI, *The United Irishmen* (Belfast, 1974)

PRONI, *The '98 Rebellion* (Belfast, 1974)

Nineteenth century (chapters 9-14)

Bassett, *County Down Guide and Directory* (Dublin, 1886)

1841 Census: Digest of Statistics for Newtownards

Day, A., McWilliams, P.(eds.) *Ordnance Survey Memoirs of Ireland: Parishes of County Down II North Down and the Ards* (Belfast, 1991)

Derry Standard, January-February 1847, The British Library, The British Museum

Devon Commission into the Occupation of Land in Ireland, 1844-45, Queen's University Library

Downpatrick Recorder, November 1846, December 1848, South Eastern Education and Library Board

Lewis,S. *Topographical Dictionary of Ireland* 1837

Londonderry Sentinel, January-February 1847, N. 13 P.R.O.N.I.

Minute Book of the Board of Guardians of Newtownards Workhouse, BG 25/A, PRONI

Newtownards Chronicle, 1873-1916, South Eastern Education and Library Board

Papers of the Rev. Mark Cassidy, D.1088, PRONI

Papers of the Rev. John Cleland, D.714 PRONI

Parliamentary Gazeteer of Ireland, 1845

Pigot's *Directory* 1824

Provincial Directory 1864

Twentieth century (chapters 15-16)

Newtownards and District Order of Service and Roll of Honour for the Unveiling and Dedication of the War Memorial, 26 May, 1934 (1934)

Petition of Newtownards Urban District Council to the Governor of Northern Ireland for the grant of a charter creating the Urban District a Municipal Borough 1937

B. Secondary sources

General

The Archaeological Survey of Co. Down   (Belfast, 1966)

Ards Historical Society, *Glimpses of the Ards* (1977), *Further Glimpses of the Ards* (1980), *Photographic Glimpses of the Ards* (1984), *A Short History of Newtownards* (1994)

Bardon,J. *A History of Ulster*   (Belfast, 1992)

Brady,C., O'Dowd, M., Walker, B. (eds.) *Ulster: An Illustrated History*, (London, 1989)

Carr,P., *The Most Unpretending of Places: A History of Dundonald* (Dundonald, 1987)

Dalton,G., Murray,P. *Northern Ireland*, (Cambridge, 1987)

Foster, R.F. (ed.) *The Oxford Illustrated History of Ireland*, (Oxford, 1989).

Griffith, E.M. 'Newtownards', *Ulster Tatler*, 1980

Kelly, G.J. *Northern Ireland: A Systematic Geography*, (Dublin, 1983)

Earliest times to the coming of the Nomans (chapters 1-2)

Adamson, I. *Bangor Light of the World* (Bangor, 1979)

Boal,F.W., Moffit,M.K. 'A partly destroyed rath in Killarn townland, Newtownards, County Down', *The Ulster Journal of Archaeology* (hereafter *UJA),* 22 (1959)

Brown, R. *Strangford Lough* (Belfast, 1990)

Bruce,F.F.*The Spreading Flame: The Rise and Progress of Christianity From John the Baptist to the Conversion of the English*, (Exeter, 1961)

Butlin,R. A. (ed.) *The development of the Irish Town* (London, 1971)

Byrne,F.J. *Irish Kings and High Kings* (London, 1973)

Carr,P.A. 'An early Mesolithic site near Dundonald, County Down', *UJA,* 48 (1985)

Carr,P.A. 'An early Mesolithic site near Comber, County Down', *UJA,* 50 (1987)

Case,H. 'Settlement patterns in the North Irish Neolithic', *UJA,* 32 (1969)

Collins,A.E.P. 'Settlement in Ulster 0-1100 A.D.', *UJA,* 31 (1968)

Hamlin,A., Lynn, C. (eds.) *Pieces of the Past: Archaeological Excavations by the Department of the Environment for N. Ireland* (Belfast, 1988)

Mac Niocall,G. *Ireland before the Vikings* (Dublin, 1972)

O' Corrain,D. *Ireland Before the Normans* (Dublin, 1972)

Richter,M. *Medieval Ireland: The Enduring Tradition* (Basingstoke, 1988)

Robinson, K., The story of Bangor Abbey (unpublished)

Norman and medieval (chapters 3-4)

Bardon,J. *Investigating Place Names in Ulster* (Belfast, 1990)

Canavan, T. (ed), *Every Stoney Acre has a Name: a celebration of the townland in Ulster* (Belfast, 1991)

Davies,O., George, A.H. 'Norman graveslabs from County Down', *UJA*, 9 (1946)

Davies,O., Quinn,D.B. 'Irish Pipe Roll 1211-2', *UJA,* 4 (1941)

Dolley,M. *Anglo-Norman Ireland* (Dublin, 1972)

Greeves,J.R.H. 'North Down at the end of the 16th century', *Belfast Natural History and Philosophical Society* (hereafter cited as *BNHPS* , 5 (1960)

Greeves, J.R.H. 'The origins of some parishes in North Down', *BNHPS* , 8 (1965)

Hughes,A.J., Hannan, R.J. *Place names of Northern Ireland, vol. 2 County Down II The Ards* (Belfast, 1992)

Lawlor,H.C., 'Mote and Mote and Bailey Castles in de Courcy's principality in Ulster', *UJA* 2 (1939)

Lawlor,H.C. 'Vassals of the Earls of Ulster', *UJA,*. 3 (1940), 4 (1941)

Lydon,J.F. *The Lordship of Ireland in the Middle Ages* (Dublin, 1972)

Mallory,J.P., McNeill,T.E. *The Archaeology of Ulster from Colonization to Plantation* (Belfast, 1991)

McNeill,T.E. *Anglo-Norman Ulster* (Edinburgh, 1980)

Morgan, H. 'The colonial venture of Sir Thomas Smith in Ulster, 1571-1575', *Historical Journal,* 28 (1985)

O'Laverty,J. *The diocese of Down and Connor,* 4 vols. (Dublin, 1878)

Orpen,G.H. *Ireland under the Normans*, 4 vols. (Oxford, 1911-20)

Orpen,G.H. 'The Earldom of Ulster', *Journal of the Royal Society of the Antiquaries of Ireland,* (hereafter *JRSAI*), 43, 44 (1913,1915)

Quinn,D.B. 'Sir Thomas Smith and the beginnings of English Colonial Theory', The *Proceedings of the American Philosophical Society,* 89 (1945)

Reeves,W. *Ecclesiastical Antiquities* (Dublin, 1867)

Young, R.M., 'The priory of St. Columba, Newtownards, County Down', *JRSAI*, 5 (1882)

Seventeenth century (chapters 5-7)

Cullen, L.M. *The emergence of Modern Ireland 1600-1900* (London, 1981)

Cregan,D.F. 'Daniel O'Neill, a Royalist Agent in Ireland, 1644-50', *Irish Historical Studies* (hereafter cited as *IHS*) 2 (1940-1)

Gillespie,R. *Colonial Ulster: the settlement of East Ulster 1600-41* (Cork, 1986)

Gillespie,R. 'The end of an era: Ulster and the outbreak of the 1641 Rising ' in C. Brady, Gillespie,R. (eds.) *Natives and Newcomers* (Dublin, 1986)

Gillespie,R. 'The origins and development of an Ulster urban network, 1609-41', *IHS* 24 (1984)

Hunter,R.J. 'Towns in the Ulster Plantation', *Studia Hibernica*, 11 (1971)

Lowe,J. 'Charles I and the Confederation of Kilkenny, 1643-9', *IHS*, vol.14, no.53 (1964)

Perceval-Maxwell,M. *The Scottish Migration to Ulster in the reign of James 1* (London, 1973, 1990)

Perceval-Maxwell, M. 'Strafford, the Ulster Crisis and the Covenanters', *IHS* (1973)

Robinson,P.S. *The Plantation of Ulster* (Dublin, 1984)

Stevenson,D. *Scottish Covenanters and Irish Confederates* (Edinburgh, 1981)

Stevenson,J. *Two Centuries of Life in Down 1600-1800* (First published 1920, reprinted Dundonald, 1990)

Eighteenth century (chapters 7-8)

Malcomson,A.P.W. *John Foster: The Politics of the Anglo-Irish Ascendancy* (Oxford, 1978)

Malcomson,A.P.W. 'The Newtown Act of 1748: revision and reconstruction', *IHS,* vol. 18 no.71 (Dublin, 1973)

Holmes,F. *Our Presbyterian Heritage* (Belfast, 1985)

Hyde,H. Montgomery 'Mount Stewart and its owners' in *Mount Stewart* (National Trust, 1976)

Hyde,H. Montgomery *The Londonderrys* (London, 1979)

Jupp, P. 'County Down elections 1783-1831', *IHS ,* vol. 18, no.70 (Dublin, 1972)

Reid,J.S. *History of the Presbyterian Church in Ireland,* 3 vols. (Belfast, 1867)

Stewart, A.T.Q. *The Narrow Ground* (London, 1989)

1798 Rebellion (chapter 8)

Derry,J.W. *Castlereagh* (London, 1976)

Dickson, C. *The Revolt in the North: Antrim and Down in 1798* (Dublin, 1960)

Elliott,M. *Partners in Revolution* (Yale, 1982)

Lyttle,W.G. *Betsy Gray* (Newcastle, 1968)

Madden,R.R. *Antrim and Down in 1798* (Dublin, 1860)

McSkimin,S. *Annals of Ulster* (Belfast, 1849)

Pakenham, T. *The Year of Liberty* (London, 1969)

Nineteenth and twentieth centuries (chapters 9-16)

Borough of Ards: The Official Guide (1989)

Bradford,R., Dillon,M. *Rogue Warrior of the SAS* (London, 1987)

Corlett,J. *Aviation in Ulster* (Belfast, 1981)

de Courcy, A. *Circe, the Life of Edith, Marchioness of Londonderry* (London, 1993)

Hall, M. *Sacrifice on the Somme* (Newtownabbey, 1993)

Harvey,W. Speech at a ceremony to mark the Fiftieth Anniversary of the granting of the Borough Charter, 23 May 1988 (unpublished)

Harvey,W. Address on the History of Newtownards, 15 December, 1993 (unpublished)

Gallagher, H.W. *Ards Hospital: The First Fifty Years* (1982)

McNeill, D.B. Early Bus Services in Ulster (unpublished)

Newtownards, The Official Guide (*c.* 1932)

Newtownards, Official town guide (1969)

Orr, P. *The Road to the Somme* (Belfast, 1987)

Stewart, A.T.Q. *The Ulster Crisis* (London, 1967)
Ulster Vintage Car Club Book of the Ards T.T. (Belfast, 1978)
Warner,P. *The Special Air Service* (London, 1971)

Local congregational histories

Centenary 1877-97 St. Patrick's Church (1977)
A History of the Congregation: First Presbyterian Church (1944)
McNeill,D.B. *Regent Street Presbyterian Church* (1987)
McNeill,D.B. *Strean Presbyterian Church 1865-1975* (1975)
Memories Between the Years 1756-1980 Regent Street Methodist Church (1980)
A Souvenir of the Opening of St. Mark's Parochial Hall (1954)
Weir,W.D. *Greenwell Street Presbyterian Church, The Story of the First Hundred Years* (1970)

Index

Farewell to the Hammer

A Shankill Boyhood
John Young Simms
Pbk, 144pp, illustrated, £4.95

A fascinating story of growing up, amidst horses, trams, cobbles and pig's feet, in the Hammer district of Belfast's Shankill Road at the height of the Great Depression.

"Each tale swells in the mind, like grain in water, until the reader finds it necessary to pause, savour its taste, and go back over it again before moving the short distance to the next..." *Sam McAughtry*

The Most Unpretending of Places

A History of Dundonald, County Down
Peter Carr
Pbk, 256pp, illustrated, £7.95

"Sparkles with compelling detail... one of the most impressive local histories available for any locality on this island, north or south."
Linenhall Review

"One word could suffice to describe this book, magnificent! ...I cannot praise it too highly. Well illustrated with photographs, studiously annotated without over-loading the text, a questioning of sources, a good index and the courage to express opinions of a controversial nature. This is what local history is all about." *Irish News*

Gape Row

Agnes Romilly White's classic comedy
Pbk, 200pp, £4.95

Can Jinanna escape the poorhouse? Will young Johnny Darragh jilt Ann? Will Mary get saddled with the awful Andy John McCready? Or will Happy Bill, the wayside preacher, nip in first and win them all for God?

A boisterous, rich, nostalgic book which immerses the reader in the cheerful chaos of everyday life in a small Irish village on the eve of the First World War.

"Captures the spirit of early twentieth century rural Ulster better than any painter of photographer could." *Sunday News*

"masterly... the dialogue goes to one's head like wine." *The Observer*

NEVER!

Fascinating Facts about Ireland
Michael Smith
Pbk, 93pp, illustrated, £3.50

Did you know ...that the only Irishman to be offered the Papacy refused it? ...that an Irish ship discovered the ghostly wreck of the *Marie Celeste*? ...that the first casualty of the Irish Civil War was a Free State sniper, smashed over the head with a teapot by an elderly Dublin woman? ...or that the skull of a Corkman is the most sacred relic of the Ashanti tribe of West Africa?

All is now revealed in this illustrated collection of amusing, amazing and arcane facts relating to Ireland and the Irish.

"A grand little book." *Ireland of the Welcomes*

"jam-packed with all sorts of scarcely believable, probably useless, but nonetheless fascinating gems of information." *The Wicklow People*

Available from bookshops, or directly from the publishers.
If ordering, please add £1 for postage and packaging.